MAKING SENSE
of the BIBLE

MAKING SENSE
of the BIBLE

A Study of 10 Key Themes Traced Through the Scriptures

H. H. Drake Williams III

Kregel
Publications

Making Sense of the Bible: A Study of 10 Key Themes Traced Through the Scriptures

© 2006 by H. H. Drake Williams III

Published by Kregel Publications, a division of Kregel, Inc., P.O. Box 2607, Grand Rapids, MI 49501.

Epigraph quotations at the beginning of each chapter are from M. Water, *The New Encyclopedia of Christian Quotations* (Grand Rapids: Baker, 2000).

Rembrandt van Rijn's *The Night Watch* courtesy of Famous Art Reproductions.com. Used by permission.

Rainbow over church photograph courtesy of Tara Smith.

All other photographs courtesy of Todd Bolen and BiblePlaces.com.

Library of Congress Cataloging-in-Publication Data
Williams, H. H. Drake.
    Making sense of the Bible: a study of 10 key themes traced through the Scriptures / by H. H. Drake Williams III.
        p.   cm.
    Includes bibliographical references and index.
    1. Bible—Criticism, interpretation, etc. 2. Bible. O.T.—Relation to the New Testament. 3. Bible. N.T.—Relation to the Old Testament. 4. Bible as literature. I. Title.
BS511.3.W55   2006   220.6—dc22   2005036164

ISBN 0-8254-4107-2

Printed in the United States of America

06 07 08 09 10 / 5 4 3 2 1

CONTENTS

PREFACE

In the Old Testament the New is concealed, in the New Testament the Old is revealed.

—Saint Augustine

A group of city guardsmen are waiting for the command from their captain, Frans Cocq. They have not yet been ordered to fall in line, and some of the men have their muskets out of order, their lances are askew, and the men are pointing or looking in different directions. Such is the portrayal in *The Night Watch*, painted in 1642, by Rembrandt van Rijn.

Rembrandt, one the most famous of the Dutch Baroque era painters, is a giant in the history of art. In the seventeenth century, he became the leading portrait painter in Holland and received many commissions for portraits as well as paintings of religious subjects. In his lifetime, he produced nearly 1,400 drawings, 300 etchings, and 600 paintings, many of which are portraits and self-portraits.

The Night Watch is one of Rembrandt's most famous works. Each individual character in the painting is a mini-masterpiece, painted with the fine care that Rembrandt gave to his single portraits. Yet the composition as a whole is greater than the sum of its individual parts.[1] In this group portrait, Rembrandt captures the personality of the entire company. Although each man appears to be going his own way, together they project a sense of vitality for their mission.

Just as Rembrandt's composition draws together seemingly discrete elements into a cohesive whole, so too the Bible assembles a collection of characters, stories, and literary styles into a masterpiece of cohesion and

Rembrandt van Rijn, *The Night Watch* (also known as *The Company of Captain Frans Banning Cocq and Willem van Ruytenburch*), 1642. Amsterdam, Rijksmuseum. (Courtesy of FamousArtReproductions.com.)

coherence. Although each book of the Bible and each theme is remarkable on its own and deserves careful individual consideration, the message of the Old and New Testaments, taken as a whole, exhibits a remarkable continuity. To read the Bible as a string of unrelated commands, promises, exhortations, and aphorisms, or to read one Testament without referring to the other, misses the greater portrait.[2] The Bible as a great work of art deserves to be considered in unity.

The goal of *Making Sense of the Bible* is to illustrate how the Old and New Testaments are interwoven in significant ways. Themes that are developed in the Old Testament can be traced into the New Testament. Moreover, what has been written in the Old Testament substantially influences our understanding of the New Testament. This continuity and coherence can be seen in the examination of ten central themes: creation, covenant, idolatry, the Messiah, Law, salvation, kingdom, the Holy Spirit, the people of God, and prophecy (with its fulfillment). Because these themes lead to important revelations about who God is, how he wants his people to relate to him, and how his great plan emerges from the beginning of time, they illustrate the divine artistry behind the pages of Holy Scripture.[3]

It is unfortunate, however, that while the Western world still exhibits a fascination for works of art, many people are not as interested in that ancient masterpiece, the Bible. Most people probably have a copy of the Bible in their homes. Some hold one in their hands each week at church, and perhaps carry one with them to a Bible study. But not everyone sees or appreciates the great beauty and intricate composition of the Bible.[4]

This lack of appreciation for the Bible is a growing trend in Western society. An October 2000 Gallup poll found that only six in ten Americans (59 percent) say they read the Bible at least on occasion. This is a noticeable decline from the 1980s, when 73 percent read the Bible on occasion. The percentage of frequent readers—that is, those who read the Bible at least once a week—decreased slightly from 40 percent in 1990 to 37 percent in 2000. In terms of frequency of readership, 16 percent of Americans say that they read the Bible every day, 21 percent say they read it weekly, 12 percent say they read the Bible monthly, 10 percent say less than monthly, and 41 percent say that they rarely or never read the Bible.[5]

Jay Leno, host of the *Tonight Show* on NBC, illustrated the decreasing knowledge of the Bible in society. Polling the audience at one of his late night shows, he said, "Name one of the Ten Commandments." Someone ventured, "God helps those who help themselves?" Leno then said, "Name one of the apostles." No one could. But almost everyone could name the four Beatles: John, Paul, George, and Ringo. Leno was not deriding the Bible, but his show that night revealed just how much American society, which is historically rooted in the Judeo-Christian Scriptures, has lost touch with the Bible.[6]

Making Sense of the Bible aims to increase appreciation of the Bible by exhibiting some of its divine artistry, as seen in the ten themes previously mentioned. Many other themes could doubtless be considered, but sampling just a few of the more prominent themes that fit together into a larger picture, displays what a great and unified masterpiece we have in the Holy Scriptures. In order to get the most from reading this book, you are encouraged to take the time to look up the Scripture references that appear in the text, as well as those that appear in the endnotes.

ACKNOWLEDGMENTS

A project such as this is accomplished not solely on one's own abilities. Thus, I wish to thank those who, in one way or another, contributed to this work.

I am thankful to Scott Hafemann, Greg Beale, I. Howard Marshall, Brian Rosner, and Paul Ellingworth for their encouragement of my study of Old Testament themes in the New Testament. Jim Weaver provided a constant source of encouragement and insight. Emily Sirindes helped with references. Tom McThenia provided helpful advice on publication, and Dave Lindstedt contributed many good suggestions during the editing process.

The members and pastors of the Central Schwenkfelder Church in Worcester, Pennsylvania, consistently encouraged me in this effort, as did the faculty at the Tyndale Theological Seminary in Badhoevedorp, The Netherlands.

As always, my wife, Andrea, and our children, Henry, Abby, and Samuel, were understanding and supportive.

This volume is dedicated to my parents and my in-laws, Mr. and Mrs. H. H. Drake Williams Jr., and Dr. and Mrs. John Gasser, thoughtful and serious students of the Bible who have encouraged me for many years. Their prayers, inspiration, and desire to study the Scriptures ultimately led to this volume. To God be the glory!

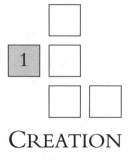

CREATION

A Whole New World

That the universe was formed by a fortuitous concourse of atoms, I will no more believe than that the accidental jumbling of the alphabet would fall into a most ingenious treatise of philosophy.

—Jonathan Swift

We must constantly remind ourselves of William Temple's great statement that "Christianity is the most materialistic of the world's great religions."

—Leighton Ford

God creates out of nothing. Therefore, until a man is nothing God can make nothing out of him.

—Martin Luther

Our first impression of God in the Bible is that of the great Creator. In the dramatic opening chapters of Genesis, the very first portrayal of God is that of the Creator of the heavens and the earth, the land, sea, animals, and human beings. His majestic and awesome works as Creator have, in fact, inspired the writing of many hymns such as "How Great Thou Art," "All Things Bright and Beautiful," "This Is My Father's World," and "For the Beauty of the Earth."

While many see God's creative ability from the early chapters of Genesis, they fail to see how the theme of creation runs throughout Scripture and influences so many other portions of the Bible.[1] An awareness of the creation theme illumines, for example, an understanding of Jesus, a

Christian's identity, and the Christian's future destiny. The first impression of God has more to say than what we might think.

CREATION IN THE OLD TESTAMENT

The Old Testament has much to say about creation. Creation ideas fill the Psalms (e.g., Pss. 8; 19; 74; 77; 89; 104; 139; 148), as well as the writings of the prophets Isaiah (40–55), Jeremiah (31:22), Ezekiel (28:13, 15), Amos (4:13), and Malachi (2:10). Passages in the wisdom literature also refer at length to creation (cf. Job 38–41; Prov. 8:22–31). Still, the first chapters of Genesis are the most prominent section of the Old Testament regarding creation. In these opening verses of the Bible are found all the key ideas concerning creation: God creates everything, God creates by his word, God creates with tremendous complexity, God's creation is ordered and good, and God's creation is destined for rest.[2] Below, each of these ideas is considered in more detail.

God Creates Everything

Genesis 1–2 speaks of God directly creating the heavens and the earth. Although scholars differ regarding the time and manner of creation, a number of points can be made from this text without engaging in debates over these issues.[3]

First, God created all things before the beginning of time. There was nothing until he created it. Genesis 1:1–2 says, "In the beginning God created the heavens and the earth. Now the earth was formless and empty, darkness was over the surface of the deep, and the Spirit of God was hovering over the waters."

This depiction is in contrast to other descriptions of the creation of the earth that are found, for example, in ancient pagan creation accounts. The Babylonian creation epic *Enuma Elish,* does not speak of God creating everything from the beginning of time.[4] Instead, this pagan account tells of how a number of gods were born and then quarreled with each other, their disagreements stemming from their several love affairs. The gods eventually battled with each other and the god Marduk won supremacy over the other lesser Babylonian gods. As he fought with the lesser gods, he killed them and then made the heavens and the earth from their corpses. This is a much different picture of creation than that presented in Genesis.

The Genesis account also differs from many current and popular understandings of the origins of life on earth. Most modern scientific suppositions say nothing of the involvement of a divine being in the act of creation. And they certainly do not portray a God who creates heaven and earth from the beginning of time.[5]

God, however, is consistently presented throughout the Old Testament as the Creator of all things. Psalm 8:1–4, for example, is quite explicit:

> O Lord, our Lord,
>   how majestic is your name in all the earth!
>
> You have set your glory
>   above the heavens.
> From the lips of children and infants
>   you have ordained praise
> because of your enemies,
>   to silence the foe and the avenger.
>
> When I consider your heavens,
>   the work of your fingers,
> the moon and the stars,
>   which you have set in place,
> what is man that you are mindful of him,
>   the son of man that you care for him?

Other Old Testament passages such as Psalm 19:1–6; 148:5; and Proverbs 8:22–27 also clearly portray God as Creator of all things.[6]

God Creates by His Word

Genesis also states the particular manner in which God created everything: he merely spoke things into existence. This is much different than our human ways of creating, in which we must manipulate things with

Sunset near Beersheba. One of many witnesses to God's creative ability. (Photograph courtesy of Todd Bolen and BiblePlaces.com.)

our hands. Unlike the baker, the gardener, or the painter, God does not need to exert himself physically, get down on his knees, or mix things with his hands, for he can speak things into existence.

Genesis 1 records ten instances of God either speaking something into existence or giving direction to something he has created (vv. 3, 6, 9, 11, 14, 20, 24, 26, 28, 29). Eight of those times, he says, "Let there be . . ." which immediately results in things being created in the world (vv. 3, 6, 9, 11, 14, 20, 24, 26). Verse 3 is a good example: "And God said, 'Let there be light,' and there was light."

The effect of his speaking things into existence can be seen by the number of times that Genesis 1 says, "And it was so" (vv. 7, 9, 11, 15, 24, 30). Never once does God struggle or become frustrated with the process of creation. Never once does he need to supplement his creation with physical labor or help from some outside agent. Effortless speech, rather than struggle or exertion, is God's way of creating (see also Ps. 33:6).

God Creates with Tremendous Complexity

Throughout the seven days of creation depicted in Genesis 1, God creates with tremendous breadth and complexity. On the first day, he creates light and separates it from darkness (vv. 3–5). On the second day, he creates the expanse of the sky and separates the waters (vv. 6–8). He creates dry land and plants on the third day (vv. 9–13). On the fourth day, he creates the luminaries (vv. 14–19). He makes the birds and the fish on the fifth day (vv. 20–23). On the sixth day, God creates humankind (vv. 24–31; 2:4–25).[7]

Each of these phases of creation is highly complex. In an article titled "The Wonders of the Natural World: God's Design," university professor Gerald R. Bergman points out how advanced God's creation is over human invention. He notes the following complexities within the animal kingdom:

- Before humans discovered and harnessed electricity, electric eels generated their own—up to 700 volts.
- Before humans invented electric lights, fireflies were flashing their signals to one another, and certain fish in the ocean depths produced light to guide their travels.
- Long before humans learned to navigate the seven seas, birds traveled from the Arctic to the Antarctic, landing at the same nesting sites year after year.
- Octopuses used jet propulsion long before humans discovered it. In its bulbous body is a muscular sac with a small opening. When an octopus expands the sac, water is sucked in, and when it vigorously contracts it, the water spurts out in a jet. By alternate expansion and contraction of this muscular sac, the octopus can jet-propel its way through the water.
- Before humans designed and built suspension bridges, spiders demonstrated engineering feats of amazing brilliance.
- Bird's nests display a high level of engineering skill in masonry, weaving, tunneling, and structural strength.
- Bees, with their wings, "air-condition" their hives.
- Beavers build large dams out of trees and mud.

- Wasps manufacture a type of paper.
- Mankind has developed radar and sonar systems, and this development is seen as a miracle of science. Yet bats do the same thing naturally. Scientists have blindfolded bats and set them loose in a room that has been strung with many thin threads. The bats were able to dart around the room without striking a single thread because in flight they emit supersonic sound pulses that hit objects and bounce back to the bat's ears.[8]

These are but a few examples of the complexity of creation from the animal kingdom. Such complexity can also be seen in the heavenly bodies, in plants, and in humans. God's creative intelligence, in fact, shows forth in many examples of great brilliance and complexity.

God's Creation Is Ordered and Good

Order can be seen in all that God creates. The separation of the days of creation, for example, reveals its orderliness. Certain things were also created on certain days. God provided order by giving boundaries to the waters (Gen. 1:9–10) and by assigning specific functions to the sun, moon, and stars (vv. 16–18), giving direction to the animals (vv. 24–25), and telling mankind to rule over creation (vv. 29–30). He also created things "according to their kinds." The repetition of that phrase reinforces the sense of order found within creation (vv. 20, 21, 24, 25). God's creation thus demonstrates obvious direction and sequence.

God's creation is also clearly good. He reviews what he has done and, seven times in the first chapter of Genesis, declares it good (vv. 4, 10, 12, 18, 21, 25, 31). At the end of his creation of mankind on day six, he described as "very good" all of his work, thus bestowing his divine pronouncement on his work of creation: "God saw all that he had made, and it was very good" (1:31).

The creation remained good, ordered, and pleasing in God's eyes until the fall of mankind. Genesis 3 says the serpent came and tempted Eve to eat from the tree of the knowledge of good and evil (vv. 1–7). From the moment that Adam and Eve disobeyed God, their relationship with him and with the rest of creation changed. The serpent was cursed so that it must travel on its belly (v. 14), and thus the relationship between mankind and the serpent was forever changed (v. 15). The woman was cursed with pain in childbirth (v. 16), and the man experienced curses from the ground (vv. 17–18). All of these curses occurred as a result of Adam and Eve's disobedience. Before the Fall, however, everything that God created was good and orderly.

God's Creation Is Destined for Rest

The final stage of God's creation was a day of rest. According to Genesis 2:2–3, rest is built into the fabric of creation:

> By the seventh day God had finished the work he had been doing; so on the seventh day he rested from all his work. And God blessed the seventh day and made it holy, because on it he rested from all the work of creating that he had done.

All of creation was accomplished on six days, and on the seventh day God rested from his work. The word used for rest in this verse is the Hebrew word *shabat,* which means "to stop" or "to cease." It is regularly used in the Old Testament, referring to completed work.[9] From *shabat,* the climax of God's week of creation, comes the word *Sabbath,* the day on which all human work is to cease.

The seventh day has further special significance in that it is the day that never ends. In the Genesis 1 account, days one through six end with the phrase, "And there was evening, and there was morning," but that phrase is missing with regard to the seventh day, giving the impression that the seventh day is never ending. One theologian commented on this aspect of the creation in Genesis when he said, "The Sabbath is the supreme goal."[10]

While in our day, the importance of the Sabbath has declined, its importance was not lost on some from the past. One such person was William Wilberforce, a renowned British politician and statesman in the 1800s who worked tirelessly for the abolition of the slave trade and the welfare of others in Great Britain. While motivated for hard work, he had this to say about the importance of the Sabbath rest: "Blessed be to God for the day of rest and religious occupation wherein earthly things assume their true size."[11] On the Sabbath, God rested from all his activities. It is the never-ending day, and the ultimate ending point of creation, and its importance was respected for generations.

OLD TESTAMENT ECHOES IN THE NEW TESTAMENT

While creation ideas are found in abundance in the Old Testament, the seminal theme of creation carries forward into the New Testament. It does so primarily in the person of Jesus Christ, but the theme of creation is present in other ways. It informs the understanding of Christians as new creations in Christ, and the Christian's hope for eternal destiny in the new heavens and the new earth.

Jesus Christ as Creator

Ask the question, "Who is Jesus?" and you're likely to receive a variety of answers. Some people think of him only as "gentle Jesus, meek and mild," the babe in the manger, or the Great Shepherd. To others, he is the embodiment of compassion, comfort, and forgiveness. Still others see him primarily as a great moral teacher, speaking in parables, preaching the Sermon on the Mount, and setting an example to emulate as we ask ourselves, "What would Jesus do?"

Rarely, however, is he described as Creator, although several passages in the New Testament refer to him in that way. The opening verses of John's Gospel (1:1–3), for example, introduce Jesus as the great Creator:

In the beginning was the Word, and the Word was with God, and the Word was God. He was with God in the beginning. Through him all things were made; without him nothing was made that has been made. In him was life, and that life was the light of men.

A number of the Epistles also refer to Jesus as the Creator. In Colossians 1:15–16, for example, the apostle Paul describes Jesus as "the image of the invisible God, the firstborn over all creation. For by him all things were created; things in heaven and on earth, visible and invisible, whether thrones or powers or rulers or authorities; all things were created by him and for him." In Hebrews 1:2, the writer refers to Jesus as the Creator: "In these last days he has spoken to us by his Son, whom he appointed heir of all things, and through whom he made the universe."

This important attribute of Jesus was a central tenet of the early church. Consider this view of Jesus from the Nicene Creed written in the fourth century A.D. It is a creed that has been recited by Christians for hundreds of years. The beginning of the creed reads,

> I believe in one God, the Father almighty, maker of all things visible and invisible: and in one Lord Jesus Christ, the Son of God, begotten of His Father before all worlds, God of God, Light of Light, very God of very God, begotten, not made, being of one substance with the Father, by whom all things were made.

Reading John 1, Colossians 1, and Hebrews 1 in relation to what has been written in Genesis 1–2, heightens our understanding of the character and attributes of Jesus. Like God the Father, Jesus is the awesome and almighty great Creator. As such, all the creative attributes of God the Father apply to Christ as well. He is the one who created everything in our world, the heavens and the earth, the plants, the animals, and us as human beings. He created with tremendous diversity, complexity, and order. His ability was such that he created by his word. Great and awesome (and yet humble) is our Savior who came to earth to dwell among that which he had created (see John 1:10–11).

New Creatures in Christ

The creation account of Genesis 1–2 not only influences our understanding of Jesus, but it also provides key ideas for understanding Christian identity. Paul's letters refer to Christians as new creations in Christ:

> Therefore, if anyone is in Christ, he is a new creation; the old has gone, the new has come! (2 Cor. 5:17)

May I never boast except in the cross of our Lord Jesus Christ, through which the world has been crucified to me, and I to the world. Neither circumcision nor uncircumcision means anything; what counts is a new creation. (Gal. 6:14–15)

These passages speak of the great benefit of being "in Christ," and their promise is a welcome blessing to all of us who need a fresh start after a sordid past. Yet, when 2 Corinthians 5:17 and Galatians 6:14–15 are read in light of the creation accounts in Genesis 1–2, our being new creations in Christ means even more. Just as God created in Genesis by his word, so too his word creates in us newness of life. And just as God spoke into a void and created tremendous things by his word, so too tremendous things result when he speaks into people's lives that are empty and void and without hope. Also, as in Genesis God created things that were good and in order, so too does he create people in Christ who are good and in order—whereas their lives were chaotic before they came to Christ. How good it is to know that God can make new creations out of nothing!

Mel Trotter (1870–1940) gained a deep appreciation of God's great creative ability. Before he became a Christian, Trotter's life was chaotic, with very little good to be found in it.

He was exposed to alcohol at an early age by his father, a bartender. Despite the earnest prayers of his mother, Mel followed his dad headlong into runaway drinking, smoking, and gambling. When he married, his habits reduced his family to poverty. To replenish his drinking money, Mel sold the family's possessions from under his wife's nose, and then he resorted to robbery to satisfy his craving for more booze.

One day he staggered home to find his wife holding the body of their young son, who had died suddenly. Over the boy's casket, Mel promised never to touch another drop of liquor as long as he lived, but his resolve barely lasted through the funeral.

Shortly after his son's death, Mel, at age twenty-seven, hopped on a freight car for Chicago. It was a bitterly cold January night, but his addiction to alcohol was stronger than his need for warmth, and he sold his shoes for some drinking money. After arriving in Chicago, he made his way to a bar on Clark Street, but he was soon evicted. He then headed toward Lake Michigan to commit suicide. Somehow, though, he took a detour and ended up at the Pacific Garden Mission. He was so drunk that the doorman had to prop him against a wall so he wouldn't fall off his chair during the evangelistic service.

Despite his inebriation, Trotter raised his hand for prayer at the close of the service and trusted Christ as his Savior. The change was instant and remarkable. Mel Trotter became a new creation, and 2 Corinthians 5:17 became his testimony verse. He began sharing it everywhere. His wife came to Chicago to join him, and in time Mel Trotter became one of the most sought-after preachers, speakers, soul-winners, and rescue workers in America.

"The greatest day I ever lived was the nineteenth of January, 1897," he once said, "when the Lord Jesus came into my life and saved me from sin. That transaction revolutionized my entire life. Don't call me a reformed drunkard. I am a transformed man, a child of God."

Mel Trotter had little if any good in his life, yet God spoke into the nothingness of Mel's life and transformed him, creating something good and in order. His life is an example of the profound renewal that takes place when a person becomes a new creation in Christ.

Destiny in Christ

The Old Testament theme of creation also adds to our understanding of our ultimate destiny as Christians. In Revelation 21:1–2, 5–7, the apostle John writes of the wonder of seeing the new creation in eternity:

> Then I saw a new heaven and a new earth, for the first heaven and the first earth had passed away, and there was no longer any sea. I saw the Holy City, the New Jerusalem, coming down out of heaven from God, prepared as a bride beautifully dressed for her husband. . . . He who was seated on the throne said, "I am making everything new!" Then he said, "Write this down, for these words are trustworthy and true." He said to me: "It is done. I am the Alpha and the Omega, the Beginning and the End. To him who is thirsty I will give to drink without cost from the spring of the water of life. He who overcomes will inherit all this, and I will be his God and he will be my son."

This passage makes much more sense when we think of it in terms of Genesis 1–2. The vocabulary found in both passages is similar. The phrase "a new heaven and a new earth" is closely related to the "heaven and the earth" that God created. The Greek translation of Genesis uses, in fact, the same words for *heaven (ouranos)* and *earth (gē)* as are used in Revelation 21.

Some in our day believe that heaven will be incredibly boring. Who could possibly enjoy an eternity spent walking on golden streets, playing a harp, and worshipping God? Others think of heaven as something they want to avoid for as long as possible. Even many longstanding Christians feel this way.

As the story goes, in one church a pastor was talking about going to heaven. In his message he said, "How many of you would like to go to heaven tonight?" Every hand went up except for that of a little boy in the balcony. The pastor tried again, "How many of you would like to go to heaven?" Every hand raised, except one—a little fellow's in the balcony. So the pastor said to him, "Son, don't you want to go to heaven?" The little boy replied, "Yeah, *someday,* but I thought you were gettin' up a load right now."[12]

Remembering Genesis 1–2 can help us appreciate our wonderful future. As in Genesis 1–2, God will create everything in the new heaven and earth. He will create it good and in order. At the beginning of time, the created world was magnificent, and in the future, the new world will be no less magnificent. The earth was created for pleasure and rest, and the new earth will be created for greater pleasure and rest in a future that will never end. When we as Christians think of our destiny in light of God's first creation—its greatness, complexity, and diversity—we can anticipate an even greater *new* creation of tremendous possibilities and potential.

Far from being bored, we will see the new creation with renewed vision, as if the scales have fallen off our eyes and we're seeing everything for the first time in all its brilliance. Perhaps our experience will be like that of William Dyke, a young man who became blind at the age of ten. Despite this handicap, he grew to be intelligent, witty, and handsome. While attending graduate school in England, Dyke met the daughter of an English admiral. The two soon became engaged. Although he had never seen her, Dyke loved his fiancée very much. Shortly before the wedding, at the admiral's insistence, Dyke submitted to special treatment for his loss of sight. Hoping against hope that the procedure would work, he wanted the gauze removed from his eyes during the wedding ceremony so that the first thing he saw would be the face of his wife. As the bride came down the aisle, Dyke's father, not knowing if the operation had been successful, started unwinding the gauze from around his son's head and eyes. When the bandage was completely removed, William Dyke looked into the face of his bride for the first time. "You are more beautiful than I ever imagined," he said. So, too, will be the beauty, the greatness, and the goodness of the new creation.[13]

So, too, the "first impression" we have of God in the Bible—as the Creator—provides a baseline for understanding his character and our world. Everything was created by God, in all its wonderful complexity. It was spoken into existence by his word, it was good and ordered, and it pointed to the Christian's ultimate resting with him.

This "impression" of God is not confined to the book of Genesis. It runs throughout the Old Testament and forward into the New Testament. There, it informs our understanding of who Jesus is, our identity (if we're Christians) as new creations in Christ, and our ultimate destiny in the new heavens and new earth.

Robert Murray McCheyne captures a wonderful glimpse of the future in a hymn he wrote based on the picture of creation found in Genesis:

> When this passing world is done,
> When has sunk yon glaring sun,
> When we stand with Christ in glory,
> Looking o'er life's finished story,
> Then, Lord, shall I fully know,
> Not till then, how much I owe.
>
> When I stand before the throne,
> Dressed in beauty not my own,
> When I see Thee as Thou art,
> Love Thee with unsinning heart,
> Then, Lord, shall I fully know,
> Not till then, how much I owe.

When the praise of heaven I hear,
Loud as thunders to the ear,
Loud as many waters' noise,
Sweet as harp's melodious voice,
Then, Lord, shall I fully know,
Not till then, how much I owe.

Even on earth, as through a glass,
Darkly, let Thy glory pass;
Make forgiveness feel so sweet;
Make Thy Spirit's help so meet;
Even on earth, Lord, make me know
Something of how much I owe.[14]

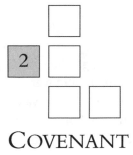

2

COVENANT

God's Promises Are Forever

The Old Covenant is revealed in the New, and the New Covenant is veiled in the Old.

—Saint Augustine

Lord, I am no longer my own, but yours. Put me to what you will, rank me with whom you will. Let me be employed by you or laid aside for you, exalted for you or brought low by you. Let me have all things, let me have nothing. I freely and heartily yield all things to your pleasure and disposal. And now, O glorious and blessed God, Father, Son, and Holy Spirit, You are mine and I am yours. So be it. Amen.

—John Wesley

Off the northwestern coast of Scotland stands a group of five hundred rugged islands called the Hebrides. In 1949, a fifty-year-old man named Duncan Campbell left the Scottish mainland to preach in the towns and villages on the Isle of Lewis, the largest of the Hebrides islands. During Campbell's itinerant ministry there, a revival swept the island that is talked about to this day. Campbell later recalled that, during those years, one could stop any passerby and find that he or she was thinking about God and the state of his or her soul.

Despite the amazing progress that Campbell made in spreading the gospel, one small town remained indifferent, a town named Arnol. Finding little response there to his preaching, Campbell invited a small group of concerned townsmen to join him for a prayer meeting. When they had assembled, he asked the local blacksmith to lead them in prayer.

"O God," said the blacksmith, "You made a promise to pour water upon him that is thirsty and floods upon the dry ground. Lord, it's not happening. I don't know how the others here stand, but Lord if I know anything about my own heart, I stand before Thee as an empty vessel. O Lord, Your honor is at stake, and I now challenge you to fulfill your covenant engagement and do what you have promised to do."

At that moment, the house began to tremble and shake. Someone whispered to Duncan, "An earth tremor." Duncan replied, "Yes," but his mind was thinking of Acts 4:31, when "after they [had] prayed, the place where they were meeting was shaken. And they were all filled with the Holy Spirit and spoke the word of God boldly."

When Duncan Campbell walked from the church, he found the whole village "alive with the awareness of God." From that moment, a mighty awakening happened that is spoken of in Scotland today as the Arnol revival.

The Arnol revival was dramatic in several respects, not the least of which was Duncan Campbell's desire to preach the good news of Jesus Christ in the Hebrides. The earth tremor and the outpouring of the Spirit that followed the prayer service were certainly remarkable as well. But perhaps the most astonishing aspect of the Arnol revival was the faith-filled prayer of the blacksmith. This humble, hardworking man, trusting in the "covenant engagement" that God made with his people, prayed that God would fulfill his promises. Clearly, the blacksmith, Duncan Campbell, and many others on the Isle of Lewis had a great trust in the God who honors covenants.[1]

In contrast to the Christians on the Isle of Lewis, many Christians today are unfamiliar with the concept of a covenant. Certainly, some Christians attend churches that have the word *covenant* in their names. Occasionally, a Christian teacher may refer to the idea of a covenant in a message or a Bible study. But many Christians are unaware that a covenant exists between God and them.

This chapter, then, explores the idea and nature of covenants in the Bible. First, *covenant* will be defined, and then some significant covenants in the Old Testament will be explored, as well as how the idea of covenant comes to fruition in the New Testament. As many theologians have noted, the reality of our covenant with God is one of the more significant truths expressed in Scripture.[2] The term appears more than three hundred times in some versions of the Bible. It is used nearly thirty times in the New Testament, including such notable instances as the Last Supper and Paul's statements about his new covenant ministry. Examples of covenants between human beings can be found in the Bible, but Scripture is most interested in the covenants between God and mankind.

WHAT IS A COVENANT?

Before considering specific places in the Old Testament where covenants are found, it is important to start with a basic understanding of the word *covenant*. A number of definitions can be found in a standard English dictionary, including "an agreement, usually a formal agreement between two or more persons." Synonyms for *covenant* include *pact, treaty,* or *contract. Covenant* can also be used in legal circles as an incidental clause in an agreement. Some churches today use *covenant* to refer to an agreement between members to support each other.

The word for *covenant* in the original languages of the Bible, however, conveys an intensified sense of "commitment," over and above that which might be found in a simple "agreement," legal, formal, or otherwise. In the Old Testament, the word translated as "covenant" is the Hebrew word *berith.* Various root words have been suggested for *berith,* including a derivation from a Hebrew word meaning "to eat bread with," which in ancient times was a sign of commitment. Thus, a sense of *intimacy* is established. Others associate *covenant* with the Akkadian preposition *běrit,* which means "between." *Běrit* may also be derived from an Akkadian word that means "bond" or "fetter." The idea of covenant is sometimes connected with the Hebrew word *hesed,* a word that means "steadfast love" or "loyal love," and is regularly used to describe God's devotion and commitment to his people. The term used for *covenant* in the Greek New Testament is *diathēkē,* meaning "settlement," "treaty," "will," or "testament." All of these words further enhance the sense of dedication found in the concept of covenant.

From this brief background, we can derive a working definition for the word *covenant. A covenant is a formal agreement between two parties characterized by dedication and commitment.*

COVENANT IN THE OLD TESTAMENT[3]

Although the Old Testament includes examples of covenants made between people, this section focuses specifically on covenants between God and his people.[4] Key ingredients from these Old Testament covenants add to the appreciation of covenants found in the New Testament.

God's Covenant with Noah

The first explicit mention of the term *covenant* in the Old Testament is found in Genesis 6.[5] In Genesis 6:18, God says to Noah, "I will establish my covenant with you, and you will enter the ark—you and your sons and your wife and your sons' wives with you." God promises to make this covenant immediately before the great flood that will kill everyone on the earth (Gen. 7–9).

What leads God to make this covenant is Noah's righteous character, which he is displaying in an evil world. God knows that the world is filled with great evil, and thus he announces to Noah that he is going to destroy everything in the earth with floodwaters. God considers Noah, however, to be a righteous man and thus promises to keep him safe despite the great flood. He commands Noah to make an ark and enter it so that he and his family may be preserved. When Noah emerges from the ark following the flood, God formalizes the covenant:

> Then God said to Noah and to his sons with him: "I now establish my covenant with you and with your descendants after you and with every living creature that was with you—the birds, the livestock and all the wild animals, all those that came out of the ark with you—every living creature on earth. I establish my covenant with you: Never again will all life be cut off by the waters of a flood; never again will there be a flood to destroy the earth."
>
> And God said, "This is the sign of the covenant I am making between me and you and every living creature with you, a cov-

enant for all generations to come: I have set my rainbow in the clouds, and it will be the sign of the covenant between me and the earth. Whenever I bring clouds over the earth and the rainbow appears in the clouds, I will remember my covenant between me and you and all living creatures of every kind. Never again will the waters become a flood to destroy all life. Whenever the rainbow appears in the clouds, I will see it and remember the everlasting covenant between God and all living creatures of every kind on the earth.

So God said to Noah, "This is the sign of the covenant I have established between me and all life on the earth." (Gen. 9:8–17)

This covenant has notable features that illustrate important elements of biblical covenants. First is a promise made by God, in this case vowing never again to flood the world. This promise is an everlasting promise (cf. Gen. 8:22).

A second element is the presence of a sacrifice. Before God institutes the covenant, Noah offers a sacrifice (Gen. 8:20), and this righteous act pleases the Lord, leading to the establishment of the covenant (v. 21).

A third element of God's covenant with Noah is the giving of a sign to remind people that the covenant is reliable. The sign of the rainbow is such a significant part of this covenant that some people even call it the "rainbow covenant." To this day, a rainbow, in fact, reminds us of God's promise. In countries that receive a lot of rain, such as Ireland and Scotland,[6] some people place a picture of a rainbow in a spot where it can be seen often as a reminder of God's faithfulness. The sign of the rainbow gives them hope that, even on the rainiest of days, the rain will eventually end. The rainbow, then, is the assurance that God's agreement with Noah is still in effect.

God's Covenant with Abraham

The next covenant found in the Old Testament is that between God and Abraham (Gen. 15; 17).[7] The importance of this covenant is evident in the repeated references to it in both the Old and New Testaments. God's covenant with Abraham includes the same three essential elements

Rainbow over the Presbyterian Church of Dún Laoghaire in Dún Laoghaire, County Dublin, Ireland. (Photograph courtesy of Tara Smith.)

found in his covenant with Noah—a promise, a sacrifice, and a sign—as well as a few other characteristic features of biblical covenants.

The promise in this covenant is threefold: land, seed, and blessing. At the time that God called him, Abraham has neither land nor children (Gen. 12). It seems impossible from a human perspective that Abraham would ever have a child—he was seventy-five years old and his wife was in her late sixties. Nevertheless, God promises Abraham that he will, indeed, have land, children, and a blessing.

In Genesis 15 and 17, God restates these promises, but this time he declares them to be part of his "covenant" with Abraham (cf. v. 18). God promises Abraham many children—and then illustrates how many by drawing Abraham's gaze up to the heavens (v. 5).[8]

If you have ever been away from the city on a clear night, perhaps out in the wilderness or on top of a mountain, you have no doubt seen the sky filled with stars. Without any lights to interfere with his view, Abraham likely saw thousands upon thousands—perhaps millions—of stars in the sky. What a tremendous thrill it must have been for this childless old man to imagine that his offspring could be as numerous as the stars.

In Genesis 15:18, God promises to Abraham a land as well:

On that day the LORD made a covenant with Abram and said, "To your descendants I give this land, from the river of Egypt to the great river, the Euphrates—the land of the Kenites, Kenizzites, Kadmonites, Hittites, Perizzites, Rephaites, Amorites, Canaanites, Girgashites and Jebusites."

These promises are restated as a covenant in Genesis 17:1–8, everlasting promises from God to Abraham.

God's covenant with Abraham also included a sacrifice. Before God initiates the covenant, Abraham brings a heifer, a goat, a ram, a dove, and a pigeon to be slaughtered. He cuts them in two and arranges them opposite each other. Although he does not divide the birds in two, he kills them and lays them opposite each other, leaving all the sacrificial animals like this so that the covenant can be ratified. When God ratified the covenant, he was in effect saying to Abraham, "May I be made like these animals if I do not fulfill the demands of the covenant." This event of sacrifice was thus an important part of the covenant promises that God gave to Abraham.[9]

The sign associated with God's covenant with Abraham was the sign of circumcision: "You are to undergo circumcision, and it will be the sign of the covenant between me and you" (Gen. 18:11). The difference between this sign and the sign of the rainbow is that circumcision was an obligation that Abraham must perform. He was to circumcise every male in his family on the eighth day after birth, and any uncircumcised males would be cut off from the covenant (17:14).

This distinctive feature of God's covenant with Abraham introduced a new essential element to the concept of covenant in the Old Testament, namely obligations or commands that God's people must keep. Without Abraham's obedience to God's commands, there could be no blessing from God or fellowship with him.

A second distinguishing feature of this covenant is that God introduced himself prior to the covenant. In Genesis 15:1, God appears before Abraham, declaring his character and describing himself as Abraham's shield and very great reward. In 17:1–2, God again appears before Abraham, saying,

"I am God Almighty; walk before me and be blameless. I will confirm my covenant between me and you and will greatly increase your numbers." This declaration of the character of God, made prior to ratifying a covenant, was an important aspect of covenants that would continue to be found throughout the Old Testament.

A similar practice of the stronger party introducing itself to the weaker was found in ancient covenants among the Hittites of Asia Minor, the Ugarits of the Mediterranean, the Mari people of the Euphrates, and the Assyrians of Mesopotamia.[10]

God's Covenant with Moses

The next significant covenant in the Old Testament is that of God with Moses, which was enacted at Mount Sinai following the Exodus from Egypt. God proposes the covenant in Exodus 19:3–6 when he speaks directly with Moses on the mountain. A list of commands (most notably the Ten Commandments) and promises (Exod. 20–23) ensues. After God establishes the conditions and promises, the covenant is ratified (Exod. 24).

As in the covenant with Abraham, God's character is set forward at the beginning of the transaction. In Exodus 20:2–6, God declares who he is to the people of Israel:

> I am the LORD your God, who brought you out of Egypt, out of the land of slavery. You shall have no other gods before me. You shall not make for yourself an idol in the form of anything in heaven above or on the earth beneath or in the waters below. You shall not bow down to them or worship them; for I, the LORD your God, am a jealous God, punishing the children for the sin of the fathers to the third and fourth generation of those who hate me, but showing love to a thousand generations of those who love me and keep my commandments.

God's character is then further portrayed in the first three of the Ten Commandments. He is the great redeemer, the holy one, the one worthy of worship, the jealous one, the disciplinarian, and the loyal one.

As with the Abrahamic covenant, certain commandments must be kept. Beyond the Ten Commandments, this covenant is filled with other commandments regarding servants, physical injuries, theft, property damage, honesty, civil and religious observations, Sabbaths, feasts, and the conquest of the Promised Land (Exod. 21:1–23:33). If God's people keep these laws, their relationship with God will be positive.

Consistent with his covenants with Noah and Abraham, God makes promises to his people. If Israel will keep the commands that God has given, they will receive certain things in return. Although Israel's inheritance of the Promised Land is never in doubt, their status in the land depends on their obedience. Notice the conditions that God established at the beginning of this covenant:

> Then Moses went up to God, and the LORD called to him from the mountain and said, "This is what you are to say to the house of Jacob and what you are to tell the people of Israel: 'You yourselves have seen what I did to Egypt, and how I carried you on eagles' wings and brought you to myself. Now if you obey me fully and keep my covenant, then out of all nations you will be my treasured possession. Although the whole earth is mine, you will be for me a kingdom of priests and a holy nation.' These are the words you are to speak to the Israelites." (Exod. 19:3–6)

If the people obey him, God will make them his "treasured possession, a kingdom of priests, and a holy nation." Blessing will result from obedience.

The Mosaic covenant also included sacrifices. In Exodus 24:4–8, Moses erects an altar at the foot of the mountain and sets up twelve stone pillars, representing the twelve tribes of Israel. After sacrificing several young bulls, he reads the laws and promises of the covenant, and all of Israel verbally agrees, saying, "We will do everything the Lord has said; we will obey" (v. 7). Moses then takes the blood of the bulls and sprinkles it on the people, thereby representing all of Israel as taking part in these sacrifices before the Lord.

The final component of the covenant is the sign showing that it is in effect:

Then the LORD said to Moses, "Say to the Israelites, 'You must observe my Sabbaths. This will be a sign between me and you for the generations to come, so you may know that I am the LORD who makes you holy. Observe the Sabbath because it is holy to you. Anyone who desecrates it must be put to death; whoever does any work on that day must be cut off from his people. For six days, work is to be done, but the seventh day is a Sabbath of rest, holy to the LORD. Whoever does any work on the Sabbath day must be put to death. The Israelites are to observe the Sabbath, celebrating it for the generations to come as a lasting covenant. It will be a sign between me and the Israelites forever, for in six days the LORD made the heavens and the earth, and on the seventh day he abstained from work and rested." (Exod. 31:12–17)

The Sabbath is the unique sign of this covenant. In later years, the prophets would point to the absence of this sign as an indication of the spiritual poverty of God's people (e.g., Jer. 17:19–27; Ezek. 20:12–14; cf. Exod. 20:8–11).

The Mosaic covenant between God and the people of Israel was renewed many times in many places. It was renewed after the people of Israel sinned by worshipping the golden calf (Exod. 34). It was renewed again on the plains of Moab after the Israelites had wandered in the desert for forty years (Deut. 29). It was revived at Shechem in the days of Joshua (Josh. 24). Various kings also renewed the covenant—King Jehoiada (2 Kings 11), King Hezekiah (2 Chron. 29), and King Josiah (2 Kings 23). It is one of the more significant covenants of the Bible, and it is one that will be explicitly addressed in the New Testament.

The covenant had to be renewed so many times throughout Israel's history because the people persisted in making partial commitments to God. Halfway commitments do not work with a God who makes covenants.

In more recent history, an entire church denomination grew up based on partial commitments to God. The Half-Way Covenant Church became popular in seventeenth-century Massachusetts as an alternative to the strictures of Puritanism. The original settlers of Massachusetts had a strong faith that caused them to sail across the Atlantic Ocean and settle in the New World. They were hoping to find freedom to worship and also to establish a pure community of like-minded people, a "city on a hill" (in accordance with Matt. 5:14). The succeeding generations, however, found that their convictions toward God had cooled, which led to the Half-Way Covenant.

The original qualifications for membership in churches in Massachusetts called for a person to affirm a conversion experience. Many people had been baptized as children but had never had a conversion experience. As a result, those without conversion experience failed to qualify for membership in the church. Instead of their being completely ostracized, however, they were formed into the Half-Way Covenant, in a sense allowing them halfway into the church. They could not vote or receive Communion, but they could have their children baptized. It appears that from their vantage point, being half a member was better than not being a member at all.

Although this compromise avoided a dilemma for the Puritans, the Half-Way Covenant did not work. Along with other factors, it eventually led to the dissolution of Puritan society. In God's economy, halfway covenants will never work. When God makes a covenant, he asks for full obedience. Halfway obedience to the covenant that Moses and the people of Israel made with God eventually led to their ruin and exile (Cf. 2 Kings 17:1–41; 24:18–25:21).

God's Covenant with David

Many years after his covenant with Moses, God made another covenant with King David, the second king of Israel. David, who composed many of the psalms that are recorded in the book of Psalms, was generally known as a righteous king, save for his adultery with Bathsheba. David was at a high point in his career and in his relationship with God at the time of the foundation of this covenant.

This covenant is preceded by David's motivation to please God. In 2 Samuel 7, David proposes to build a house for the Lord. He observes that, although he dwells in a great palace, the presence of God, as symbolized by the ark of the *Mosaic* covenant, remains in a tent (v. 2). God appears to Nathan the prophet, God's spokesman at that time, and refuses to allow David to build the Lord's temple. God wanted instead David's son Solomon to build the temple (2 Sam. 7:13). Instead of allowing David to build a house for the Lord, the Lord promises to build David's "house."

As in previous covenants, the character of God is displayed before the covenant is made:

> Now then, tell my servant David, "This is what the LORD Almighty says: I took you from the pasture and from following the flock to be ruler over my people Israel. I have been with you wherever you have gone, and I have cut off all your enemies from before you." (2 Sam. 7:8–9)

God reminds David that it is he who led David to the position of king, and that God has been with David and has been his great protector.

The covenant with David also contains many promises. David is promised a great name, victory over his enemies, a special relationship with God, and a special line that will receive this inheritance (2 Sam. 7:9–16; cf. Ps. 89:23, 26).

Many strong similarities are evident between this covenant and the covenant made with Abraham. Promises of a "great name" (Gen. 12:2), victory over enemies (Gen. 22:17), a special relationship with God (Gen. 17:7–8), and a special line that will receive this inheritance (Gen. 21:12) harken back to the promises given to Abraham. A further similarity between these two covenants is the requirement that the descendants of Abraham and David keep God's laws (Gen. 18:19; 2 Sam. 7:14). Finally, both covenants promise that a special descendant will lead to international blessing (Gen. 22:18; 2 Sam. 7:12–14; Ps. 72:12).

God's covenant with David is likely a continuation and expansion of his covenant with Abraham,[11] which may account for the lack of an explicit sign. Neither circumcision, the Sabbath, nor the rainbow are present in the Davidic covenant, nor does it contain specific commandments.

The Promised New Covenant

In the book of Jeremiah, the "new covenant" is first put clearly on display.[12] God's people have failed miserably to keep the Mosaic covenant, and as a consequence, Jeremiah prophesies doom and gloom. The prophecies of Jeremiah are, in fact, so gloomy that the prophet is often called "the weeping prophet" or the "prophet of loneliness" (Jer. 9:1; 13:17; 16:2). For more than forty years, he endures persecution while he proclaims judgment on God's people in the land of Judah.[13]

Then, as his countrymen were being deported to Babylon because of their disobedience to God, Jeremiah offers a bright ray of hope, the promise of a new covenant:

> "The time is coming," declares the LORD,
>   "when I will make a new covenant
> with the house of Israel
>   and with the house of Judah.
> It will not be like the covenant
>   I made with their forefathers
> when I took them by the hand
>   to lead them out of Egypt,
> because they broke my covenant,
>   though I was a husband to them,"
>   declares the LORD.
> "This is the covenant I will make with the
>   house of Israel
>   after that time," declares the LORD.
> "I will put my law in their minds
>   and write it on their hearts.
> I will be their God,
>   and they will be my people.
> No longer will a man teach his neighbor,
>   or a man his brother, saying, 'Know the LORD,'
> because they will all know me,
>   from the least of them to the greatest,"
>   declares the LORD.
> "For I will forgive their wickedness
>   and I will remember their sins no more."
>   (Jer. 31:31–34)

The new covenant contains many of the same elements as former covenants. As with the Mosaic covenant, an aspect of law is found, although this time the law will be within their minds and hearts (Jer. 31:33). Also, God's people will possess special blessings. In this case, they will have a special, committed, covenant relationship with God, who says, "I will be their God, and they shall be my people" (v. 33; cf. Exod. 19:4–7). Although the new covenant signals a break with the past, "the newness of the new covenant must not stand in absolute contradiction to the previous covenants," writes O. P. Robertson. "A factor of continuity must be recognized."[14]

A number of features are, however, truly new in the new covenant. God will now, for example, put his law in people's minds and write it on their hearts (Jer. 31:33). Previously, the law was given for people to read, but in the new covenant God's law will be part of the Israelites' heartfelt living as their hearts are transformed. A second new feature is the complete removal of sin (v. 34). Previously, a yearly atonement for sin had to be offered by a priest (cf. Lev. 16). In the new covenant, the atonement for sin is complete, so that God will no longer remember sin. A third feature of the new covenant is the intimate relationship it affords with God. Previously, every person had to be taught about the Lord. In the new covenant, everyone will know the Lord, "from the least of them to the greatest" (Jer. 31:34). All of these promises speak of the greatness and newness of this covenant.

The covenants presented in the Old Testament are not static—they develop. The covenant with David develops the covenant with Abraham. The new covenant prophesied in Jeremiah's time develops and then supersedes the covenant with Moses.

COVENANT IN THE NEW TESTAMENT

With an understanding of covenants in the Old Testament, portions of the New Testament now become illuminated. The New Testament, for example, reveals that Jesus is the fulfillment of the Old Testament covenants. Other passages of the New Testament indicate that Jesus is also the initiator of the new covenant, which was prophesied by Jeremiah. This new covenant with Jesus is superior to and surpasses the earlier covenants.

Covenant in the Gospels

Although the word *covenant* does not appear in the Gospels until the time that Jesus institutes the Lord's Supper, covenantal ideas are found in many places. The Gospels repeatedly present Jesus as the climax of the Old Testament promises of the covenant. He, for example, is the fulfillment of the promises made in previous covenants, such as the Abrahamic covenant. Matthew introduces this idea by tracing Jesus' genealogy directly back to Abraham: "A record of the genealogy of Jesus Christ the son of David, the son of Abraham" (Matt. 1:1). Matthew 1:17 concludes the genealogy of Jesus by saying, "Thus there were fourteen generations in all from Abraham to David, fourteen from David to the exile to Babylon, and fourteen from the exile to Christ." By tracing Jesus' origin to Abraham—and doing so twice within his genealogy—Matthew points to Jesus as a fulfillment of the covenant with Abraham.

Other places in the Gospels indicate that Jesus is the promised seed of Abraham. Mary rejoices about this promised seed after hearing the good news from the angel that she would bear the Christ child. During her song of praise, she credits God with fulfilling the promises he made to Abraham (Luke 1:55). A few verses later, Zechariah, the father of John the Baptist, also rejoices in the birth of Jesus, referring to him as the seed of Abraham (vv. 72–73). In the gospel of John, Jesus himself, after a long discourse about who Abraham is, points out that he is the seed in which Abraham rejoiced (John 8:56).

Jesus is seen, then, to be not only a fulfillment of the covenant given to Abraham, but he is also portrayed as a fulfillment of the promise given to David. His royal connection to David, spoken of in 2 Samuel 7, is established in the opening genealogy of Matthew, in the same verses that declare him to be the seed of Abraham (Matt.1:1, 17). Other passages, too, refer to Jesus as a royal son. In his song anticipating the birth of Jesus, Zechariah states that Jesus is the horn of the house of David (Luke 1:69–70). Later in Jesus' ministry, a Canaanite woman, whose daughter needs healing, associates Jesus with King David: "Lord, Son of David," she calls out to Jesus, "have mercy on me!" (Matt. 15:22).

Not only are promises from previous covenants fulfilled in Jesus, but he is also the one in whom the commands to Moses are fulfilled and surpassed. Of the many passages in the Gospels that speak of this fulfillment,[15] Matthew 22:34–40 presents a strong example. The Sadducees and Pharisees question Jesus concerning the greatest commandment. He replies that the greatest commandment is to love the Lord with all of your heart, soul, and mind, and the second greatest commandment is to love your neighbor as yourself. He then relates his answer to the obligations that were given in the covenant with Moses: "All the Law and the Prophets hang on these two commandments" (v. 40). By his answer, Jesus shows that his commands, rather than annulling and surpassing the previous commands, fulfill them.

As Old Testament covenants promised God's withdrawing of blessing for disobedience, so too is rejection by Jesus the ultimate curse for disobedience. Many places in the Gospels refer to those who do not believe as being cursed for their unbelief,[16] but perhaps the most striking statement of the rejection of disobedient Israel is in the parable of the tenants (Matt. 21:33–46; Mark 12:1–12; Luke 20:9–19). Jesus relates this parable in the temple courts, surrounded by the Jewish leaders and the masses. The parable is about a man who owns and plants a vineyard, which he then rents to some farmers to take care of. After allowing the farmers to tend the vineyard, he sends servants to collect his share of the fruit. Instead of handing over the owner's share, the tenants seize the servants and treat them poorly, beating one and killing another. The owner then hopes that the tenants will respect his son. When he sends his son, however, the tenants seize him and kill him.

After telling the parable, Jesus asks the people what the owner of the vineyard should do. They reply that the farmer ought to terminate his relationship with the tenants and give the vineyard to someone else. At this point, Jesus concludes the parable by pointing to the Jewish leaders who reject him, stating in plain terms that condemnation will fall upon them: "Therefore I tell you that the kingdom of God will be taken away from you and given to a people who will produce its fruit. He who falls on this stone will be broken to pieces, but he on whom it falls will be crushed" (Matt. 21:43–44). By his statement, Jesus shows that rejection of him surpasses the curses of previous covenants.

Jesus also initiates the blessings of the new covenant, which are identical to the blessings prophesied by Jeremiah. Jesus is the one through whom salvation will come to all of the nations.[17] He is also the one through whom people receive the promised forgiveness of sins. These ideas can be found in many passages in the Gospels.[18]

The new covenant relationship can be seen to be formally initiated at the Last Supper when Jesus presents the cup to his disciples saying, "This cup is the new covenant in my blood; do this whenever you drink it, in remembrance of me" (Luke 22:20; 1 Cor. 11:25; cf. Matt. 26:28; Mark 14:24). When this act is seen in relation to Jesus' overall ministry, it contains many covenantal elements. For example, just as God presented his character before initiating the Old Testament covenants, so too Jesus presented himself to his disciples for three years in his public ministry before the Last Supper. During his ministry, Jesus gave his disciples a significant number of commands, a second component of covenants. And as prophesied of the new covenant, he presented the promise of forgiveness of sins (Matt. 26:28). Consistent with the terms of previous covenants, Jesus sealed the new covenant with a sacrifice, his own sacrifice. Finally, the new covenant has a distinguishing sign, the eating of a meal. This sign is to be enacted regularly among Christ's followers reminding them of the new covenant relationship that now exists (cf. 1 Cor. 11:23–26).[19]

Reading the Gospels in light of Old Testament passages about covenants reveals that the Gospels are substantially influenced by Old Testament covenant ideas. Jesus is the fulfillment of the covenants of Abraham and David. He is also the initiator of the eagerly anticipated new covenant foretold by Jeremiah.

Covenant in Paul's Writings

Old Testament ideas about covenants also influence the reading of Paul's letters. Paul, in fact, used the word *covenant* nine times in his letters (Rom. 9:4; 11:27; 1 Cor. 11:25; 2 Cor. 3:6, 14; Gal. 3:15, 17; 4:24; Eph. 2:12). Most of these references are to Old Testament covenants in effect for the Jewish people. In these instances, Paul's letters affirm the durability of the arrangements that God has made.

Paul also speaks in his letters of the great blessings that come to God's people as a result. Consider Ephesians 2:11–12, for example. The passage is found in a section of Paul's writings that declares the blessing of being in Christ. These blessings are now available to Gentiles and Jews. Before coming to Christ, however, the Gentiles did not have the blessing of a committed covenant relationship with God:

> Therefore, remember that formerly you who are Gentiles by birth and called "uncircumcised" by those who call themselves "the circumcision" (that done in the body by the hands of men)— remember that at that time you were separate from Christ, excluded from citizenship in Israel and foreigners to the covenants of the promise, without hope and without God in the world.

The most significant mention of covenant in Paul's writings occurs in 2 Corinthians 3, where it speaks explicitly of the new covenant. This passage states that Paul's new-covenant ministry is superior to any previous covenant arrangement. The allusions to the new covenant from Jeremiah 31 are apparent. Not only does this 2 Corinthians passage specifically use the words *new covenant* (3:6), ideas from Jeremiah 31 are also found in 2 Corinthians 3:3 and 3:6:

> You show that you are a letter from Christ, the result of our ministry, written not with ink but with the Spirit of the living God, not on tablets of stone but on tablets of human hearts. . . . He has made us competent as ministers of a new covenant—not of the letter but of the Spirit; for the letter kills, but the Spirit gives life.

The image of the Holy Spirit writing on the hearts of God's people in a permanent way is clearly reminiscent of the new covenant prophecy in Jeremiah 31.[20]

With the backdrop of Jeremiah 31 in view, the greatness of Paul's new-covenant ministry is displayed. Because Paul's message, the message of the new covenant, was announced from the time of Jeremiah, it is not just one more message in the world. Instead, Paul's message surpasses even that of the prophets of the past, and also Moses, who brought letters and stone tablets to God's people.

Paul's ministry, then, offers a ministry to people's hearts. His message is one of life, permanence, and the Spirit of God, just as Jeremiah prophesied. His message speaks of a covenant that is superior to the other covenants, even the covenant of Moses written on stone tablets (2 Cor. 3:7–18).

Letters on stone tablets represent an authority that is often rebelled against. How much better it is for laws of obedience to be written on human hearts.[21]

Covenant in Hebrews

The influence of Old Testament ideas about covenants extends beyond the Gospels and Paul's letters. These ideas also influence the book of Hebrews, which has the highest concentration of covenant ideas in the New Testament. The term *covenant* is used sixteen times, and the letter ends with a benediction that mentions the word *covenant* (cf. Heb. 13:20).

The influence of covenant ideas in Hebrews is likely due to the Jewish audience to whom the letter was written. They would have been familiar with all the nuances of the Old Testament covenants. In a letter in which the writer is trying to persuade Jewish Christians not to desert their Christian faith, the writer establishes the new covenant in Christ as superior to the older covenants that the Jews respected.

Over and over again, the writer to the Hebrews returns to the idea that Jesus is superior to the covenant made with Moses (also called "old covenant" in Hebrews). Hebrews 7:22, for instance, states, "Jesus has become the guarantee of a better covenant"; 8:6 states, "But the ministry Jesus has received is as superior to theirs as the covenant of which he is mediator is superior to the old one, and it is founded on better promises"; 12:23–24 says, ". . . You have come to God, the judge of all men, to the spirits of righteous men made perfect, to Jesus the mediator of a new covenant, and to the sprinkled blood that speaks a better word than the blood of Abel."

The covenant in Jesus is further superior to the old covenant because it is identified as the new covenant prophesied by Jeremiah. The writer to the Hebrews makes this identification explicit by twice citing excerpts from Jeremiah 31:31–34 (Heb. 8:8–12; 10:16–17). It is exceptionally rare for a New Testament writer to cite the same passage twice in the same book. Clearly, then, the writer to the Hebrews is trying to drive home the point that it is Jesus who gives us the new covenant, which is superior to the previous covenants.

Although the new covenant is superior to previous covenants, the central element—that of sacrifice—remains the same. Just as the Old Testament covenants were sealed by a blood sacrifice, so too the blood of Jesus Christ initiates the new covenant. Hebrews 9:14 says, "How much more, then, will the blood of Christ who through the eternal Spirit offered himself unblemished to God, cleanse our consciences from acts that lead to death, so that we may serve the living God." The precious blood of the Son of God was the critical element that initiated this long-ago-promised covenant.

The new covenant, then, hearkens back to the old covenants in that it is a formal agreement characterized by God's dedication and commitment. Begun by the sacrifice of Jesus Christ, it involves commands that his people are to follow, and God's promise of forgiveness of sins. The sign of the covenant is the Lord's Supper.

Cecil Frances Alexander, writing in the 1800s, captures the essence of the new covenant—Christ's great sacrifice, the promises he makes to Christians, and the obligation for obedience—in a great old hymn:

> There is a green hill far away,
> Without a city wall,
> Where the dear Lord was crucified,
> Who died to save us all.
>
> We may not know, we cannot tell
> What pains He had to bear;
> But we believe it was for us
> He hung and suffered there.
>
> He died that we might be forgiven,
> He died to make us good,
> That we might go at last to heaven,
> Saved by His precious blood.

There was no other good enough
To pay the price of sin;
He only could unlock the gate
Of heaven, and let us in.

O dearly, dearly has He loved,
And we must love Him too,
And trust in His redeeming blood,
And try His works to do.[22]

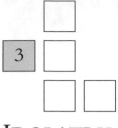

IDOLATRY

No Gods but God

> There is nothing so abominable in the eyes of God and of men as idolatry, whereby men render to the creature that honor which is due only to the Creator.
>
> —Blaise Pascal

> My sin was this, that not in him but in his creatures—myself and others—I sought for pleasures, honors, and truths, and so fell headlong into sorrows, confusions, errors.
>
> —Saint Augustine

According to the Westminster Shorter Catechism, "What is the chief end of man?"

"Man's chief end is to glorify God and to enjoy him forever."

Enjoying God for who he is has been the goal of God's people for centuries. That goal, however, has continually been challenged for many reasons.

One of those reasons is idolatry. From ancient times, God's people were influenced by the worship of idols by foreign nations. In fact, according to biblical scholars M. Halbertal and A. Margalit, "The central theological principle in the Bible is [the rejection of] idolatry."[1] Although the idols differed from time to time and place to place, both Old and New Testament authors argued against idolatry in the strongest of terms.

IDOLATRY IN THE OLD TESTAMENT

Idolatry was a perpetual problem for God's people. In the Old Testament, God's people were exposed to idols in the land of Egypt. Then, when they conquered the Promised Land, they came upon numerous idols in Canaan. Even after their kingdom had been established, they still encountered idols from neighboring cultures such as the Assyrians, Babylonians, and Philistines.[2] Knowing that his people would be tempted to worship idols, God prohibits them from doing so, for several reasons.

Idols Are Characteristic of Heathen Nations

First, worshipping idols is an activity characteristic of heathen nations who do not know God. The land of Egypt, where God's people lived for more than four hundred years before the Exodus, was a land of many gods, which are described as "detestable, filthy idols of wood and stone, of silver and gold" (Deut. 29:17). Moreover, the many nations in and around the Promised Land worshipped a multitude of gods—deities that were crafted in the shapes of bulls, mighty warriors, pillars, female figures, and other forms. These idols were usually made of gold, silver, and bronze, and had nothing to do with the one true God who had called his people to follow only him (cf. 5:6–7).

Identification with other gods, which was characteristic of other nations, was clearly a compromise for God's people, as seen in Ezekiel 20:32–33:

> You say, "We want to be like the nations, like the peoples of the world, who serve wood and stone." But what you have in mind will never happen. As surely as I live, declares the Sovereign LORD, I will rule over you with a mighty hand and an outstretched arm and with outpoured wrath.

According to Deuteronomy 8:19–20, following other gods will lead to the same fate suffered by foreign nations:

If you ever forget the LORD your God and follow other gods and worship and bow down to them, I testify against you today that you will surely be destroyed. Like the nations the LORD destroyed before you, so you will be destroyed for not obeying the LORD your God.

Even when God's people were separated from the Promised Land and sent into exile, they were not to worship idols. In Daniel 3, we are told that Shadrach, Meshach, and Abednego refused to bow down and worship the golden image that King Nebuchadnezzar forced all others to worship. Rather than bowing before this image, they chose instead to take a stand. As a consequence, they became known as young men who would not serve foreign gods (v. 12). Instead of worshipping the idols, they were willing to be thrown into a fiery furnace, stating boldly before the king,

O Nebuchadnezzar, we do not need to defend ourselves before you in this matter. If we are thrown into the blazing furnace, the God we serve is able to save us from it, and he will rescue us from your hand, O king. But even if he does not, we want you to know, O king, that we will not serve your gods or worship the image of gold you have set up. (Dan. 3:16–18)

In Daniel 6, Daniel himself refused to worship King Darius, the king of Babylon, and instead chose to be thrown into the lions' den. Like his friends, Daniel maintained his identity as a follower of God by not worshipping foreign gods.

Daniel, his three countrymen, as well as others, remembered that separation from idols and false gods was the first of the Ten Commandments. It was also a distinguishing characteristic for God's people: "I am the LORD your God who brought you out of Egypt, out of the land of slavery. You shall have no other gods before me" (Exod. 20:2–3).

Idolatry Offends a Deeply Committed God

God was deeply committed to his people and expected commitment from them in return. Little wonder, then, that the worship of idols was deeply offensive to him. The watchword of Israel's faith, the *Shema*, expresses the exclusive devotion that was to be found toward God: "Hear, O Israel: The LORD our God, the LORD is one. Love the LORD your God with all your heart, and with all your soul, and with all your strength" (Deut. 6:4–5).

The *Shema* was repeated many times daily by the Jews, recited early in the morning and again in the evening. Priests in the temple recited it even more often. Young Jewish boys were taught the first verse of the *Shema* from the time that they could speak. At the time of Christ, in the first century A.D., this confession of the Jewish faith, this declaration of full and exclusive devotion to God alone, was recited daily (cf. Mishnah, *Berakoth*, i.1).[3]

Such devotion to God was clearly appropriate, because God was clearly devoted to his people. The Bible, in fact, depicts God's devotion to Israel in the intimate terms used of a marriage. The Old Testament declares God as one who is married to his people. In a variety of places in the Prophets, especially Jeremiah, Ezekiel, and Hosea (Jer. 3:20; 31:32; Ezek. 16:32, 45; Hos. 2:2, 7, 16), God is called a husband to his people.

God thus experiences the emotions of betrayal when his people are disloyal and seek after other gods. The great hurt that God feels as a committed, loving husband is expressed in several places, including Jeremiah 3:20: "But like a woman unfaithful to her husband, so you have been unfaithful to me, O house of Israel, declares the LORD." Ezekiel 16:30–32 also describes the Lord's pain like that of a jilted lover:

How weak-willed you are, declares the Sovereign LORD, when you do all these things, acting like a brazen prostitute! When you built your mounds at the head of every street and made your lofty shrines in every public square, you were unlike a prostitute, because you scorned payment. You adulterous wife! You prefer strangers to your own husband!

Hosea 2 also reveals the deeply committed love of God for his people. In this passage, as in Jeremiah 3:20 and Ezekiel 16:30–32, God describes his people as an adulterous wife who has pursued other lovers, forgetting that God, her true husband, has provided all that she needs. Rather than disowning her, however, God's deep commitment will, Hosea proclaims, triumph. He will correct her by exposing her wrong ways and will then bring her back to himself so that she will call him "husband" once again. He will once more show love to the one called "not my loved one" so that she will say to God, "You are my God."

John Calvin in his *Institutes of the Christian Religion,* an important book on the basis of Protestant Christianity, had this to say regarding the deep commitment of the Lord as husband to his people:

> God very commonly takes on the character of a husband to us. . . . As he performs all the duties of a true and faithful husband, of us in return he demands love and conjugal chastity. That is, we are not to yield our souls to Satan, to lust, and to the filthy desires of the flesh, to be defiled by them. . . . The more holy and chaste a husband is, the more wrathful he becomes if he sees his wife inclining her heart to a rival. In like manner, the Lord, who has wedded us to himself in truth (cf. Hosea 2:19–20), manifests the most burning jealousy whenever we, neglecting the purity of his holy marriage, become polluted with wicked lusts. But he especially feels this when we transfer to another or stain with some superstition the worship of his divine majesty, which deserved to be utterly uncorrupted. In this way we not only violate the pledge given in marriage, but we also defile the very marriage bed by bringing adulterers to it.[4]

God's response to his people's faithlessness is related to his jealous nature as the husband to his people. Although it might seem inappropriate and offensive to attribute jealousy to God, this characteristic is nonetheless described in many places (e. g., Num. 25:11; Deut. 4:24; 6:16; 29:20; Josh. 24:19; 1 Kings 14:22; Ezek. 8:3–5; Nah. 1:2). God's jealousy, however, is not like human jealousy, which might say, "I want what you have, and I hate you because I do not have it." It is rather zeal to protect the deep love relationship that God has with his people (cf. Exodus 20:4–6).[5]

Idols Are Worthless

No matter how well they are crafted, how much value the materials have, or how many people revere them, false gods and idols are useless. The prophet Jeremiah (10:3–5) describes them thus:

> For the customs of the peoples are worthless:
>> they cut a tree out of the forest,
>> and a craftsman shapes it with his chisel.
> They adorn it with silver and gold;
>> they fasten it with hammer and nails
>> so it will not totter.
> Like a scarecrow in a melon patch
>> their idols cannot speak;
> they must be carried
>> because they cannot walk.
> Do not fear them;
>> they can do no harm
>> nor can they do any good.

The prophet also describes idols as scarecrows, mere figures placed in the fields to scare off birds or other animals. No matter what the craftsmen do to adorn these creations with silver or gold, idols are lifeless figures. Like scarecrows, their appearance suggests that they have the ability to protect and even work in the field in which they stand. In reality, however, their appearance is completely misleading. They are lifeless and can do nothing.

Other passages in the Old Testament, such as Psalm 135:15–18, ridicule man-made idols:

> The idols of the nations are silver and gold,
>> made by the hands of men.
> They have mouths, but cannot speak,
>> eyes, but they cannot see;
> they have ears, but cannot hear,
>> nor is there breath in their mouths.

> Those who make them will be like them,
>   and so will all who trust in them.

Although idols may be fashioned to look like human beings, says the above psalm, and although they have mouths, eyes, and ears, these organs do not function. There is no spark of life within them. They may look as if they can do what someone needs or asks, but they actually are frauds. Those who worship such things will become like them, without life and feeling (cf. Ps. 115:3–8).

Isaiah 44:9–20 states the worthlessness of idols even more forcefully. In these verses, the prophet urges the people to turn away from idols, which are "worthless, blind, ignorant, and profitless" (vv. 9–11). Moreover, rather than giving strength to those who revere them, they take strength from those who create them—the blacksmiths who fashion them give from "the sweat of their brows"; the carpenter is weakened, felling trees and crafting them (vv. 12–14). Idols also take from people's wealth because these materials could have been used in much better ways. Wood, for example, could be used for firewood to keep a person warm or for the baking of bread (vv. 15–16).

Finally, the worship of idols leads to the ultimate result, that of self-deception:

> From the rest he makes a god, his idol;
>   he bows down to it and worships.
> He prays to it and says,
>   "Save me; you are my god."
> They know nothing, they understand nothing;
>   their eyes are plastered over so they cannot see,
>   and their minds closed so they cannot understand.
> No one stops to think,
>   no one has the knowledge or understanding to say,
> "Half of it I used for fuel;
>   I even baked bread over its coals,
>   I roasted meat and I ate.
> Shall I make a detestable thing from what is left?
>   Shall I bow down to a block of wood?"

He feeds on ashes, a deluded heart misleads him;
he cannot save himself, or say,
"Is not this thing in my right hand a lie?"
(Isa. 44:17–20)

No matter how realistic idols may appear, says Isaiah, they are of no value, and they lead to delusion (cf. Hab. 2:18–19).[6]

Idolatry Is Associated with Other Vices

Other drawbacks and evils, too, are associated with the worship of idols. They bring a host of other problems with them, such as sexual impropriety, greed, and gluttony.

The first time, in fact, that God's people fall into idolatry after the giving of the Ten Commandments they revel in other vices associated with idolatry. In Exodus 32, the people of Israel were encamped at the base of Mount Sinai. When Moses was delayed from returning from the top of the mountain, the people decided to build for themselves an idol— a golden calf. After it was built, God's people "rose early and sacrificed burnt offerings and presented fellowship offerings. Afterward they sat down to eat and drink, they got up to indulge in revelry" (Exod. 32:6). The reference to revelry is likely a reference to adultery.[7] Other vices, such as pride (v. 9) and violence (v. 17), also emerged when the golden calf idol was worshipped.[8]

Exodus is not the only book in the Old Testament in which other evils are connected with idolatry. The book of Hosea, for example, regularly associates idolatry with immorality:

They consult a wooden idol
and are answered by a stick of wood.
A spirit of prostitution leads them astray;
they are unfaithful to their God.
They sacrifice on the mountaintops
and burn offerings on the hills,
under oak, poplar and terebinth,
where the shade is pleasant.

> Therefore your daughters turn to prostitution
> and your daughters-in-law to adultery.
> (Hos. 4:12–13)

In Old Testament times, sacrifices to heathen gods were offered on the mountaintops and were accompanied by immoral ceremonies. Other passages, too, within the book of Hosea associate the ideas of adultery and idolatry (Hos. 2:2–3; 5:3).

Other vices connected to idolatry include false stories, lies, child sacrifice, pride, and greed (Deut. 12:31; Ps. 52:6–7; Isa. 2:11–12; Jer. 10:9; 14:14). Indeed, it can be said, as the early Jewish book of Wisdom states, "The worship of idols . . . is the beginning and cause and end of every evil" (Wisdom of Solomon 14:27).

Idolatry Leads to Ultimate Condemnation

Condemnation by God is the ultimate result of idolatry. Many texts describe idol worship as abhorrent in the sight of God (cf. Lev. 26:30; Deut. 12:31; 13:13–14; 18:9–12; 20:18; 27:15; 32:16–22), and those who ally themselves with idols as being destroyed:

> The images of their gods you are to burn in the fire. Do not covet the silver and gold on them, and do not take it for yourselves, or you will be ensnared by it, for it is detestable to the Lord your God. Do not bring a detestable thing into your house or you, like it, will be set apart for destruction. Utterly abhor and detest it, for it is set apart for destruction. (Deut. 7:25–26)

Even people who seem to be successful in life receive divine criticism if they stray into idolatry. The portrayal of the rulers of God's people in 1 and 2 Kings is especially revealing in this regard.[9] King Omri, for example, accomplished much in his life.[10] He founded a dynasty that lasted some fifty years, and during his reign he experienced success over enemies such as the Philistines and the Moabites. He built strong alliances with Judah and Phoenicia, and he bought the hill of Samaria, where he constructed a new capital city. Later, it would take the Assyrians three years of siege warfare to subdue Samaria and the northern kingdom of Israel.[11] Despite all of his successes, however, Omri is remembered as an evil person:

> But Omri did evil in the eyes of the LORD and sinned more than all those before him. He walked in all the ways of Jeroboam son of Nebat, and in his sin which he had caused Israel to commit, so that they provoked the LORD, the God of Israel, to anger by their worthless idols. (1 Kings 16:25–26)

IDOLATRY IN THE NEW TESTAMENT

Idolatry was also a problem in New Testament times. The worship of Greek and Roman gods extensively influenced the culture.[12] Near the center of the ancient city of Ephesus, for example, there stood a magnificent structure devoted to the goddess Artemis. This building was enormous for its time, measuring nearly 420 feet in length (128 m.) and 240 feet in width (73 m.). Its roof was about 60 feet (18 m.) high and was supported by 117 columns. When it was built in 550 B.C., it was the largest building in the Greek world, and was constructed entirely of marble. Its splendor and beauty earned it a place among the seven wonders of the ancient world.

Within this temple, the moon goddess was continuously served by a host of devoted people: receptionists, supervisors, drummers, cleaners, chambermaids, acrobats, flute players, and bearers of scepters. Nearby were living quarters for these many people who worked and lived in the great edifice. A sizable portion of Ephesus was employed at the temple, and thus the worship of Artemis significantly affected the economy of the city.

Two festivals were held each year on her behalf. The first, called the Artemisia, was held in the early spring. Large musical, athletic, and theatrical events were accompanied by sacrifices to the goddess. A second festival, celebrating the birth of Artemis, took place at the end of spring. One of the highlights of this festival was a religious procession through the city, during which the people would sing, "Great is Artemis of Ephesus."

Both of these festivals were well attended, and pilgrims in great numbers came from far away. After the celebration, these pilgrims would take home with them silver statues of the goddess that they had purchased, and many of these statues were placed in miniature shrines or altars throughout Asia Minor.[13]

Second century marble statue of Artemis, in Ephesus, Turkey. She was the chief deity of Ephesus and her temple was one of the Seven Wonders of the Ancient World. (Photograph courtesy of Todd Bolen and BiblePlaces.com.)

The response of the New Testament writers to the idolatry of their time bears some resemblance to the perspective of the Old Testament prophets. Reading the Epistles with the Old Testament in view helps to make sense of some key New Testament passages.

Idols Are Characteristic of Those Who Do Not Know God

Many times in the New Testament, idols and idol worship are portrayed as opposite to Christian conversion. The apostle Paul, in his letters to the Corinthians, urges separation from those who worship idols:

What agreement is there between the temple of God and idols? For we are the temple of the living God. As God has said: "I will live with them and walk among them, and I will be their God, and they will be my people. Therefore come out from them and be separate, says the Lord. Touch no unclean thing; and I will receive you. I will be a Father to you, and you will be my sons and daughters, says the Lord Almighty." (2 Cor. 6:16–18)

Paul contends that Christians should not associate with anyone who claims to be a follower of Christ but continues in idolatry (cf. 1 Cor. 5:9–11).[14] It is noteworthy that Paul would urge the Corinthian Christians not to follow idols, because the Corinthian church was composed largely of Gentile converts, who would be less familiar than Jewish Christians with Old Testament ideas regarding idolatry. Paul, however, sets forward to the Gentile Christians a consistent standard regarding idols: those who worship idols have nothing to do with being God's people.

According to Paul, ridding oneself of idols is a distinguishing characteristic of God's people. He makes this especially clear in his first letter to the Thessalonians. He had been with the Thessalonians as a missionary for only a few weeks, because a riot had developed in the city in response to his ministry there (cf. Acts 17:1–9). Nevertheless, he praises them for their conversion and its fruits. He knows that they had been converted because he knows that they had turned away from idols:

Therefore we do not need to say anything about it for they themselves report what kind of reception you gave us. They tell how you turned to God from idols to serve the living and true God, and to wait for his Son from heaven, whom he raised from the dead—Jesus, who rescues us from the coming wrath. (1 Thess. 1:8–10)

Many Christians in our day would no doubt think of other ways to express their Christian conversion, such as attending church regularly, praying a sinner's prayer, or giving to those in need. But of the many characteristics that Paul could have used to describe conversion, he highlights turning away from idols (cf. Acts 14:15).

Not only was it important to rid oneself of idols, abstaining from meat sacrificed to them was also an imperative for Christians. It was, in fact, one of only a few restrictions placed upon the Gentile Christians by the first church council (Acts 15). The council was called to respond to a dispute over the rite of circumcision. Some Jewish Christians believed that circumcision was necessary in order to be considered a Christian (vv. 1–6). Thus, they sought to impose this Jewish custom on Gentile Christians of the day. As Paul, Barnabas, Peter, James, and the other apostles and elders discussed the issue, they determined that one did not need to be circumcised to be a Christian. It was a yoke that was not necessary for them to bear (vv. 10–11). As the council continued to debate, they settled on a short list of restrictions that would apply to both Jewish and Gentile Christians. One of these was abstaining from food polluted by idols (vv. 20, 29). Thus, idolatry, as well as practices associated with it, were deemed to be outside the boundaries of the church from early times.

Idolatry Offends a Deeply Committed God

Consistent with the teaching of the Old Testament, the worshipping of idols is portrayed in Revelation 2, and in the prophecies given to the churches of Pergamum and Thyatira, as a deep offense to God. Christ commends both churches for a variety of characteristics, including their perseverance and their witness in the midst of persecution. He then chastises them, however, for allowing their people to eat foods offered to idols (vv. 14, 20).

The judgment handed out to these churches as a result of their idolatry is severe. For the church in Pergamum, God promises to come and war against his people, fighting against them with the sword of his mouth (Rev. 2:16). The judgment for the church in Thyatira is even more dramatic. John records it in verses 22–23:

So I will cast her [that woman Jezebel] on a bed of suffering, and I will make those who commit adultery with her suffer intensely, unless they repent of her ways. I will strike her children dead. Then all the churches will know that I am he who searches hearts and minds, and I will repay each of you according to your deeds.

Remains of Zeus altar near ancient Pergamum (modern-day Bergama). Located in western Turkey 16.5 mi. (26.5 km) inland from the Aegean Sea, Pergamum was a large city of importance in the Roman province of Asia Minor. The emperor, Athena, Asclepius, and many other deities were worshipped there. (Photograph courtesy of Todd Bolen and BiblePlaces.com.)

Despite the good that these churches were doing, the sin of idolatry carried more weight. It was deeply offensive to the Lord, who is the owner of these churches (Rev. 1:17–19).

Idols Are Worthless

The New Testament writers also view idols as worthless. In the Corinthian letters, where Paul says the most about idols, the apostle asserts, "About eating food sacrificed to idols: we know that an idol is nothing at all in the world and that there is no God but one" (1 Cor. 8:4). Consistent with the teaching of the Old Testament, Paul states that, although idols look like they can act as people, they cannot. No idol in the world really is of any value because there is only one true God.

In 1 Corinthians 12:2, Paul again speaks of the worthlessness of idols:

"You know that when you were pagans, somehow or other you were influenced and led astray to mute idols." He believes that the Corinthians, with their minds now illuminated as Christians, ought clearly to recognize that idols have no ability at all.

In a further reference to the worthlessness of idols, Paul speaks during an encounter on the mission field, recorded in the book of Acts. During his first missionary journey, he and Barnabas are in Lystra, where they are mistaken for gods (Acts 14:8–18). The Lystrans bow down and worship the two men, calling Paul the Greek god Hermes, because he is the one speaking, and Barnabas, Zeus. Instead of responding to the people's flattery, or using the authority it confers upon them to proclaim the gospel with greater authority, Paul and Barnabas oppose the Lystrans' belief in idols, affirming that idols are worthless. They say, "Men, why are you doing this? We too are only men, human like you. We are bringing you good news, telling you to turn from these worthless things to the living God, who made heaven and earth and sea and everything in them" (v. 15). It seems, though, as if the Lystrans are unable to grasp what Paul and Barnabas are saying. Instead, the crowd continues trying to offer sacrifices to them (v. 18). Nevertheless, Paul and Barnabas, make it clear by their reaction to the crowd that idols are useless and have nothing to do with the Christian message.

Idolatry Is Associated with Other Vices

In both the Old and New Testaments, idolatry was not depicted as an isolated sin. As previously stated, the thriving economy in Ephesus was based on the worship of Artemis, suggesting that greed is associated with idolatry in that city. The point is made explicit in Ephesians 5:5 where greed is directly identified with idolatry (cf. Col. 3:5).

Other sins connected with idolatry in Paul's writing include gluttony: "Their destiny is destruction, their god is their stomach, and their glory is in their shame. Their mind is on earthly things" (Phil. 3:19). In Galatians 5:19–21, idolatry is associated with other such vices as fornication, witchcraft, sorcery, quarreling, and drunkenness; and in Romans 1, a whole host of vices are connected with idolatry:

Although they claimed to be wise, they became fools and exchanged
the glory of the immortal God for images made to look like mor-
tal man and birds and animals and reptiles. Therefore God gave
them over in the sinful desires of their hearts to sexual impurity
for the degrading of their bodies with one another. They exchanged
the truth of God for a lie, and worshipped and served created things
rather than the Creator—who is forever praised. Amen. Because
of this, God gave them over to shameful lusts. Even their women
exchanged natural relations for unnatural ones. In the same way
the men also abandoned natural relations with women and were
inflamed with lust for one another. Men committed indecent acts
with other men, and received in themselves the due penalty for
their perversion. Furthermore, since they did not think it worth-
while to retain the knowledge of God, he gave them over to a de-
praved mind, to do what ought not to be done. They have become
filled with every kind of wickedness, evil, greed and depravity. They
are full of envy, murder, strife, deceit and malice. They are gossips,
slanderers, God haters, insolent, arrogant and boastful; they in-
vent ways of doing evil; they disobey their parents; they are sense-
less, faithless, heartless, ruthless. Although they know God's
righteous decree that those who do such things deserve death, they
not only continue to do these very things but also approve of those
who practice them. (Rom. 1:22–32)

Both the Old and New Testaments are clear: idolatry is the root of a
whole host of evils. Augustine of Hippo noted this too, when he sought
for idols, he fell headlong into sorrows, confusions, and many errors.[15]

Idolatry Leads to Ultimate Condemnation

Finally, as in the Old Testament, the New Testament makes it clear
that those who trust in idols will ultimately be condemned. In 1 Corinthians 6:9–10 Paul states this plainly:

Do you not know that the wicked will not inherit the kingdom
of God? Do not be deceived: Neither the sexually immoral nor

idolaters nor adulterers nor male prostitutes nor homosexual offenders nor thieves nor the greedy nor drunkards nor slanderers nor swindlers will inherit the kingdom of God.

The final chapters of Revelation also group idolaters with those who will not inherit the kingdom of God. They are part of those outside of the new creation and the New Jerusalem and are destined for the "fiery lake of burning sulfur. This is the second death" (Rev. 21:8; 22:15).[16]

Both Old and New Testaments are united in the view[17] that no more serious charge is issued in the Bible than that of idolatry. Idols are characteristic of those who do not know God. They are offensive to God, worthless, associated with other vices, and deserving of ultimate condemnation. Although the presence of idols was everywhere during biblical times, and their supposed power was great, both the Old and New Testaments warn against and condemn the worship of idols.

Idols are no less destructive in our day, as seen in the following story from a Christian counselor:

I was talking to a guy recently—he and his wife were having troubles with their daughter—we talked about that and that was fine, and then we were talking about what the difficulties were and that was fine, and we were getting on and then it came around to how much of the problem was dad, and dad was working fifteen hours a day, seven days a week. People were ringing him up in the middle of the night and things like that. He looked physically ill. He said, "It's just the work," and I said, "Well, can't you cut it down? It doesn't look to be doing you much good." He said, "Yes, but I've got to keep going at it." I said, "What if you just say, 'That's it, forget it, I'm going somewhere else'?" He said, "I did that last year and they just put my pay up by 25 percent and how do you walk away from that?[18]

Christians in the twenty-first century must guard against idols of the heart.[19] Gods of money, astrology, possessions, fame, popularity, technology, physique, and achievement are plentiful and powerful in today's

society. Many supposed substitutes for God are available in modern culture—found not in pagan temples, per se, but on the altars of human
hearts.[20] John's simple admonition to the church is as relevant today as
ever: "Dear children, keep yourself from idols" (1 John 5:21).

Instead of following idols, may God's people focus on the true char-
acter and attributes of God found in Scripture and recorded in song.
One such beautiful hymn is Johann Schütz's "Sing Praise to God Who
Reigns Above":

> Sing praise to God who reigns above,
> The God of all creation,
> The God of power, the God of love,
> The God of our salvation;
> With healing balm my soul He fills,
> And every faithless murmur stills
> To God all praise and glory.
>
> What God's almighty power hath made,
> His gracious mercy keepeth;
> By morning glow or evening shade
> His watchful eye ne'er sleepeth;
> Within the kingdom of His might,
> Lo! all is just and all is right:
> To God all praise and glory.
>
> The Lord is never far away,
> But, through all grief distressing,
> An ever present help and stay,
> Our peace, and joy, and blessing;
> As with a mother's tender hand,
> He leads His own His chosen band:
> To God all praise and glory.
>
> Thus, all my gladsome way along,
> I sing aloud His praises,

That men may hear the grateful song
My voice unwearied raises,
Be joyful in the Lord, my heart,
Both soul and body bear your part:
To God all praise and glory.[21]

THE MESSIAH

Unto Us a Child Is Born

See! in yonder manger low,
Born for us on earth below,
See! the tender Lamb appears
Promised from eternal years.
Hail, thou ever-blessed morn!
Hail, redemption's happy dawn!
Sing through all Jerusalem,
"Christ is born in Bethlehem!"
                    —Edward Caswall

This is he whom seers in old time
Chanted of with one accord,
Whom the voices of the prophets
Promised in their faithful word;
Now he shines, the long-expected;
Let creation praise its Lord,
Evermore and evermore.
                    —Prudentius

Christmastime is one of the most anticipated times of the year. For many people in America, the holiday season begins with the arrival of Santa Claus at the annual Thanksgiving Day parade in New York City. For others, the season begins when television advertisements announce bargains for the Christmas shopping season. Many anticipate the day by decorating their homes in the holiday spirit, displaying wreaths, candles, and lights. Many communities adorn their streets with Christmas lights and decorate public Christmas trees.

Because we have young children in our family, our home is abuzz with Christmas activities: cookies to bake, Christmas lights to place in the windows, holiday music to enjoy, and gifts to wrap. We must watch certain holiday classics such as *How the Grinch Stole Christmas* and *Rudolph the Red-Nosed Reindeer,* and of course we look forward to selecting our Christmas tree and trimming it with lights, tinsel, and holiday ornaments.

Although we greatly anticipate Christmas each year, our expectancy pales in comparison to the yearning for the coming of the Messiah that characterized the nation of Israel in the years leading up to the birth of Christ. His advent was foretold from the earliest chapters of the Old Testament, and the hope of his arrival reached a high point at the time of Jesus' birth.[1]

OLD TESTAMENT PERSPECTIVES OF THE MESSIAH

The Old Testament—the story of God's work among his covenant people, Israel—contains many passages that point to the coming Messiah. This present section examines the descriptions of the Messiah found in the first thirty-nine books of the Bible, and considers his anticipated roles.[2]

The Ultimate Hope of God's People Is Found in the Messiah

The earliest passage that alludes to the Messiah as the great and ultimate hope of God's people is found in Genesis 3. There, God responds to the catastrophe of sin in the Garden of Eden. After pronouncing his judgment on Adam and Eve, God turns his attention to the serpent: "Cursed are you above all the livestock and all the wild animals! You will crawl on your belly and you will eat dust all the days of your life. And I will put enmity between you and the woman, and between your offspring and hers; he will crush your head, and you will strike his heel" (Gen. 3:14–15). Although God had already created—and declared good—creatures that move along the ground (1:24–25), here he specifically demotes the serpent to crawl on its belly and eat the dust of the earth, a sign of subjugation.[3] God promises that the crushing of the enemy will take place through the offspring of Eve—a reference to the coming Messiah.

Further reasons can be cited for finding the hope of the Messiah in Genesis 3:15. The Jewish community viewed this prediction as a messianic text three hundred years before Jesus Christ was born.[4] The New Testament, too, alludes to this text as messianic.[5] Early church fathers as well, including Justin and Irenaeus, viewed this text as the first messianic prophecy of the Old Testament. Modern scholars, too, have viewed this as a messianic prophecy. One called verse 15 the "mother prophecy" that gave birth to all of the promises.[6] Another sees it as "the germ of promise which unfolds in the history of redemption."[7]

As the history of God's people developed, more promises were made about the Messiah, many of which anticipated that he would be the ultimate hope of God's people.[8] An explicit promise is found, for example, in 2 Samuel 7. There, the prophet Nathan gives to King David a response, following the king's wish to build a temple for God. The dialogue between the prophet and the king occurs after David had been given rest on all sides from his enemies in Canaan and in the surrounding countries. He had recently built a cedar palace for himself and was prospering, but then he realizes that the ark of God was still dwelling in a tent with curtains that were hundreds of years old. David seeks to rectify this situation by making plans for an elaborate house for the Lord. At first, Nathan agrees that David should build a temple, but that night he receives different instructions from the Lord. David is not to build a house for God; instead, God will build a house out of David (v. 13).

Although David is not to build the temple, his desires are good, and God promises to bless him in great ways. Some of these ways involve David's name being made great, a permanent place for God's people to dwell, rest from all enemies, and offspring from David to succeed him (2 Sam. 7:9–12). One of God's promises to David is that the promised Messiah will emerge from David's seed. That seed will build a house for God, and David's house and his kingdom will continue forever (vv. 12–16; 23:1–7).

Not even the most renowned of human dynasties, some of which lasted for hundreds of years, had the promise from God that they would last forever. The Babylonian Empire, for example, contributed advances in social structure, economic organization, arts and crafts, science and literature, and a judicial system that influenced the entire ancient world. But even though its heyday lasted approximately 1,200 years, from the eighteenth century B.C. to the sixth century B.C., the empire was eventually supplanted.

Likewise, the ancient Greek Empire lasted from the third millennium B.C. until the first century B.C., but it, too, fell. Although the Greeks made tremendous advances in the areas of philosophy, government, and the arts, many of which are still felt today, the empire no longer exists.

Nor does the Roman Empire exist, which at its zenith encompassed the entire Mediterranean region, as well as large portions of Western and Eastern Europe. Even though the empire itself has long vanished, it lasted five centuries and contributed much to Western civilization, influencing the cultural and political shape of Europe down to the present day.

The Ming Dynasty in China spanned about two centuries. It made countless contributions to Chinese art and culture and is known for its porcelain and ceramic art.

There was a time when the sun never set on the British Empire, which at its height in the early 1900s encompassed more than 20 percent of the world's land mass and more than 400 million people. British influence extended to all continents, shaping the economies of nations such as Australia, South Africa, and the United States.

Despite the greatness of all these dynasties, every one eventually passed away and was replaced. So when God promised David an eternal kingdom through the promised Messiah, David rightly and understandably was overwhelmed (2 Sam. 7:18–19). From his house would come the ultimate hope and charter for all humanity.[9]

That ultimate hope to be brought by the Messiah can be seen in many of the prophetical books.[10] Isaiah, though, contains the largest number of such passages,[11] 9:2–7 being particularly explicit. There, although God's people are in danger of being conquered by surrounding nations, Isaiah's prophecy assures them of victory. The prophet also encourages those who are walking in the shadow of darkness that they will see a great light. The yoke that burdens them and the bar across their shoulders will be shattered. Instead of warfare and slavery, they will be delivered to an everlasting peace (vv. 2–5). All this is due to the ultimate hope of the Messiah's birth, which verses 6–7 so eloquently states:

> For to us a child is born,
> to us a son is given,
> and the government will be on his shoulders.
> And he will be called
> Wonderful Counselor, Mighty God,
> Everlasting Father, Prince of Peace.
> Of the increase of his government and peace
> there will be no end.
> He will reign on David's throne
> and over his kingdom,
> establishing and upholding it
> with justice and righteousness
> from that time on and forever.
> The zeal of the LORD Almighty
> will accomplish this.

The names by which the Messiah will be known are significant in that they explain the great hope of God's people. The term "Wonderful Counselor" means the one whose very being is a wonder through and through.[12] In *Mighty God* is the promise that the child to be born will be the God of power and might. As "Everlasting Father," he is eternal and the one who created all things. As "Prince of Peace," his rule will be one without war or conflict. Great will be his power and his presence, his being the ultimate expectation for God's people.

Roles of the Messiah Are Set Forward in the Old Testament

Not only does the Old Testament describe the Messiah as the ultimate hope of God's people, it also foreshadows critical roles that the Messiah will fulfill—prophet, king, and priest.

The role of the Messiah as prophet of God can be seen in Deuteronomy 18:15, 18:

The LORD your God will raise up for you a prophet like me from among your own brothers. You must listen to him. . . . I will raise up for them a prophet like you from among their brothers; I will put my words in his mouth, and he will tell them everything I commanded him.

These words are spoken following the forty years that Israel wandered in the desert, as the time of Moses' leadership is passing. The interpretation has been mixed, however, regarding the identity of the prophet whom Moses envisioned. Some have wondered if Deuteronomy is speaking of one prophet, a class of prophets, or both.[13] Although Deuteronomy 18:15, 18 occurs in the portion of the book where classes of individuals like judges, kings, priests, and false prophets are considered, the passage uses the singular form of the word *prophet* rather than the plural, thus suggesting one prophet.[14] Moreover, the uniqueness of Moses as a prophet (cf. Num. 12:6–8; Deut. 34:10–12) makes it seem that only the Messiah could fulfill the expectations given in Deuteronomy 18:15, 18. Seen in this way, the prophesied Messiah of Deuteronomy 18 would be like Moses. His communication would be directly with God, he would lead and deliver his people, and he would speak God's word authoritatively.

Not only was the Messiah expected to be a prophet, he was also expected to be a king. This role as the great ruling king of God's people is set forward in a number of places.

The Psalms contain many passages in which the Anointed One, understood to be the Messiah, was proclaimed as the ultimate hope for God's people. Although a number of texts could be considered,[15] the following two psalms, Psalms 2 and 110, speak most clearly of the Messiah's reign. One scholar has even noted that these two particular psalms resemble a coronation ceremony.[16]

Psalm 2 shows the Anointed One of God, the Messiah, as the supreme king over all. His rule and authority are set forward in verses 4–9:

> The One enthroned in heaven laughs;
>   the Lord scoffs at them.
> Then he rebukes them in his anger
>   and terrifies them in his wrath, saying,

"I have installed my King
on Zion, my holy hill."
I will proclaim the decree of the LORD:
He said to me, "You are my Son;
today I have become your Father.
Ask of me,
and I will make the nations your inheritance,
the ends of the earth your possession.
You will rule them with an iron scepter;
you will dash them to pieces like pottery."

The Messiah's authority, power, and dominion are so overarching that all of the nations will be his inheritance. His rule will be so strong that the nations can be shattered into pieces like pottery by his iron scepter (Ps. 2:8–9).

This great kingly rule of the Messiah can also be seen in Psalm 110, which speaks of the Messiah's dominion. The first two verses clearly speak of this authority:

The LORD says to my Lord:
"Sit at my right hand
until I make your enemies
a footstool for your feet."
The LORD will extend your mighty scepter from Zion;
you will rule in the midst of your enemies.

Such is the power of the Messiah that the nations, even with all of their strength, are merely something for him to rest his feet upon.

The Messiah as king can also be seen in the writings of the prophets. Once again, a number of texts could be cited, but for the sake of brevity Isaiah 11 will be considered as representative.[17] In this passage is prophesied a spirit of justice, counsel, and knowledge resting upon the Messiah as he rules as king:

A shoot will come up from the stump of Jesse;
from his roots a Branch will bear fruit.

The Spirit of the LORD will rest on him—
    the Spirit of wisdom and of understanding,
    the Spirit of counsel and of power,
    the Spirit of knowledge and of the fear of the LORD—
and he will delight in the fear of the LORD.

He will not judge by what he sees with his eyes,
    or decide by what he hears with his ears;
but with righteousness he will judge the needy,
    with justice he will give decisions for the poor of the earth.
He will strike the earth with the rod of his mouth;
    with the breath of his lips he will slay the wicked.
Righteousness will be his belt
    and faithfulness the sash around his waist.

                                                    (Isa. 11:1–5)

A distinguishing characteristic of the Messiah's dominion is how powerful and peaceful his rule will be. Animals that normally devour each other will be at peace. Not only will animals not devour each other, they will even be friends; the wolf will live with the lamb and the leopard will lie down with the goat (Isa. 11:6). Young children will even put their hands into a viper's nest without harm (vv. 8–9). So dominant will be the Messiah's kingly reign that "they will neither harm nor destroy" (v. 9).

A third role of the Messiah is that of priest. In Old Testament times, the priests functioned as intermediaries between God and his people, bringing sacrifices to atone for sin. The Messiah as priest is foretold in Psalm 110:4: "The LORD has sworn and will not change his mind: 'You are a priest forever in the order of Melchizedek.'"

Here the psalm refers to the account in Genesis 14 in which the righteous priest Melchizedek appears to Abraham. Melchizedek is described in that passage as a priest of the most high God (v. 18). Likewise, the Messiah will be a priest of God most high.

The book of Zechariah, too, declares that the Messiah will be a priest. Zechariah 6:12–13 is most explicit in this regard:

Tell him this is what the LORD Almighty says: "Here is the man whose name is the Branch, and he will branch out from his place and build the temple of the LORD. It is he who will build the temple of the LORD, and he will be clothed with majesty and will sit and rule on his throne. And he will be a priest on his throne. And there will be harmony between the two."[18]

Here the Messiah is presented as the ideal priest, the one who will build the temple of the Lord. He will sit and rule as not only priest, but as prophet and king. No other person in the Old Testament was expected to fulfill all three roles.

Descriptions of the Messiah Are Set Forward in the Old Testament

The Old Testament provides a number of descriptions of the type of person the Messiah will be. The lengthiest description is from Isaiah's prophecy, depicting him as a servant, the unassuming helper of God's people. This picture is most clearly drawn from four passages that have been called the "servant songs" (Isa. 42:1–4; 49:1–6; 50:4–9; 52:13–53:12).

The meaning of these passages has been greatly debated. The main question focuses on whether God's servant is the nation of Israel or the Messiah. Although some elements of these verses could be construed as referring to the nation of Israel, the better conclusion is that these passages refer to a single person—especially in light of Isaiah 53:4–6, 10–12, which refers to one person influencing many others. It seems most likely, too, that only a single person, rather than an entire nation, could bear infirmities, sorrows, punishments, and wounds as atonement for the iniquities of others.[19]

A portrait of the expected Messiah can thus be deduced from Isaiah 42:1–7: he will be tender and merciful, "He will not shout or cry out, or raise his voice in the streets" (v. 2); he will be gentle, "a bruised reed he will not break, and a smoldering wick he will not snuff out" (v. 3).

Isaiah 49:5–6 exhibits further attributes of the Messiah, portraying him as the great unifier of Israel and of all the nations:

And now the LORD says—
  he who formed me in the womb to be his servant
to bring Jacob back to him
  and gather Israel to himself,
for I am honored in the eyes of the LORD
  and my God has been my strength—
he says:
"It is too small a thing for you to be my servant
  to restore the tribes of Jacob
  and bring back those of Israel I have kept.
I will also make you a light for the Gentiles,
  that you may bring my salvation to the ends of the earth."

Isaiah 50:4–9 reveals that the Messiah will experience suffering. He will offer his back to be beaten, his beard to be pulled out. In a culture where beards were symbolic of manhood, this would be truly degrading. Furthermore, he would be mocked and spat upon (Isa. 50:5–6). Yet despite his suffering, the servant will trust in the Lord, and as a result, he will not be disgraced or put to shame. The Sovereign Lord will help and sustain him despite the suffering (v. 9).

The final servant song, Isaiah 52:13–53:12, is the lengthiest, witnessing to both the suffering and triumph of the servant. Polycarp, the early church father (A.D. 69–115), called this fourth servant song the "golden *passional* of the Old Testament evangelist," indicating that he saw the passion events of the Gospels depicted here.

Isaiah 52:13 speaks of the servant's success: "See my servant will act wisely; he will be raised and lifted up and highly exalted." At the end of the song, the triumph of the servant can also be seen: "He will see the light of life and be satisfied; by his knowledge my righteous servant will justify many, and he will bear their iniquities" (53:11), and he will be given "a portion among the great" (v. 12).

Between the bookends of success and triumph, references to the suffering of the servant are found in the middle of the song. He is rejected and despised by men, "a man of sorrows, and familiar with suffering . . . [and] stricken by God" (Isa. 53:3–4). Indeed, men hide their faces from him; he carries infirmities and sorrows. He is to be pierced for our transgressions, and crushed for our iniquities. He experiences punishment and wounds for his followers. Verses 7–9 describes his oppression, trial, and death on behalf of his people.

The servant passages provide a concrete picture of the Messiah. On the one hand, they suggest an unassuming Messiah who is humble and gentle, who suffers on behalf of his people, who goes to great extremes for them. On the other hand, they present a Messiah who will triumph. God will exalt him and lift up his name, unifying the Jewish nation and drawing Gentiles from the ends of the earth to know him.

The Old Testament also presents a second picture of the Messiah—as the Son of Man.[20] This image emerges from Daniel 7, in which the prophet experiences a vision. He is terrified by four great beasts: a lion, a bear, a leopard, and a ten-horned beast, each of which represents a different kingdom (Dan. 7:1–8).

Fear dominates in this vision until the Ancient of Days, the Lord himself, comes and takes his seat. His appearance is awe inspiring—clothing white as snow, his throne aflame with fire and its wheels ablaze. The fire pours forth like a river from his throne, and thousands upon thousands attend him as he opens a set of books. This vision presents a picture of the Lord of the universe rendering worldwide judgment (Dan. 7:9–12).

At this point, "one like a son of man" appears before the throne and is given great authority over all peoples and nations. People of every language worship him, and his dominion is proclaimed to be an everlasting dominion that will not pass away. The extent of his rule expresses his divinity, yet at the same time, his depiction as a "son of man" suggests his humility as well.

A number of passages in the Old Testament, though relatively few, also describe the Messiah as a stone or cornerstone. In Isaiah 28:16, he is set forward as the precious and decisive cornerstone, and those who trust in this cornerstone will not be shaken even when the world is in turmoil. Other Old Testament passages, such as Psalm 118:22–23; Daniel 2:34, 44–45; and Zechariah 3:9, describe the Messiah as the foundation of the true temple, the one who crushes other kingdoms, and who is the foundation for an everlasting kingdom.[21]

A NEW TESTAMENT PERSPECTIVE ON THE MESSIAH

Throughout the New Testament, the Messiah can be seen in the person of Jesus Christ. Whereas the Old Testament is, in effect, a compilation of books about the anticipated Messiah, the New Testament, in which Jesus is everywhere visible, is a collection of books about Jesus.[22] When the themes of messianic anticipation are considered in the New Testament, then, they show that Jesus is the fulfillment of the great expectation written of in the Old Testament.

Jesus Christ Is the Ultimate Hope of God's People

Whereas the Old Testament portrays the Messiah as the ultimate hope of God's people, the New Testament repeatedly presents Jesus Christ as the fulfillment of that ultimate hope. The opening chapters of some of the Gospels, for example, particularly Luke and John, portray Jesus' birth as the long anticipated event for God's people.[23] In Luke, Gabriel the angel's words to Zechariah and to Mary reveal that something significant is happening.[24] Gabriel appears to the priest Zechariah, declaring that his son will "turn the hearts of the fathers to their children and the disobedient to the wisdom of the righteous—to make ready a people prepared for the Lord" (1:17). Shortly thereafter, Gabriel appears to Mary, telling her of the coming birth of Jesus, who will be "great and called the Son of the Most High" (vv. 32–33). What Gabriel says indicates that the hope of God's people will soon be fulfilled with Jesus' birth.

The book of Luke further indicates that the great hope of God's people is about to be fulfilled. In the song Mary sings, responding to the news that she will be the mother of Jesus, she glorifies God for the grandeur of what will occur (1:46–55). When in 2:29–32 the infant Jesus is brought to the temple to be presented to the Lord, he is seen by the righteous priest Simeon. After encountering Jesus, Simeon declares that he can depart in peace; he has seen Jesus, who is the salvation for all people.

In the opening of John's Gospel, many verses point to Jesus as the hope of God's people. John 1:4 says that the Word is the life and the light of men, a description repeated in verse 9. In verse 14, Jesus is described as full of grace, glory, and truth: "The Word became flesh and made his dwelling among us. We have seen his glory, the glory of the One and Only who came from the Father, full of grace and truth." Likewise, verse 18 declares that Jesus is the one who makes known God the Father.

The Gospels are not the only place in the New Testament where Jesus is presented as the ultimate fulfillment of God's promise to his people. The apostle Paul also presents Jesus as the fulfillment of the longings of God's people. Christ's life and resurrection are of "first importance" to Paul (1 Cor. 15:3–5), and he emphasizes that Christ is "the beginning and the firstborn from among the dead, so that in everything he might have the supremacy" (Col. 1:18). Jesus is the one who fully embodies God and the one who brings fullness and completeness to every believer (2:9–10).

In Philippians 3:8, Paul declares, "I consider everything a loss compared to the surpassing greatness of knowing Christ Jesus, my Lord, for whose sake I have lost all things. I consider them rubbish [*skubalon*], that I may gain Christ." The New International Version understates the meaning of *skubalon* as "rubbish." It is better translated "dung" or "garbage." All of Paul's birth privileges, his achievements as a Jew and a Pharisee, he counts as utterly worthless compared to the greatness of knowing Jesus. Indeed, Jesus is Paul's ultimate hope, the one "through whom all things came and through whom we live" (1 Cor. 8:6).

Many other passages throughout the New Testament point to Jesus as the greatest hope for God's people,[25] and nothing in the New Testament better underscores that hope than the heavenly throne scene in Revelation 5. People from every tongue, tribe, and nation gather around the throne in heaven, bowing down and praising the Lamb of God. Angels cry to him in a loud voice, "Worthy is the Lamb who was slain, to receive power and wealth and wisdom and strength and honor and glory and praise!" (v. 12). Every creature in heaven and on earth then sings to Jesus, "To him who sits on the throne and to the Lamb be praise and honor and glory and power for ever and ever!" (v. 13). In this climactic scene at the end of time, Jesus is presented as the ultimate hope for all creation.

The grandeur and the wonder of the person of Jesus the Messiah fulfills, too, the expectations of humans through the ages. This has been captured in art as well as splendid music, none more so than that by composer George Frideric Handel in his masterpiece called simply *Messiah*. Its appeal endures today, more than 250 years later, and it is widely regarded as one of the finest oratorios of the eighteenth century.

Handel wrote this grand composition after reading portions of the Old and New Testaments compiled by a friend. With his mind and his soul moved by the power of these texts, he immediately secluded himself and worked night and day on his musical response, often forgetting to eat. From time to time, his servants could hear his sobs as he labored. He finished the original libretto and score in only twenty-four days. Following the composition of the piece he said, "I think I did see all heaven before me and the great God himself."[26]

Jesus Christ Fulfills the Prophesied Roles of the Messiah

In the New Testament, Jesus fulfills the roles expected of the promised Messiah: prophet, priest, and king.

Jesus Christ as Prophet

The Gospels—by making note of his supernatural insight, his pronouncements of doom on some, and his ability to speak directly the voice of God—portray Jesus as a prophet.[27] A Samaritan woman, a blind man whom Jesus healed, some of the people at the feeding of the five thousand, and two of Jesus' disciples all, in fact, recognize Jesus as a prophet.[28]

Jesus, as well, presents himself as a prophet. The clearest example occurred at the outset of his ministry in Nazareth, when Jesus went to the synagogue and was given a scroll to read, that of the prophet Isaiah (Luke 4:18–19):

> The Spirit of the Lord is on me,
>   because he has anointed me
>   to preach good news to the poor.
> He has sent me to proclaim freedom for the prisoners
>   and recovery of sight for the blind,

to release the oppressed,
to proclaim the year of the Lord's favor.

In choosing to read this Scripture from Isaiah 61:1–2, and then applying it to himself, he declares that he is both prophet and the fulfillment of this prophecy.

In Luke 4:24–25, Jesus draws a parallel between himself and the prophets Elijah and Elisha. He states, "No prophet is accepted in his hometown."[29] This pronouncement of himself as a prophet, however, draws the crowd's anger, as they realize what Jesus is saying,

Jesus also claims that his words are from God: "My teaching is not my own. It comes from him who sent me" (John 7:16). This assertion is more or less repeated in 14:10: "The words I say to you are not just my own. Rather, it is the Father, living in me, who is doing his work." Also, in the same way that Old Testament prophets declared their prophetic authority by saying, "Thus says the Lord," Jesus underscores his authority and emphasizes the importance of his words by introducing them with the phrase, "I tell you the truth."[30]

Jesus Christ as Priest

Jesus in his role as priest is seen most clearly in the book of Hebrews. In this epistle—written to Jewish believers who were wondering whether to hold on to their Christian faith or revert to Judaism—the writer in several places portrays Jesus as a high priest. He is described as a "merciful and faithful high priest" (Heb. 2:17), the "high priest whom we confess" (3:1), and a high priest who can "sympathize with our weaknesses" (4:14–15).

The superiority of his priesthood is set forth in Hebrews 5–10—a remarkable claim considering that the Jewish Christian audience would be well familiar with the venerated position of the high priest. Hebrews 5:5 describes Jesus as the high priest of the heavenly temple, and Hebrews 6:20 and 7:3 portray Jesus as an eternal priest, given his office not by natural descent but by God himself (7:11–26). Various passages in Hebrews portray Jesus as not only a priest, but superior to any priest who had come previously (8:6; 9:11, 25–27; 10:11–14).

Jesus Christ as King

Jesus Christ in his role as king is foreshadowed in the Gospels, with their many accounts of miracles showing his power over sickness, blindness, demons, and death. His status is emphasized at the Mount of Transfiguration when his glory is revealed as superior over even Moses and Elijah. His ride into Jerusalem on Palm Sunday—which followed the practice of previous kings, that of having palms laid before them as they entered the city—also points to Jesus as a king.[31]

Other books in the New Testament also speak of Christ as king. Paul indicates that Jesus is the one to whom every knee will bow (Phil. 2:10), and describes Jesus as "above all rule and authority, power and dominion" (Eph. 1:21; see also, 1 Cor. 15:24–27). Paul proclaims him, too, as the "King of kings and Lord of lords" (1 Tim. 6:15). The apostle John as well asserts that Jesus is king (cf. Rev. 4–5; 17:14).[32]

Old Testament Pictures of the Messiah Are Used to Describe Jesus

The Old Testament descriptions of the Messiah are also applied to Jesus in the New Testament. Although scholars debate the particular meaning of various descriptions, Jesus clearly associated himself with the Old Testament messianic pictures of the servant, the cornerstone, and the Son of Man. The New Testament writers also refer to Jesus in these ways.[33]

Jesus Christ as Servant

In addition to four references of Jesus as servant found in the book of Acts,[34] a variety of other passages in the New Testament associate Jesus with the servant songs of Isaiah.[35] Allusions to Isaiah 53:11–12, for example, can be understood from Jesus' statements in Mark 10:43–45:

> Whoever wants to become great among you must be your servant, and whoever wants to be first must be slave of all. For even the Son of Man did not come to be served, but to serve, and to give his life as a ransom for many.

Other Old Testament elements in regard to Jesus are expressed in the form of direct quotations from the servant passages of Isaiah. In Matthew 8:17 his healing ministry is explained as fulfilling Isaiah 53:4: "He took up our infirmities and carried our sorrows." His withdrawal from the light of public attention is understood in the light of Isaiah 42:1–4, which is quoted in full in Matthew 12:15–21. His death among the lawless is understood in reference to Isaiah 53:12, which is quoted in Luke 22:37. The unbelief of the Jewish nation is explained in John 12:38 by a citation from Isaiah 53:1.

Jesus Christ as the Cornerstone

Speaking to the chief priests and the Pharisees in the temple, Jesus quotes Psalm 118:22–23 in describing himself as the precious cornerstone that was rejected by humanity (Matt. 21:42; cf. Mark 12:10–11; Luke 20:17–18). Peter and John clearly articulated this messianic connection in their witness for Jesus before the Jewish officials of the Sanhedrin: "He is 'the stone you builders rejected, which has become the capstone'" (Acts 4:11). In their letters, Paul and Peter, both citing Isaiah 28:16—Paul in Romans 9:33 and Peter in 1 Peter 2:6–8—also refer to Jesus as the precious cornerstone.[36]

Jesus Christ as the Son of Man

The New Testament refers to Jesus as the Son of Man more than eighty times. It is, in fact, the title most often used in the Gospels to refer to Jesus. As an allusion to his role as the Messiah, Jesus uses the phrase *Son of Man* in reference to his present authority for the forgiveness of sins (Mark 2:10), his lordship of the Sabbath (e.g., v. 28), and his impending suffering, death, and resurrection.[37] He also speaks of his future coming in glory, which is clearly reminiscent of the prophet Daniel's vision of "one like a son of man, coming with the clouds of heaven" (Dan. 7:13).[38]

Other New Testament writers, too, speak of Jesus as the Son of Man, particularly emphasizing his power and authority.[39] Luke in Acts 7 records Stephen, the first Christian martyr, as declaring that Jesus is the Son of Man. Immediately before his stoning, Stephen looks into heaven and sees the glory of God, and "the Son of Man standing at the right hand of God" (v. 56). In Revelation 1:13–16, the apostle John sees Jesus as

> someone 'like a son of man,' dressed in a robe reaching down to his feet and with a golden sash around his chest. His head and hair were white like wool, as white as snow, and his eyes were like blazing fire. His feet were like bronze glowing in a furnace, and his voice was like the sound of rushing waters. In his right hand he held seven stars, and out of his mouth came a sharp double-edged sword. His face was like the sun shining in all its brilliance.

John's response is to fall at the Lord's feet in worship as he rightly recognizes the authority that Jesus possesses as the Son of Man.[40]

These three descriptions of Jesus—as servant, cornerstone, and Son of Man—refer to Old Testament expectations of the Messiah. By using such terminology, Jesus, his disciples, and the writers of the New Testament clearly and deliberately tap into the messianic expectation promised from generations ago.

As prophesied in the Old Testament, the Messiah was to be the ultimate hope for God's people, fulfilling the roles of prophet, priest, and king. All of these expectations are fulfilled in Jesus as he is described in the New Testament.[41]

Truly, the great unfolding mystery and the ancient love song found in the Old Testament portrays our wonderful Savior in marvelous ways.[42] Some Christmas carols recall the great anticipation of the Messiah's being fulfilled with the appearance of Jesus Christ. One such carol is "Lo, How a Rose E'er Blooming," dating from the fifteenth century. It combines the messianic anticipation from the book of Isaiah with the reality of his appearance as is found in the Gospels:

> Lo, how a Rose e'er blooming
> From tender stem hath sprung!
> Of Jesse's lineage coming
> As men of old have sung.
> It came a Flower bright,

Amid the cold of winter,
When half-spent was the night.

Isaiah 'twas foretold it,
The Rose I have in mind;
With Mary we behold it,
The virgin mother kind.
To show God's love aright
She bore to men a Savior,
When half-spent was the night.

This Flower, who fragrance tender
With sweetness fills the air,
Dispels with glorious splendor
The darkness everywhere.
True man, yet very God,
From sin and death he saves us
And lightens every load.[43]

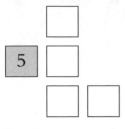

LAW

Regulating the Good Life

If the Spirit of grace is absent, the law is present only to convict and kill.
—Saint Augustine

It may be true that the law cannot make a man love me. But it can keep him from lynching me, and I think that's pretty important.
—Martin Luther King Jr.

The ancient empire of the Babylonians was known for its great system of laws, the code of Hammurabi. Formed in 1726 B.C. by the Babylonian king, this collection of laws dealt with property rights, loans, legal procedure, and personal injury. It also contained articles for the protection of all classes of Babylonian society, including the weak, poor, women, slaves, and children. It was a particularly humane code for its day and attests to the law and justice of Hammurabi's rule and the greatness of the Babylonian Empire.

Many centuries later, another great set of laws formed the backbone of another influential society. On June 15, 1215, King John of England sealed the Magna Carta, a series of promises to his subjects that he would govern England justly, and deal with his vassals in agreement with feudal law. No person, not even the king, would be above the law. The Magna Carta laid the foundation of British law and testified to the strength of the British Empire.

Similarly, the U. S. Constitution has guided the American republic

A copy of the Code of Hammurabi, unearthed by French archaeologists in Susa (in modern-day Iran) in the winter of 1901–1902. (Photograph courtesy of Todd Bolen and BiblePlaces.com.)

since 1787, outlining principles of political representation, the powers of the president, procedures for election to office, the role of the legislature, and the powers of the federal courts. This code of laws upholds American society and is an example of law for many developing countries in the world.

The greatest set of laws, however, was initially presented to the nation of Israel in a dramatic way at Mount Sinai—with smoke, fire, and lightning. These regulations eventually became the guiding principles of the nation of Israel (Exod. 19:16–20:26). Many of these laws, such as the Ten Commandments, are still widely known and revered throughout the world.[1]

Although the Law was a defining feature of ancient Israel, many neglect it in our day. Many within Western society question its relevance for contemporary law, and even some Christians consider it relatively unimportant. Many have never read the Old Testament Law and thus have little appreciation for it, this despite its importance in the flow of human history and its significance to the Christian faith, which follows in the footsteps of Judaism. This chapter considers key themes in the Law and their influence on our understanding of the New Testament.[2]

The Law in the Old Testament

The Hebrew word for Law *(tôrâh)* occurs 214 times in the Old Testament. As given to Moses by God, the Law occupies large sections of four of the first five books of the Old Testament. Much of the historical and prophetical books, too, are given over to accounts of the consequences of respect (or lack of respect) for the Law. The Law clearly, then, is a major component of the Old Testament.[3]

The Law Was a Great Possession of God's People

In the Old Testament, the Law is greatly valued, the treasured possession of God's people. Numerous times in the Old Testament, the Law is portrayed as Israel's unique and special possession.

In Moses' final speech to the nation of Israel, for example, found in Deuteronomy 4:7–8, he says, "What other nation is so great as to have their gods near them the way the LORD our God is near us whenever we pray to him? And what other nation is so great as to have such righteous decrees and laws as this body of laws I am setting before you today?" Later in that same chapter, Moses proclaims again the great privilege of possessing the Law:

> Ask now about the former days, long before your time from the day God created man on the earth; ask from one end of the heavens to the other. Has anything so great as this ever happened, or has anything like it ever been heard of? Has any other people heard the voice of God speaking out of fire, as you have, and lived? Has any god ever tried to take for himself one nation out of another nation, by testings, by miraculous signs and wonders, by war, by a mighty hand and an outstretched arm, or by great and awesome deeds, like all the things the LORD your God did for you in Egypt before your very eyes? (Deut. 4:32–34)

Later, too, in Israel's history, God's people proclaim the value of the Law. In Psalm 147:19–20, the psalmist proclaims, "He has revealed his word to Jacob, his laws and decrees to Israel. He has done this for no other nation; they do not know his laws. Praise the Lord." Other places in the Old Testament express that possessing the law makes God's people wiser than their enemies (e. g., Deut. 4:6; Ps. 119:98–99).[4] Possession of the Law is, then, considered a unique blessing for God's people.

Great benefits, too, are found in adhering to the Law. According to Psalm 19:7–11,

> The law of the LORD is perfect,
> reviving the soul.
> The statutes of the LORD are trustworthy,
> making wise the simple.
> The precepts of the LORD are right,
> giving joy to the heart.
> The commands of the LORD are radiant,
> giving light to the eyes.
> The fear of the LORD is pure,
> enduring forever.
> The ordinances of the LORD are sure
> and altogether righteous.
> They are more precious than gold,
> than much pure gold;
> they are sweeter than honey,
> than honey from the comb.
> By them is your servant warned;
> in keeping them there is great reward.

This psalm declares that the fruit of following the Law makes one spiritually wealthy: "the ordinances of the Lord . . . are more precious than gold." Gold, of course, has always been a much desired commodity. The gold rush in Australia in 1851 led to the tripling of that country's population in the next nine years. New Zealand saw its population double in six years when gold was discovered in 1861. Johannesburg, South Africa, was founded as a result of a gold rush in 1886. San Francisco in 1849 grew from a small town to a city of 25,000 people in one year's time as people rushed west to find gold.

People will also endure a tremendous amount of hardship to find gold.

For those who traveled west across the United States in 1849, they endured heat, difficult terrain, and a lack of food and water in the hopes of striking it rich in California. Once they reached the mother lode, gold miners would spend ten hours a day in knee-deep, ice cold water, digging, sifting, and washing. They endured this backbreaking work in hopes that they would find the precious commodity of gold.

By comparison, though, the Law of God is of far greater worth than anything else that can be owned in this world.

A phylactery is a small box containing passages from the Law. During prayer, one was bound on the forehead and the other on the arm—fastened so as to be near to the heart. (Photograph courtesy of Todd Bolen and BiblePlaces.com.)

The Law Regulated One's Relationship with God and Others

Unlike most laws which simply regulate conduct between people in society, the Law of God describes as well the proper ways in which God's people should relate to him.

The first four commandments of the Decalogue (the Ten Commandments) regulate the people's relationship with God (Exod. 20:1–17; Deut. 5:6–21). They are to have no other gods before God, they are not to have idols or take God's name in vain, and they are to keep the Sabbath holy (set apart). The other six commandments regulate relationships with other people—exhorting them to honor their parents and prohibiting them from committing murder, adultery, stealing, false witnessing, and coveting. These commandments exemplify the essence of the Law.

A second section of the Law, which also regulates the relationship between the people and God, might be called the Book of the Covenant (Exod. 20:22–23:33).[5] It provides specific instructions for worship and the conduct of certain festivals (20:22–26; 23:14–19). The Law also includes regulations concerning the rights of slaves, retaliation for personal injury, rules relating to livestock, theft, dishonesty, property damage, seduction (22:16–17), and the protection of rights (21:2–23:13). This section concludes with a statement that addresses the relationship of God to his covenant people as they prepare to enter the Promised Land (23:20–33).

A third section of the Law concerns ethical and religious matters (Deut. 12:1–26:19), including the establishment of a central place of worship (12); avoidance of idolatry (13); injunctions concerning food, tithes, the Sabbath year, festivals, and leaders (14:1–17:13); laws regarding criminals, wars, manslaughter, marriage and family life (19:1–22:30); directives regarding congregational life, protection for the weak, and first fruits (23:1–26:19).

Leviticus 17–26, which encompasses a fourth section of the Law, has been called by some scholars "the holiness code."[6] This section comprises laws necessary for worship and life in the covenant community, including laws governing sacrifices, sexual relationships, religious and ethical laws, standards for priests, consecration of seasons and festivals, and the conduct of Sabbath and Jubilee years (Lev. 17:1–25:55). This section concludes with a listing of blessings for obedience and punishments for disobedience (26:1–46).

The final section of the Law addresses ceremonial law. Scattered throughout Exodus, Leviticus, Numbers, and Deuteronomy, these ceremonial laws governed the religious rituals, fasts, and feasts of the community.[7] Elaborate rituals governed the ways in which God's people could approach him, because approaching God in the wrong way could lead to disaster.[8]

Seen together, these five sections of the Law promote right conduct before God and between people.

THE FIVE SECTIONS OF THE LAW

1. Ten Commandments (Exod. 20:1–17; Deut. 5:6–21)
2. Book of the Covenant (Exod. 20:22–23:33)
3. Government of Israel (Deut. 12:1–26:19)
4. "The Holiness Code" (Lev. 17–26)
5. Ceremonial Law (found throughout Exodus, Leviticus, Numbers, Deuteronomy)

God's Blessing or Curse Results from One's Obedience or Disobedience to the Law

The Law provided clear standards for God's people to follow. If they kept the commandments, they would receive blessing; if they disobeyed, they would be cursed. This may be hard for many to understand in our day and age where laws are broken with few ramifications. It is abundantly clear, however, that in Old Testament times, God's blessing or curse resulted from one's obedience or disobedience to the Law.

At the end of Deuteronomy, in his final speech to the people of Israel, Moses restates much of the Law and concludes by declaring the benefits of fulfilling the Law and the consequences of disobeying it. Some of the blessings include prosperity in their dwelling places, an abundance of children and food, safety in travel, victory over enemies, a great name, rain in its season, wealth, and honor (Deut. 28:3–13). The consequences of not following the Law are detailed in Deuteronomy 28:15–68, a section even lengthier than the one on blessings. These curses include disasters, pestilence, sickness, drought, a lack of food, defeat by enemies, dishonor, confusion, theft, loss of family members, boils, exile, locusts, and poor harvests (vv. 16–42). Disobedience ultimately would lead to slavery to other nations, plagues like those from Egypt, exile, abandonment, and misery (vv. 47–68). These curses would come upon the people, pursuing and overtaking them until they were destroyed.

Specific examples of blessings for following the Law can be found in the book of Joshua. Before God's people enter the Promised Land, Joshua promises success if the nation will meditate day and night on God's Law (Josh. 1:8). Throughout this book, which documents the illustrative battles and victories of God's people, they conquer fortified cities such as Jericho when they follow the Law. They achieve victories over the Amorites, Canaanites, Hittites, Perizzites, Jebusites, and Hivites. At the end of his life, Joshua attributes these victories to Israel's adherence to the Law. In one of his final speeches, he says,

> Be very strong; be careful to obey all that is written in the Book of the Law of Moses, without turning aside to the right or to the left. . . . You are to hold fast to the Lord your God, as you have until now. The Lord has driven out before you great and powerful nations; to this day no one has been able to withstand you. One of you routs a thousand, because the Lord your God fights for you, just as he promised. So be very careful to love the Lord your God. (Josh. 23:6–11)

Success for following the Law can also be seen in various accounts of the Jewish kings. When a king led the people in obedience to the Law, the nation prospered. The account of King Josiah most notably reveals the blessings that resulted from following the Law. In the eighteenth year of Josiah's reign, some of his officials discover the book of the Law while the house of the Lord is being repaired. Upon hearing the Law, King Josiah tears his clothes in grief and declares,

> Go and inquire of the Lord for me and for the people and for all Judah about what is written in this book that has been found. Great is the Lord's anger that burns against us because our fathers have not obeyed the words of this book; they have not acted in accordance with all that is written there concerning us. (2 Kings 22:13)

Josiah subsequently examines the commandments and decrees found in the Law and follows them with all of his heart and soul. He also influences the entire nation to follow these decrees. He deposes idolatrous priests, destroys idols, destroys high places, and removes shrines. He also celebrates the Passover and establishes the practices of the book of the Law (cf. 2 Kings 23). As a result, his rule is blessed and he is remembered as a king who turned to the Lord with all his heart, soul, and mind (v. 25).[9]

As surely as blessings for keeping the Law can be seen in the history of God's people, so too, can be seen the consequences of ignoring the Law or rebelling against it. In 2 Chronicles 12, King Rehoboam is said to have abandoned the Law of the Lord—which is equivalent to abandoning the Lord himself (vv. 1, 5). As a direct result of his turning away from the Law and the Lord, Rehoboam is attacked by King Shishak of Egypt, who captures many of the cities of Judah and then rules over the kingdom. Shishak carries off the treasures of the temple and the royal palace. The enemies of God's people rule over the nation of Israel as a direct result of King Rehoboam's disregard for the Law of the Lord.

The consequences of rebellion against God's Law can also be seen in the account of other kings of Israel and Judah. King Manasseh of Judah, for example, did many evil things in the sight of the Lord. Besides building idols to put on the high places surrounding the nation, he also built altars in the Temple, the place where God's name alone was supposed to dwell. He practiced soothsaying and augury, activities specifically condemned by God's Law (cf. Lev. 19:26; Deut. 18:14). As a result of Manasseh's disobedience, God brought fearful judgment on the nation, promising to bring great evil and to cast his people into exile (2 Kings 21:1–16). Because of his disobedience of the Law, Manasseh eventually was confined in manacles and taken into captivity (2 Chron. 33:11).[10]

Manasseh's deliberate breaking of the Law had, even beyond his death, major ramifications on God's people. The penalties for his defiance of the Law of God could not be completely overcome by Josiah's good efforts (2 Kings 23:26). Judah's exile into Babylon over 50 years later is directly related to the evil deeds performed by King Manasseh:

> Surely these things happened to Judah according to the LORD's command, in order to remove them from his presence because of

the sins of Manasseh and all he had done, including the shedding of innocent blood. For he had filled Jerusalem with innocent blood, and the LORD was not willing to forgive. (2 Kings 24:3–4)

Manasseh's flagrant disobedience to the Law (and God's judgment of such behavior) can be seen in the lives of other kings, such as Ahab, Jehoahaz, Menahem, Hoshea, Amon, Jehoiakim, and Jehoiachin.[11] Deliberate disobedience to the Law led to God's extending his hand of judgment.

The Law Is Ultimately to Be Fulfilled by New Hearts

Although the Law was recorded plainly in the Old Testament, Israel's history is filled with examples of the people's refusing to follow it. Still, the Old Testament contains promises that God's people will eventually fulfill the Law, despite their past. In Deuteronomy 30:6, 8, for example, Moses prophesies,

The Lord your God will circumcise your hearts and the hearts of your descendants, so that you may love him with all your heart and with all your soul, and live. . . . You will again obey the LORD and follow his commands I am giving you today.

The promise of a new heart to obey God's commandments is repeated elsewhere in the Old Testament:

I [the Lord] will give them an undivided heart and put a new spirit in them; I will remove from them their heart of stone and give them a heart of flesh. Then they will follow my decrees and be careful to keep my laws. They will be my people, and I will be their God (Ezek. 11:19–20; cf. 36:26–27).

The prophet Jeremiah declares a similar promise:

"The time is coming," declares the LORD,
  "when I will make a new covenant
with the house of Israel
  and with the house of Judah.

> It will not be like the covenant
> I made with their forefathers
> when I took them by the hand
> to lead them out of Egypt,
> because they broke my covenant,
> though I was a husband to them,"
> declares the LORD.
> "This is the covenant I will make
> with the house of Israel
> after that time," declares the LORD.
> "I will put my law in their minds
> and write it on their hearts.
> I will be their God,
> and they will be my people."[12]
>   (Jer. 31:31–33)

Many passages in the Old Testament promise a new heart to God's people so that in the future they would be able to keep the Law completely. Their hearts of stone would be replaced by hearts of flesh.

The promise of a new heart cannot help but offer encouragement. As an analogy, consider the fine medical care available in most Western societies. Today, many people have access, for example, to donated organs. Many live in hope that they will soon receive a new lung, kidney, or even a heart that will help to extend their lives. Indeed, some, after having received a donated organ, have lived another twenty years or more with an improved quality of life. Organ donation thus provides hope to many people whose health is failing. Likewise, the new heart that God promised his people gave them hope for the future. Even when they found themselves falling short of God's perfect standards, the promise of a new heart encouraged them in anticipating the day when the Law of God would be written on their hearts.

THE LAW IN THE NEW TESTAMENT

Although the emphasis on the Law is found largely in the Old Testament, its influence is found many places in the New Testament. The Greek word for "law," *nomos,* occurs more than 150 times in the New Testament, and many other New Testament passages assume knowledge of the Law from the Old Testament.

The Law Is a Valuable Commodity

The value of the Old Testament Law in a New Testament context is amply conveyed in the Gospels. Jesus, for example, declares the importance of the Law in the Sermon on the Mount:

> Do not think that I have come to abolish the Law and the Prophets; I have not come to abolish them but to fulfill them. I tell you the truth until heaven and earth disappear, not the smallest letter, not the least stroke of a pen, will by any means disappear from the Law until everything is accomplished. (Matt. 5:17–18; cf. Luke 16:17)

Jesus' declaration is extraordinary in light of the intricate nature of the written Hebrew language. The Hebrew letter, *yodh*, for example, represented by a ׳, is such a small letter that its omission might easily be overlooked in a handwritten document. The difference between the letters *daleth* (ד) and *resh* (ר) involves a slight stroke of the pen; the omission of such a stroke could happen fairly easily. In a language filled with jots and tittles, it would be very easy, then, for the "least stroke of a pen" to disappear. Jesus' claim that this will not happen with respect to the Law demonstrates his view that the Law has lasting value.[13]

Jesus deliberately observed the Law in his conduct. He attended the major feasts in Jerusalem, paid the half-shekel temple tax (Matt. 17:24–27), and wore the prescribed edge on his robe (9:20; cf. Num. 15:38–41). He also observed Passover, even his last one, at which he knew that on the next day he would die (Matt. 26:17–19; cf. Num. 9:1–14).

At other times in the Gospels, Jesus appears to contradict the Law, particularly with regard to Sabbath observance. In Matthew 12, for example, he is accused of breaking the Law by having the disciples pick heads of grain on the Sabbath. On a later Sabbath, Jesus heals a man with a withered hand, emphasizing the importance of caring for people in need rather than adhering strictly to the human traditions of the day. A closer look at both of these instances shows that Jesus did not contradict the Law. Rather, he contradicted the religious traditions that the Pharisees were advocating (vv. 1–13). Looking after one's own physical needs and attending to the needs of others is obedience to a higher principle.

The book of Acts reveals the high value that many of the early Christians ascribed to the Law. The church in Jerusalem was particularly law observant, as shown in Acts 21:20, which states that thousands of Christian Jews were "zealous for the law." Many Christian Jews continued to function as priests (Acts 6:7), practice circumcision (11:2–3), attend Jewish festivals (20:16), and participate in temple ceremonies and sacrifices (2:46; 3:10; 21:23–26). They also continued to observe food regulations that were originally set forward in the Law (10:9–16).[14]

Peter had a vision in which he was instructed three times to kill and eat meat that was considered unclean according to the Law. He refused because of his respect for the Law (Acts 10).[15] This same respect for the Law can be seen in the lengthy debates among the church leaders regarding the application of the Law to Gentile Christians. In Acts 15, which records the only church council mentioned in the Bible, the place of the Law in the lives of Gentile believers is the key issue—namely, do Gentiles who have become Christians need to keep the Law like the Jews? After much discussion among the elders, and testimony from such witnesses as Paul and Barnabas, James, the leader of the church in Jerusalem and a Jewish Christian, declares the council's decision:

> It is my judgment, therefore, that we should not make it difficult for the Gentiles who are turning to God. Instead, we should write to them, telling them to abstain from food polluted by idols, from sexual immorality, from the meat of strangled animals and from blood. For Moses has been preached in every city from the earliest times and is read in the synagogues on every Sabbath. (Acts 15:19–21)

The apostle Paul's respect for the Law can be seen in his letters to the Romans and the Galatians. In Romans 3:2, he speaks of the privilege of the Jewish people in being entrusted with the "oracles of God." In Romans 9:4–6, he affirms that the Law of God was part of Israel's great heritage. He devotes eight chapters in Romans, his most systematic letter, to discussion of the Law and its proper place.[16] Indeed, he claims, "we uphold the Law" (3:31).[17]

Most of Paul's letter to the Galatians is spent discussing the Law. From the middle of the second chapter through the fifth chapter, he argues against those in Galatia who want a larger role for the Law. As in Romans, because the place of the Law is significant, it cannot be dismissed with a short statement.[18]

Some of the Law Continues to Regulate Christian Behavior

In the New Testament, the ceremonial Law is ultimately set aside in favor of new covenant practices. This is so because Christ in his sacrifice fulfilled the requirements of the ceremonial Law once and for all. The other provisions of the Law, however, continue to exert their influence over the lives of God's people.

In many instances, Jesus used the Law to teach proper behavior. He argued from the Law, for example, concerning the greatest commandments:

One of the teachers of the law came and heard them debating. Noticing that Jesus had given them a good answer, he asked him, "Of all the commandments, which is the most important?" "The most important one," answered Jesus, "is this: 'Hear, O Israel, the Lord our God, the Lord is one. Love the Lord your God with all your heart and with all your soul and with all your mind and with all your strength.' The second is this: 'Love your neighbor as yourself.' There is no commandment greater than these." (Mark 12:28–31; cf. Matt. 22:36–40; Luke 10:26–30)

In the Sermon on the Mount, Jesus again uses the Law as a basis for Christian ethics:

You have heard that it was said to the people long ago, "Do not murder, and anyone who murders will be subject to judgment." But I tell you that anyone who is angry with his brother will be subject to judgment. Again, anyone who says to his brother, "Raca," is answerable to the Sanhedrin. But anyone who says, "You fool!" will be in danger of the fire of hell. (Matt. 5:21–22)

Jesus did not discard the Law but used it as a building block for Christian instruction, doing so in other sections of the Sermon on the Mount (Matt. 5:27–48).[19]

Paul, too, used the Law as a means to regulate Christian behavior. In Romans 13:9, for example, he cites a number of the Ten Commandments: "Do not commit adultery," "Do not murder," "Do not steal," "Do not covet." In Ephesians 6:2, he cites another of the Ten Commandments: "Honor your father and mother."

On other occasions, Paul drew directly from Leviticus and Deuteronomy for instruction about revenge, idolatry, and provision.[20] The commandments against idolatry, for example, can be heard in his encouragement to Christians not to eat food offered to idols (1 Cor. 8–10).[21]

James, as well, used the Old Testament Law to regulate Christian conduct. James 2:11, for example, quotes two of the Ten Commandments, "Do not kill" and "do not commit adultery," and the book of James repeats these same ideas in 4:1–4. Leviticus 19, a portion of the Law concerning ritual holiness and purity, also influences large sections of James's epistle.[22]

The Value of the Law Magnifies the Greatness of Christ

When the Law is seen as a valuable commodity, it magnifies the greatness of Jesus Christ, because he surpasses even the Law. As valuable as the Law is in the New Testament, Jesus Christ is of greater importance, and his completed work is exalted over the place of the Law.

Christ's superiority over the Law is made plain in many passages in the Gospels, Paul's letters, and in the book of Hebrews. By his own words, Jesus indicated that his mission surpassed the Law. In Luke 16:16 he states, "The Law and the Prophets were proclaimed until John [the Baptist]. Since that time, the good news of the kingdom of God is being preached, and everyone is forcing his way into it."[23] His statement indicates that the time of the Law and the Prophets has been fulfilled and is now surpassed in him. Since the time of John the Baptist, who announced the coming of Jesus (cf. 3:1–22), the Law and the Prophets were subsumed by the new mission of Jesus Christ.

Paul, who more than any author in the New Testament has the most to say about the Law, also saw Christ as being exalted above the Law. In Romans, Paul explains that the Law cannot save, but that Jesus can (cf. 2:12–27; 3:19–20; 3:23–24; 6:23). In 10:4, Paul states the purpose of the Law: "Christ is the end of the law so that there may be righteousness for everyone who believes." In this verse, the word used for *end* is the Greek word *telos*, which can mean "end," but can also be translated "completion," "achievement," or "purpose."[24] Christ, then, becomes the completion, achievement, or purpose for which the Law was established. So although the Law is glorious, Christ is more glorious still.

In Galatians, Paul further establishes Christ's surpassing value by comparing him with the Law. Galatians 3:24–25 states the purpose of the Law as secondary to Christ.[25] It was put in place to *lead us* to Christ (or as some versions translate it, the Law was our "schoolteacher").[26] The schoolteacher or disciplinarian is, of course, valuable. Such a person instructs or prepares children in how to conduct themselves. Good schoolteachers train their students in reading and writing, preparing them for life beyond the schoolroom. Sometimes that instruction can be harsh, as it was in schools many years ago, so that the student learns with pain. Despite sometimes delivering pain, the good schoolteacher prepares the student in the best way possible for the future. So, too, from Paul's perspective, the Law is a good schoolteacher that prepares Christians to walk in freedom with Christ.

The corrective value of the Law has been stated well by others throughout history. C. H. Spurgeon, the great Baptist preacher, expresses well the purpose of the Law: "The heart is like a dark cellar, full of lizards, cockroaches, beetles, and all kinds of reptiles and insects, which in the dark we see not. But the Law takes down the shutters and lets in the light, and we see the evil." Samuel Bolton rightly says about the Law, "When you see that men have been wounded by the Law, then it is time to pour in the gospel oil. It is the sharp needle of the Law that makes way for the scarlet thread of the gospel."

John Calvin, noting that Christ is superior to the Law, wrote, "In the maxims of the law, God is seen as the rewarder of perfect righteousness and the avenger of sin. But in Christ, his face shines out, full of grace and gentleness to poor, unworthy sinners." The Law corrects and prepares so that one may be led to Christ.

The book of Hebrews, too, places Christ in an exalted place in relation to the Law. In a letter with many references to the Old Testament Law, the writer repeatedly proclaims Christ as greater. He is the greater revelation, servant, priest, hope, and mediator than the Law and its systems.[27] Indeed, compared to what was originally set forth in the Law, Christ ushered in a great change in the way God interacts with his people.

Regarding Jesus in relation to the Law, Hebrews provides the particularly imaginative illustration of an object to its shadow (Heb. 10:1).[28] If one sees a shadow, there must be something casting the shadow, whether a building, a tree, or a person. Depending on the angle of the sun, the shadow may be long or short, defined or fuzzy. The shadow is, of course, a poor representation of the object, because the shadow is two dimensional and opaque. Only the object itself can fully represent itself. The writer of Hebrews makes it plain that Jesus is the true object and the Law is the shadow. As glorious as the Law is, Jesus is more glorious still.

No New Testament writer or figure disputed the greatness that the Law held for God's people who lived during the time of the Old Testament. The person of Jesus Christ, however, far surpasses it.

The Law Is Fulfilled When It Is Written upon Hearts

The Old Testament promises in many places that the Law would be fulfilled by obedient hearts. God himself would place his Law in the hearts of people, and as a result, God's people would be obedient and receive no more condemnation.[29]

In the New Testament, the Law is portrayed as having great value, pointing people to Christ, and elevating Christ in his glory. But God's people will not be able to follow the Law until God writes it on their hearts. Apart from Christ's gracious work, the Law functions as an unwilling ally of sin: "The sting of death is sin, and the power of sin is the law" (1 Cor. 15:56). It brings condemnation and death (e.g., 2 Cor. 3:6; Gal. 3:10, 21–22) and, as Paul testifies in Romans 7:9–12, it even brings misery:

Once I was alive apart from law; but when the commandment came, sin sprang to life and I died. I found that the very commandment that was intended to bring life actually brought death. For sin, seizing the opportunity afforded by the commandment, deceived me, and through the commandment put me to death. So then, the law is holy, and the commandment is holy, righteous and good.

Only when the Law is written on their hearts will people be able to follow it. Saint Augustine states this need, saying, "The law was given, in order to convert a great into a little man—to show that you have no power of your own for righteousness and might thus, poor, needy, and destitute, flee to grace."

The promise of a new heart prophesied in the Old Testament is found in the New Testament, particularly in 2 Corinthians 3: "You show that you are a letter from Christ, the result of our ministry, written not with ink but with the Spirit of the living God, not on tablets of stone but on tablets of human hearts"(v. 3).[30] These Old Testament promises are further suggested in verse 6: "He has made us competent as ministers of a new covenant—not of the letter but of the Spirit; for the letter kills but, the Spirit gives life." According to Paul, Christians show themselves to be walking examples of the Law. The Holy Spirit has written the Law on the tablets of human hearts rather than on stone tablets.[31] As a result, Christians receive the benefits of the most glorious ministry of the Spirit (vv. 7–12). Although the way Moses received the Law was spectacular, it is amazingly divine for God to write his Law in a Christian's heart. Only the Lord himself could do something so magnificent.[32]

There's a great difference, after all, between knowing something in our hearts and knowing something only in our heads. Anyone can read a cookbook or a manual on how to do home repair, but it's an entirely different thing to put theory into practice, working out that knowledge and thus demonstrating to others an experiential knowledge of cooking or carpentry. This is a reasonable parallel to what Paul describes in 2 Corinthians 3. The letter of the Law taught people how they ought to behave. Because it also exposed people's weaknesses again and again, it brought death (vv. 6, 9). Now, however, the Law has been written on human hearts, and it brings life and freedom (vv. 6, 17). Further, it re-sults in Christians demonstrating "ever-increasing glory" as they know in their heads and experience in their hearts the true Law of God that leads to their transformation "into his likeness" (v. 18).

The Law at times may seem outdated or oppressive, but as it becomes a living presence in our hearts its power can truly be seen, as this hymn so aptly describes:

> O Word of God Incarnate,
> O Wisdom from on high,
> O Truth unchanged, unchanging,
> O Light of our dark sky,
> We praise Thee for the radiance
> That from the hallowed page,
> A lantern to our footsteps,
> Shines on from age to age.
>
> The Church from her dear Master
> Received the gift divine,
> And still that light she lifteth,
> O'er all the earth to shine;
> It is the golden casket
> Where gems of truth are stored;
> It is the heaven-drawn picture
> Of Christ, the living Word.
>
> It floateth like a banner
> Before God's host unfurled;
> It shineth like a beacon
> Above the darkling world;
> It is the chart and compass
> That o'er life's surging sea,
> 'Mid mists and rocks and quicksands,
> Still guides, O Christ, to Thee.

O make Thy Church, dear Saviour,
A lamp of purest gold,
To bear before the nations
Thy true light, as of old;
O teach Thy wandering pilgrims
By this their path to trace,
Till clouds and darkness ended,
They see Thee face to face.[33]

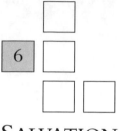

6

SALVATION

Amazing Grace!

> Rock of Ages, cleft for me,
> Let me hide myself in thee.
> Let the water and the blood,
> From thy wounded side which flowed,
> Be of sin the double cure,
> Save from wrath and make me pure.
> —A. M. Toplady

> My only hope of salvation is in the infinite, transcendent love of God manifested to the world by the death of his Son upon the cross. Nothing but his blood will wash away my sins. I rely exclusively upon it. Come, Lord Jesus! Come quickly!
> —Benjamin Rush,
> Signer of the American Declaration
> of Independence

For many Christians, there is no greater matter than personal salvation. The main concern of many evangelistic and mission organizations today is to see the evangelization of as many people as possible.

The enthusiasm to share the message of salvation can be clearly heard in the words of popular evangelists of our day. Luis Palau, for example, dreams for "an international revival of Christianity." He would love "to see the nations truly reawaken where not just a few thousand, but millions hear the Good News and discover Christ."

Billy Graham has said, "There is no more urgent and critical question in life than that of your personal relationship with God and your eternal salvation." On another occasion, he said, "The most important thing that we have to settle in this life is our eternal salvation. Those who ignore God's warnings and invitations do so at great peril." Indeed, personal salvation is of great importance.

It is unfortunate at times that when many respond to the message of salvation, they often do not take time to understand the importance of the underpinnings of their salvation: redemption, atonement, and justification. As long ago as 1915, in a lecture at Princeton Seminary, B. B. Warfield, the great theologian, noted with regard to words like *redemption*, that western Christians were "at the death bed of a word." He said, "It is sad to witness the death of any worthy thing—even of a worthy word [like redemption]. . . . Sadder still is the dying out in the hearts of men of the things for which the words stand."[1] Certainly, in our day this could be said of the word *redemption*, but also for *atonement* and *justification*.

This chapter, then, considers Old Testament elements behind these three key words, and thus lends understanding to the use of these words in the New Testament. It is hoped that by tracing each of these elements through the Old and the New Testament, the greatness of salvation will be truly understood.

OLD TESTAMENT CONCEPTS REGARDING SALVATION

Redemption

In American culture, perhaps the most common use of the word *redemption* is in a financial sense—as the repurchase of shares of stock. We also might think of redemption in terms of liberation, emancipation, or recovery. Slaves, animals, and property can all be redeemed.

The Old Testament uses *redemption* in the sense of buying something back, but other elements of redemption have deeper import. First, redemption was bound up in the law of the kinsman-redeemer. A kinsman-redeemer was a close male relative, such as a brother, uncle, father, or cousin, who was concerned about the welfare of his family. He would buy back a relative out of financial problems or out of slavery (Lev. 25:23–34, 48–52; cf. Jer. 32:7–8). He also would redeem the life of a murdered relative by destroying the killer (Num. 35:19; 2 Sam. 14:11). In this way, the kinsman-redeemer would function as an "avenger of blood."

The kinsman-redeemer could also support his family in many other ways. He could marry a deceased relative's widow to produce an heir (Ruth 2:20; 3:9, 13; 4:1–14), in this way intervening to help strengthen the family. The redeemer could also support a needy relative in a lawsuit (Job 19:25; Prov. 23:11) or help pursue justice for someone who was illegally imprisoned (Ps. 72:14; Jer. 50:34). In all of these situations, the kinsman-redeemer protected the family against weakness and worked to restore any losses.

In the Old Testament, a kinsman-redeemer was not always required in order for redemption to occur. A firstborn male who was offered to the Lord could, for example, simply be redeemed for a price (Exod. 13:2, 13; 22:29f.; cf. Luke 2:23). The life of an animal or the payment of a certain sum of money could be substituted for a person's life (Exod.13:13; 34:20). A human son, for example, could be redeemed by paying five shekels, which was to be given to the priests (v. 13, 15; Num. 18:15f.; cf. 3:44–51).[2] This was called "redemption money" (Num. 3:51). Land or a home could also be redeemed for a price, thus not requiring the intervention of the kinsman-redeemer (cf. Lev. 27:14–25).

The best example of redemption in the Old Testament is found in the book of Exodus, when God is the redeemer who frees his people from the nation of Egypt. In Exodus 6:6–8 he speaks with Moses about his plan of redemption:

> I am the Lord, and I will bring you out from under the yoke of the Egyptians. I will free you from being slaves to them, and I will redeem you with an outstretched arm and with mighty acts of judgment. I will take you as my own people, and I will be your God. Then you will know that I am the Lord your God, who brought you out from under the yoke of the Egyptians. And I will bring you to the land I swore with uplifted hand to give to Abraham, to Isaac and to Jacob. I will give it to you as a possession. I am the Lord.

In Exodus, God's people are redeemed from slavery and bondage, which in Exodus 1:11–14 is described as ruthless and oppressive with forced labor. This cruel treatment is mentioned in other accounts in Exodus as well (5:6–23). When many years later the Israelites look back on their time in Egypt, it would be remembered, in fact, as one of slavery and bitter bondage (cf. Deut. 7:8; 13:5; Mic. 6:4).

A second element here of redemption is that God, not a human kinsman, is the redeemer, bringing his people out of slavery. Exodus 6:1 says, "Then the LORD said to Moses, 'Now you will see what I will do to Pharaoh: Because of my mighty hand he will let them go; because of my mighty hand he will drive them out of his country.'"

In Exodus 13:3, Moses reminds the people of God's redemption of them: "Commemorate this day, the day you came out of Egypt, out of the land of slavery, because the LORD brought you out of it with a mighty hand. Eat nothing containing yeast" (cf. v. 9). Elsewhere, too, in the Old Testament, the strength of God's hand is seen as ultimately responsible for his people's freedom (cf. 15:6; Deut. 9:26; Neh. 1:10; Ps. 77:17).

A third element of redemption is God's commitment to his people. He redeems Israel based on his prior covenant relationship with them as the "God of their ancestors."[3] This commitment is seen most clearly in the calling of Moses at the burning bush (Exodus 3). In that encounter, God appears to Moses and announces his commitment to the people of Israel. He is the God of Abraham, Isaac, and Jacob, the God of the ancestors of Israel (2:24; 3:6).[4] Because of his commitment to their forefathers, God will free his people from the burden of slavery and bring them to the land that he promised to Abraham, Isaac, and Jacob (6:7–8).

This pattern of redemption—that God will purchase his people from slavery, based on his covenant relationship with them—is repeated throughout the Old Testament. In the second half of Isaiah, for example, God as Redeemer surfaces again, being called Redeemer thirteen times in Isaiah 40–66.[5] As in the book of Exodus, God honors his covenant and with a strong hand brings his people out of bondage (cf. 43:15–17; 51:10–11; 52:3–6, 9; 54:10; 59:21; 60:16–17). Great is this picture of redemption in the Old Testament.

In more recent history, one man who understood the joy of redemption was Philip Bliss, one of America's greatest hymn writers. By the time he was thirty-eight, he had written such hymns as "Hold the Fort," "Almost Persuaded," "Let the Lower Lights Be Burning," "Hallelujah! What a Savior!" and the music to "It Is Well with My Soul."

Besides being a hymn writer, Bliss was also known as a genuine person. His employer and publisher, W. F. Root, said of him, "It is rare indeed to find both mind and body alike so strong, healthy, and beautiful in one individual as they were in him. . . . His smile went into his religion and his religion into his smile. His Lord was always welcome and apparently always there in his open and loving heart."[6]

On December 29, 1876, Philip Bliss and his wife died in a train wreck in Ashtabula, Ohio. That night, eighty-seven souls fell into eternity in eleven railcars of raging fire. Of the 161 passengers, ninety-two died—either killed outright or later dying of injuries sustained in the crash—and sixty-nine others were injured. At that point in American history it was the worst railroad tragedy ever to have occurred. Although the bodies of Philip Bliss and his wife were not found, his suitcase was recovered. Inside was found a sheet of lyrics that speak of the wonders of redemption, a redemption that marked Philip Bliss's disposition so well:

> I will sing of my Redeemer
> And his wondrous love to me;
> On the cruel cross he suffered
> From the curse to set me free.
>
> Sing, O sing of my redeemer,
> With his blood he purchased me;
> On the cross he sealed my pardon,
> Paid the debt and made me free.[7]

The hymn speaks of being brought out of a lost estate by Christ's sacrificial love. It also exudes great joy. The lyrics were set to music, and it remains another favorite of the remarkable songwriter who knew redemption so well.[8]

Atonement

In our day, the word *atonement* is most often used when a mistake has been made or when forgiveness is needed. It may be used to refer to a special act required for missing an anniversary, coming late to work, or miscalculating a sum of money, and is performed when someone hopes to make up for something that went wrong.

The Old Testament elements of atonement, however, have far deeper meaning than simply making personal reparation after a mistake.[9] First, atonement is a necessary remedy for all human sin, and the Old Testament is replete with the idea that humanity is in dire need. 1 Kings 8:46, for example, says that "there is no one who does not sin" (cf. 2 Chron. 6:36). Ecclesiastes 7:20 declares, "There is not a righteous man on earth who does what is right and never sins." Psalm 14:2–3 says, "The LORD looks down from heaven on the sons of men to see if there are any who understand, any who seek God. All have turned aside, they have together become corrupt; there is no one who does good, not even one." These are but a sampling of the many verses in the Old Testament that indicate humanity's need for atonement (cf. Job 14:4; Prov. 20:9).[10]

A second element in biblical atonement is its requirement of a sacrifice involving the shedding of blood. The strong connection between sacrifice, blood, and atonement is, in fact, well established in the Old Testament.[11] Blood sacrifice is especially explicit in Leviticus 16, which details the sacrifices held each year on the Day of Atonement,[12] a significant event in the life of Israel in which the entire nation would have their sins cleansed.[13] In the elaborate atonement ritual, the high priest offered the blood of a bull for his own sin (16:6, 11), and he sacrificed a goat for the sins of the people (v. 9). The blood from the bull and goat were then applied to the Ark of the Covenant, sprinkled on what was called the "atonement cover" (vv. 13–15). Next, the high priest took more blood from these animals and sprinkled it seven times on the horns of the altar (vv. 18–19). The shedding of blood, then, was clearly essential for the atonement of sins.[14]

The sacrifice of other specific animals was also necessary for the atonement to be done properly. In addition to the bull and the goat, two rams were brought by the high priest—one for himself as a burnt offering, and one for the people. For the congregation, he brought two male goats as a sin offering and a ram as a burnt offering.[15] The animals were sacrificed in a particular order, according to the Law, and the incense and burning coals had to be placed in the correct spot.[16] The high priest also wore sacred garments, including a linen coat, linen breeches, linen girdle, and a linen miter (cf. Lev. 16:23, 32). He was also required to bathe before he dressed so that he would be clean before putting on the priestly garments.

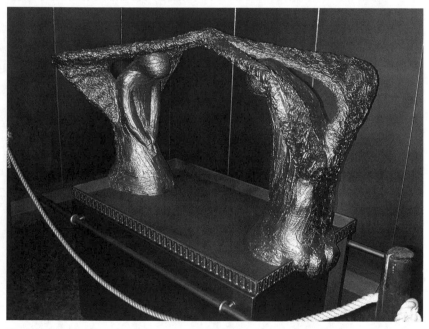

The Ark of the Covenant lay in the Holy of Holies of the Temple of Jerusalem. It was 2.5 cubits (3' 9") in length and 1.5 cubits (2' 3") in breadth and height. According to some sources, it contained Aaron's rod, a pot of manna, and the stone tablets of the Decalogue. (Photograph courtesy of Todd Bolen and BiblePlaces.com.)

After the goats entered the sanctuary, the high priest laid his hands on one of them—called the *scapegoat*—symbolizing that Israel's sins were upon that goat. The scapegoat was then led out into the wilderness, taking the sins of the people out of their midst.

After completing the ritual of atonement, the high priest left his garments in the Most Holy Place, washed again, and then burned an offering for himself and the people. Even the person who released the scapegoat had to wash and bathe as part of this highly detailed ceremony.[17]

Justification

Like *redemption* and *atonement,* the word *justification* has a modern connotation that falls far short of the biblical definition. In our contemporary parlance, when we are accused of something, we might try to "justify" ourselves by providing an explanation or rationalization for our behavior. The Old Testament understanding of justification, however, is based squarely on the concept of *righteousness.*[18]

The first element of justification—the need for righteousness—is found in numerous Old Testament passages, such as Malachi 4:1–6:

> "Surely the day is coming; it will burn like a furnace. All the arrogant and every evildoer will be stubble, and that day that is coming will set them on fire," says the LORD Almighty. "Not a root or a branch will be left to them. But for you who revere my name, the sun of righteousness will rise with healing in its wings. And you will go out and leap like calves released from the stall. Then you will trample down the wicked; they will be ashes under the soles of your feet on the day when I do these things," says the LORD Almighty. "Remember the law of my servant Moses, the decrees and laws I gave him at Horeb for all Israel. See, I will send you the prophet Elijah before that great and dreadful day of the LORD comes. He will turn the hearts of the fathers to their children, and the hearts of the children to their fathers; or else I will come and strike the land with a curse."[19]

A second element of Old Testament justification involved God's mercy, with which he must intervene in order to justify sinful human beings. At times, he chooses to intervene apart from any human merit.[20] At other times, God's people plead for mercy so that they might be justified (Dan. 9:16–18).

Specific individuals in the Old Testament also turned to God and asked for mercy so that they might be justified. David, for example, turns to the Lord and asks for mercy and righteousness, acknowledging his guilt and wrongdoing and pleading for forgiveness (Pss. 32:3–5; 51:2–12). David's renewed right standing results from a contrite heart—"The sacrifices of God are a broken spirit; a broken and contrite heart, O God, you will not despise" (v. 17)—but it is God who justifies (32:5).

A third element of justification in the Old Testament is its forensic character. In other words, it is God who declares, or adjudges, people as righteous. He can do so, despite the guilty condition in which they currently find themselves. In Isaiah 45:19, God says straightforwardly, "I, the LORD, speak the truth; I declare what is right" (cf. v. 21). Other Old Testament texts imply that God can declare a lasting righteousness for his people (cf. Ps. 72:1; Isa. 51:6–8). God's righteousness is available to those who place their faith in him despite their circumstances (cf. Hab. 2:4).

Perhaps one of the best examples of God's declaring his people righteous can be seen in the calling of Isaiah (Isa. 6). In this passage, Isaiah suddenly comes upon the Lord in the temple. There he encounters seraphs calling out, "Holy, holy, holy is the LORD Almighty; the whole earth is full of his glory" (v. 3). Isaiah is immediately overwhelmed by his own sinfulness and the sin of his people, and calls out, "Woe to me! . . . I am ruined! For I am a man of unclean lips, and I live among a people of unclean lips, and my eyes have seen the King, the LORD Almighty" (v. 5). Rather than leaving Isaiah in this state, feeling his guilt and unworthiness, one of the seraphs approaches Isaiah with a coal from the altar. The angel then touches Isaiah's lips with the coal, signifying that he has been declared righteous (v. 7).

One final element of justification found in the Old Testament is its relationship to creation.[21] Not only does God by his mercy declare people righteous, but his righteousness also influences creation. This is most clearly seen, again, in the book of Isaiah. There, righteousness and creation is connected in verses such as Isaiah 45:8: "You heavens above, rain down righteousness; let the clouds shower it down. Let the earth open wide, let salvation spring up, let righteousness grow with it; I, the LORD, have created it." Other passages in Isaiah also connect creation with righteousness as well as with salvation:

> But Israel will be saved by the LORD
>> with an everlasting salvation;
> you will never be put to shame or disgraced,
>> to ages everlasting.

> For this is what the LORD says—
> he who created the heavens,
>> he is God;
> he who fashioned and made the earth,
>> he founded it;
> he did not create it to be empty,
>> but formed it to be inhabited—
> he says:
> "I am the LORD,
>> and there is no other."[22]
>> (Isa. 45:17–18)

God sometimes establishes right order within creation, at which time his justice and righteousness are revealed. At the time of the Flood, God recognized Noah's righteousness and preserved him, declaring him to be righteous despite the wickedness on the earth (Gen. 6:9; 7:1). And then God creates a whole new world (Gen. 9).[23]

In summary, the Old Testament reveals a contention between God and humanity. It is God, however, who justifies people by his mercy, at times declaring his people righteous. His righteousness, too, is often connected with a renewed creation.

INTO THE NEW TESTAMENT: OLD TESTAMENT ECHOES OF SALVATION

The message of salvation is a prominent feature in the New Testament. There, redemption, atonement, and justification are even more central than in the Old Testament. When these words are considered in the New Testament, however, much of their Old Testament understanding can still be heard.

Redemption

Redemption is mentioned frequently in the New Testament, the word itself being used ten times, and the verb *redeem* occurring eight times. When these New Testament passages are considered in light of Old Testament elements of redemption, our understanding of its significance deepens.

Old Testament redemption involves the payment of a great price. The New Testament continues that understanding in verses such as Mark 10:45: "For even the Son of Man did not come to be served, but to serve, and to give his life as a ransom for many." Titus 2:14 reminds us that Jesus Christ "gave himself for us to redeem us from all wickedness and to purify for himself a people that are his very own, eager to do what is good." In both cases, Jesus' life is the great price paid for redemption.

Other texts, such as 1 Peter 1:18–19, emphasize, too, that Jesus gave his lifeblood to secure redemption: "For you know that it was not with perishable things such as silver or gold that you were redeemed from the empty way of life handed down to you from your forefathers, but with the precious blood of Christ, a lamb without blemish or defect" (cf. 1 Cor. 6:20; Heb. 9:12).

Galatians 3:13 emphasizes further that, by dying on the cross, Jesus endured the curse of a criminal's gruesome death: "Christ redeemed us from the curse of the law by becoming a curse for us, for it is written: 'Cursed is everyone who is hung on a tree.'" In the first century, death on a cross was an enormous penalty, involving great pain. Victims of crucifixion suffered the pain of having nails driven into the hands and feet, lacerated veins, crushed tendons, swollen arteries, particularly in the head and stomach, raging thirst, and exposure to the sun and insects. Also the victim suffered the humiliation of physical exposure as well as the knowledge of inevitable death.[24] Great, indeed, was the price that Jesus paid for the redemption of God's people.[25]

As in the Old Testament, redemption in the New Testament is pictured in relation to slavery. Galatians 4:4–7 is a case in point:

But when the time had fully come, God sent his Son, born of a woman, born under law, to redeem those under law, that we might receive the full rights of sons. Because you are sons, God sent the Spirit of his Son into our hearts, the Spirit who calls out, "Abba, Father." So you are no longer a slave, but a son; and since you are a son, God has made you also an heir.

Colossians 1:13–14 also mentions the slavery from which God's people have emerged: "He has rescued us from the dominion of darkness and brought us into the kingdom of the Son he loves, in whom we have redemption, the forgiveness of sins." Christ's work of redemption means that Christians will emerge from darkness to light and go from slaves to sons.

Finally, when redemption is considered in the New Testament, it displays the great benefits that accrue to those who have been redeemed. Ephesians 1, for example, elaborates on the blessings found with redemption. It leads to giving praise, receiving forgiveness, the Holy Spirit's presence, and future inheritance in glory (vv. 7–8, 13–14).

God's people, in fact, sing of the greatness of their redemption in Revelation 5. In this scene at the end of time, God's people sing with joy around the throne of Christ:

And when he had taken it, the four living creatures and the twenty-four elders fell down before the Lamb. Each one had a harp and they were holding golden bowls full of incense, which are the prayers of the saints. And they sang a new song: "You are worthy to take the scroll and to open its seals, because you were slain, and with your blood you purchased men for God from every tribe and language and people and nation. You have made them to be a kingdom and priests to serve our God, and they will reign on the earth." (Rev. 5:8–10)

The enormity of benefit that comes with being purchased by God is evident in this triumphant hymn. God's people are not only released from slavery, but they were bought with a great price, namely the precious blood shed by Christ on the cross. Blessing of inestimable value and awesome wonder are found among those who sing the greatness of God, the Redeemer (cf. Rev. 14:1–4).

Atonement

Unlike the language of redemption, which is found in many places in the New Testament, specific uses of the word *atonement* are few and far between. In the NIV translation of the New Testament, the word *atonement* occurs only three times (Rom. 3:25; Heb. 2:17; 9:5), and *atoning* occurs twice (1 John 2:2; 4:10). The Old Testament understanding of atonement, however, comes through loud and clear in these New Testament passages.

As in the Old Testament, the necessity of atonement to satisfy the wrath of God toward human sin can clearly be seen. Throughout the first three chapters of Romans, for example, human sinfulness is on display. In Romans 1:18–32, Paul declares that all people are sinful because they exchange the truth of God for idols and lies. The sense of guilt and accountability build through Romans 2, in which we learn that not even the one who believes he is keeping the Law is innocent. Romans 3 brings the argument to a climax by presenting humanity's utter sinfulness and the consequent judgment that is due. Romans 3:12–20 states the gravity of humanity's sin:

All have turned away, they have together become worthless; there is no one who does good, not even one. Their throats are open graves; their tongues practice deceit. The poison of vipers is on their lips. Their mouths are full of cursing and bitterness. Their feet are swift to shed blood; ruin and misery mark their ways, and the way of peace they do not know. There is no fear of God before their eyes. Now we know that whatever the law says, it says to those who are under the law, so that every mouth may be silenced and the whole world held accountable to God. Therefore no one will be declared righteous in his sight by observing the law; rather, through the law we become conscious of sin.

At this point, Paul introduces the means by which this guilt and condemnation can be wiped away. Jesus Christ, by his atoning death on the cross, satisfies this wrath and justice of God:

God presented him as a sacrifice of atonement, through faith in his blood. He did this to demonstrate his justice, because in his forbearance he had left the sins committed beforehand unpunished—he did it to demonstrate his justice at the present time, so as to be just and the one who justifies those who have faith in Jesus. (Rom. 3:25–26)

The apostle John also speaks of atonement in this way. Unlike Paul, John does not devote three chapters to a discussion of the wrath of God, but he does imply that fear of God accompanies sin:

"My dear children, I write this to you so that you will not sin. But if anybody does sin, we have one who speaks to the Father in our defense—Jesus Christ, the Righteous One. He is the atoning sacrifice for our sins, and not only for ours but also for the sins of the whole world" (1 John 2:1–2).

As the atoning sacrifice, Jesus Christ erases the threat and punishment resulting from wrongdoing before a holy God (cf. 1 John 4:10).[26]

Echoes of the Old Testament can be heard again in the references to atonement in the book of Hebrews. Just as the Old Testament gives specific instructions for performing the necessary sacrifices, so, too, the book of Hebrews explains in detail how the sacrifice that appeases the wrath of God must be a specific one: the person of Jesus Christ. Jesus had to be fully man in every way so that he could be like his brothers (Heb. 2:17). He had to conduct himself more faithfully than Moses (Heb. 3) and fulfill the role of the perfect and great high priest expected from generations past (cf. Heb. 5, 7). Because of Christ's faithfulness and sacrifice, the wrath we deserve as a result of our sin has been atoned for forever (cf. Heb. 10).

The wrath of God is not a popular subject to discuss. The power of atonement to appease the wrath of God can be seen, however, in the following story:

A boy and his father were walking through a Kansas wheat field. On every side, wheat stretched out as far as the eye could see.

After the two had walked for a little while, the boy saw smoke in front of him, indicating that a fire was burning up ahead and moving toward him and his father.

The fire grew and seemed to be advancing at an alarming rate. The boy knew that he could not outrun the windswept flames.

With the flames and smoke approaching rapidly, the boy began to panic. His father, however, remained calm as he reached into his pocket and pulled out a pack of matches. Lighting a match, the man dropped it into the wheat behind him and his son. Soon, the second fire began moving away from the boy and his dad, burning a patch of ground behind them.

Just before the large fire reached the boy and his father, they stepped backward onto the ground where the second fire had already been. This ground was safe from the wrath of the advancing fire because the wheat that would have burned had already been consumed by the fire the father had set.

In a sense, Christ's work of atonement is like this. The fire of God's wrath has been poured out on the world and threatens to burn up everything in its path. But the death of Jesus Christ fully satisfied the wrath of God, and as we stand on Christ's finished work, we need not fear the coming wrath.

Justification

As with the concept of *redemption,* the language of justification can be found in many places in the New Testament. It is especially prominent in Paul's letters, particularly Romans and Galatians.[27]

In Romans, Paul establishes and builds upon the Old Testament theme of the contention between God and humanity. Paul devotes the first three chapters of the letter to the sinfulness of all humanity. Theologian D. Martin Lloyd-Jones summarized these chapters as follows: "Everyone needs to be saved, however great, however illustrious. We are all sinners. We are all born in sin."

Having established the centrality of the conflict between God and humanity, Paul explains how justification—that is, God's righteous judgment on sinners—is the answer to the problem of sin:

> But now a righteousness from God, apart from law, has been made known, to which the Law and the Prophets testify. This righteousness from God comes through faith in Jesus Christ to all who believe. There is no difference, for all have sinned and fall short of the glory of God, and are justified freely by his grace through the redemption that came by Christ Jesus. (Rom. 3:21–24)

Four times in Romans 3:22–31, Paul speaks of justification as the solution for the hostility between God and humanity. Being justified before God resolves the tension so that there is no condemnation (Rom. 5:9, 16; 8:33).

The New Testament understanding of justification contains a second similarity with the Old Testament, in that God justifies people as a result of his mercy and grace. Many times in his writings, Paul emphasizes that justification does not come as a result of works. In Romans 4:1–12, he shows how the patriarch of the Jewish faith, Abraham, was justified as a result of God's grace, and later Paul states that justification is God's gift (5:15–17; 6:23).

In Galatians, Paul also states emphatically that justification does not come as a result of following the Law but, again, by grace through faith (3:11). Paul understands this to apply to himself as a Jew and to Gentiles:

> We who are Jews by birth and not "Gentile sinners" know that a man is not justified by observing the law, but by faith in Jesus Christ. So we, too, have put our faith in Christ Jesus that we may be justified by faith in Christ and not by observing the law, because by observing the law no one will be justified. (Gal. 2:15–16)

Indeed, if anyone is seeking to be aligned with the Law, that person has become alienated from Christ and fallen away from Christ (Gal. 5:4). Justification comes as a result of God's grace and is activated by human faith (cf. Acts 13:39; Eph. 2:8–9; Phil. 3:1–9).

As in the Old Testament, God grants a justifying righteousness when people turn to him by faith. Romans 1:16–17 indicates that justifying righteousness is, in fact, available to all who have faith:

> I am not ashamed of the gospel, because it is the power of God for the salvation of everyone who believes: first for the Jew, then for the Gentile. For in the gospel a righteousness from God is revealed, a righteousness that is by faith from first to last, just as it is written: "The righteous will live by faith."

Later, in Romans 10:9–10, Paul states explicitly that people are justified after they turn to God in faith.

As in the Old Testament, the New Testament speaks of God's declaring people as righteous. This can be seen in numerous passages in Paul's letters, where God "counts," or "reckons," people as righteous when he justifies them.[28] This accounting or reckoning of people as righteous carries a forensic connotation, borrowing from legal terminology, wherein a person is declared righteous by a judge. In Paul's understanding of justification, God is the righteous judge who pronounces his justice as the Lord of the universe.[29]

In Galatians 3:6, Paul writes, "Consider Abraham: 'He believed God, and it was credited to him as righteousness.'" In Romans 4:5, Paul explains how righteousness is declared: "However, to the man who does not work but trusts God who justifies the wicked, his faith is credited as righteousness." Other places in Paul's writings indicate that justification results in a new status given before the Lord.[30]

When God justifies, he gives his righteousness to his people as a gift. G. F. Handel, the great composer, writes of the blessing of being declared righteous by grace through faith: "What a wonderful thing it is to be sure of one's faith! How wonderful to be a member of the evangelical church, which preaches the free grace of God through Christ as the hope of sinners! If we were to rely on our works—my God, what would become of us?"[31]

Finally, as in the Old Testament, the concept of creation is connected with that of justification. In 2 Corinthians 5:17–21, for example, Paul speaks of the Christian as a "new creation" in Christ and then immediately ties this to God's righteousness:

Therefore, if anyone is in Christ, he is a new creation; the old has gone, the new has come! All this is from God, who reconciled us to himself through Christ and gave us the ministry of reconciliation: that God was reconciling the world to himself in Christ, not counting men's sins against them. And he has committed to us the message of reconciliation. We are therefore Christ's ambassadors, as though God were making his appeal through us. We implore you on Christ's behalf: Be reconciled to God. God made him who had no sin to be sin for us, so that in him we might become the righteousness of God.

Other passages connect God's creating work in believers with their justification as in the Old Testament, but perhaps none more succinctly than Ephesians 2:8–10: "For it is by grace you have been saved, through faith—and this not from yourselves, it is the gift of God—not by works, so that no one can boast. For we are God's workmanship, created in Christ Jesus to do good works, which God prepared in advance for us to do." In the good works produced in a believer's life as a result of justifying faith, we see that created righteousness goes hand in hand with declared righteousness.

Merlin Carothers, author of the book *Prison to Praise*, tells of the great joy that came into his life when he understood that he had been declared righteous by a higher power. He likened it to a time when he went AWOL while serving in the army during the Second World War. A judge sentenced Carothers to five years in prison, but told him he could avoid prison by returning to serve in the army for five more years. If Carothers left the army before those five years were completed, he would have to spend the rest of his term in prison. Carothers chose to serve in the army but was discharged before the end of the five years. When he dutifully returned to the prosecutor's office to find out where he would spend the remainder of his sentence, he found to his surprise and delight that he had received a full pardon from President Harry Truman. "Your record is completely clear," the prosecutor explained. "It is just as if you never were involved with the law."

Carothers went on to live a life devoted to the Lord, serving as an army chaplain and writing many inspirational books. Being declared righteous meant that Carothers was free to serve the Lord in newness of spirit.

For all of us, a newness of spirit comes as a result of salvation, a gift of grace that is central to the Christian faith, and encompasses redemption, atonement, and justification. Both the Old and New Testament speak of the grandness of our salvation.[32]

Although the meaning of words such as *redemption, atonement,* and *justification* seem to be lost today on many Christians, it is evident that those words were well understood by Christians of the New Testament era. It is also evident that they were understood by the hymn writers of yesteryear, including Philip Bliss, whose "Hallelujah, What a Savior!" includes the ideas of redemption, atonement, and justification:

> Man of sorrows! what a name
> For the Son of God, who came
> Ruined sinners to reclaim:
> Hallelujah! what a Saviour!
>
> Bearing shame and scoffing rude,
> In my place condemned he stood,
> Sealed my pardon with his blood;
> Hallelujah! what a Saviour!
>
> Guilty, vile, and helpless, we;
> Spotless Lamb of God was he;
> Full atonement! can it be?
> Hallelujah! what a Saviour!
>
> Lifted up was he to die,
> "It is finished!" was his cry:
> Now in heav'n exalted high:
> Hallelujah! what a Saviour!
>
> When he comes, our glorious King,
> All his ransomed home to bring,
> Then anew this song we'll sing:
> Hallelujah! what a Saviour![33]

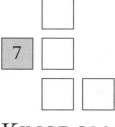

KINGDOM

Jesus Rules over All

Let the proud seek and love earthly kingdoms, but blessed are the poor in spirit for theirs is the kingdom of heaven.
—Saint Augustine

The only significance of life consists in helping to establish the kingdom of God.
—Leo Tolstoy

Over the years, Christians have done many remarkable things when they were motivated to seek God's kingdom first. John Wanamaker, for example, the well-known founder of the Wanamaker Department Stores in the Northeast United States, became motivated to seek God's kingdom in his business as well as in other activities. Wanamaker was active in Christian causes, serving as president of the world's largest Sunday school, speaking widely, and advising evangelical leaders such as D. L. Moody. Later, he was named postmaster general of the United States.

When someone asked Wanamaker how he could hold all of these posts at once, he said, "Early in life I read, 'Seek ye first the kingdom of God, and his righteousness, and all these things shall be added unto you.' The Sunday school is my business, and the rest are the things." Pursuing God's kingdom was an important part of John Wanamaker's life.

Richard Greene of Cary, North Carolina, also placed great importance on seeking God's kingdom first. While he was in college, he was troubled with his bills. While balancing his checkbook one day, he grew agitated and afraid. "Where will the extra money come from?" he said aloud. "Please, Lord, help me pay these bills."

When he finished balancing his checkbook, he noted that he had six dollars and thirty-three cents left. Then, when he looked at his pocket calculator, his mind focused in a new way on the digits—6.33. He remembered a verse he'd just discovered: Matthew 6:33. He recited the verse to himself, "But seek ye first the kingdom of God, and his righteousness; and all these things shall be added unto you" (KJV). Then he laughed, and took it as a message from the Lord. Shortly afterward, he received an unexpected scholarship. Later, a friend handed him a check for his month's rent. God provided his needs throughout college, and today Richard is director of public relations for Trans World Radio, beaming the message of Scripture (including Matt. 6:33) around the world.[1]

The encouragement to seek God's kingdom is clearly set forward in Matthew 6:33, and is supported in many portions of the New Testament. In particular, Matthew, Mark, and Luke, refer to "the kingdom," "the kingdom of God," and "the kingdom of heaven" nearly one hundred times.[2] Jesus uses the term *kingdom* fifty-two times in Matthew, eighteen times in Mark, forty-one times in Luke, and three times in John.[3] Indeed, the New Testament deals much with the idea of God's kingdom.[4]

Because the Old Testament deals less frequently with the idea of God's kingdom, some people have come to believe that the Old Testament has little to say about it.[5] This chapter, however, considers how Old Testament ideas about the kingdom provide a framework for understanding the New Testament.[6] What will become clear is the greatness of the kingdom that Jesus came to bring in this world, and what it means to seek it.

Old Testament Antecedents of God's Kingdom

At first glance, studying God's kingdom in the Old Testament appears to be a fruitless pursuit because the phrase "kingdom of God" does not appear in the Old Testament.[7] The *idea* of the kingdom of God, however, is found in many places in the Old Testament. God is often depicted as a king, for example, and in many places his promised kingdom is presented as well.[8]

God Is King over All Creation

In the earliest chapters of the Old Testament, God is presented as the Lord of all creation. After each day during his creating, he declares that what he has created is "good" or "very good." By creating things out of nothing, appointing the sun and the moon to rule the night and the day, and then pronouncing them good, God reveals himself as not only the Creator but also the ruler of all that is created.[9]

Other Old Testament passages also reveal that God not only creates but is sovereign over all creation. A number of psalms, for example, celebrate God's kingship as the great Creator:

> For great is the LORD and most worthy of praise;
>   he is to be feared above all gods.
> For all the gods of the nations are idols,
>   but the LORD made the heavens.
> Splendor and majesty are before him;
>   strength and glory are in his sanctuary.
>
> Ascribe to the LORD, O families of nations,
>   ascribe to the LORD glory and strength.
> Ascribe to the LORD the glory due his name;
>   bring an offering and come into his courts.
> Worship the LORD in the splendor of his holiness;
>   tremble before him, all the earth.
> Say among the nations, "The LORD reigns."
>   The world is firmly established, it cannot be moved;
>   he will judge the peoples with equity.
>
> (Ps. 96:4–10)

This psalm is representative of others in which God's dominion is based upon his role as Creator.[10] Other passages in the Prophets and Writings also reveal the sovereignty and rule that God possesses as a result of his creative ability.[11]

Perhaps the passage that contains the most memorable illustration of God's reign over the entire world can be found in Daniel 4. In this chapter,

King Nebuchadnezzar, the king of the powerful Babylonian empire, gloats over his superiority over all of the earth. As he sleeps one night, he has a dream that deeply disturbs him. In the dream, he sees a tree that grows very large with its top appearing to touch the sky and visible to all of the earth. It is a beautiful tree, giving shelter to the beasts of the field and the birds of the air—and every creature is fed by it. But then a messenger comes from heaven and calls for the tree to be cut down, its branches trimmed, and its leaves and fruit scattered. All that is to remain are the stump and its roots. Then, King Nebuchadnezzar hears a command given for a man to live among the animals and plants, drenched with the dew of heaven. The man will be given the mind of an animal until seven times pass him by and the man recognizes that God is sovereign over all the kingdoms of men, giving them to whom he wishes.

After Daniel interprets the dream, it becomes a reality for King Nebuchadnezzar. As he gloats over the kingdom of Babylon one night, he is driven away from civilization and eats grass like cattle. His body is drenched with dew from heaven, his hair grows like the feathers of an eagle, and his nails are like the claws of a bird. In this humiliating state, he then turns to the true king of the world and praises him, saying,

> His dominion is an eternal dominion;
>   his kingdom endures from
>   generation to generation.
> All the peoples of the earth
>   are regarded as nothing.
> He does as he pleases
>   with the powers of heaven
>   and the peoples of the earth.
> No one can hold back his hand
>   or say to him: "What have you done?" . . .

Now I, Nebuchadnezzar, praise and exalt and glorify the King of heaven, because everything he does is right and all his ways are just. And those who walk in pride he is able to humble. (Dan. 4:34–35, 37)

In the above passage, Nebuchadnezzar recognizes, as should all creation, that God alone is the great ruler over all of creation.

God Is Especially Ruler over Israel

God, then, is presented as King over the entire world. His rule is especially realized, though, in his relationship with his people, Israel (Exod. 19:5–6; Deut. 9:26; 33:5),[12] that nation being seen as his dominion.[13]

Evidence of God's rule and authority over Israel can be seen in many places in the Old Testament. When God demands, for example, that Pharaoh set the people of Israel free, he is speaking as one ruler to another, through Moses, his intermediary.[14] Likewise, in the conquest of the Promised Land, God acts as the ruler of Israel, in the book of Joshua playing the role of divine general leading his people to conquer the land.[15] When the Promised Land has been conquered, God, as their ruler, apportions it to his people (Josh. 13–22).

When in 1 Samuel 8 the nation of Israel requests a human king, they are directly challenging God's divine kingship over them. Until then, Samuel has been serving as God's intermediary and the righteous judge of Israel, but the people desire an earthly king as the other nations around them have. Distressed by this request, Samuel prays to the Lord, and the Lord's response indicates that he has considered himself as king over Israel since the days of Egypt:

And the LORD told him: "Listen to all that the people are saying to you; it is not you they have rejected, but they have rejected me as their king. As they have done from the day I brought them up out of Egypt until this day, forsaking me and serving other gods, so they are doing to you. Now listen to them; but warn them solemnly and let them know what the king who will reign over them will do." (1 Sam. 8:7–9)

Even after God allows a human king to rule over Israel, the nation prospers only when the people obey the Law established by God, their true King.[16] When the human kings follow the ways of the Lord, righteousness, peace and prosperity result. The best example of a righteous king was King David (cf. 1 Sam. 13:14; Acts 13:22), and as a result of David's desire to follow God, the nation was prosperous and increased throughout much of his reign.

Subsequent kings who followed in God's ways also had peaceful and prosperous kingdoms. Hezekiah's righteous behavior, for example, led to prosperity for Israel:

> Hezekiah trusted in the LORD, the God of Israel. There was no one like him among all the kings of Judah, either before him or after him. He held fast to the LORD and did not cease to follow him; he kept the commands the LORD had given Moses. And the LORD was with him; he was successful in whatever he undertook. (2 Kings 18:5–7)

The same can be said of King Josiah. When he restored the words of God's Law to the land of Israel and encouraged the nation to follow the Lord, the nation prospered (2 Kings 22–23; 2 Chron. 34–35).

Conversely, those kings who did evil and rebelled against the Lord found his blessings of righteousness, peace, and prosperity removed. The unrighteous behavior of kings such as Manasseh, Jehoahaz, Jehoiachin, Jehoiakim, and Zedekiah led to a decline in the kingdom of Israel. Their lack of regard for God's rule, which indicated they were at odds with God himself, also diminished the Lord's rule within the nation of Israel.

Great Anticipation of God's Kingdom

The manifest kingdom of God is eagerly anticipated in the Old Testament. The prophets look forward to a day when God's rule is fully realized in the nation of Israel. At that time, God's rule will extend to the nations;[17] God's righteousness will be found among the people;[18] and his peace will pervade all things (which means not only the absence of war among humanity but also peace in the animal kingdom).[19] Most importantly, peace will be extended, existing not only between God and his people, but to others as well.[20]

The anticipated effect of the coming kingdom is perhaps summarized best by the prophet Isaiah:

This is what Isaiah son of Amoz saw concerning Judah and Jerusalem:

> In the last days the mountain of the LORD's
>   temple will be established
>   as chief among the mountains;
> it will be raised above the hills,
>   and all nations will stream to it.
>
> Many peoples will come and say,
> "Come, let us go up to the mountain
>   of the LORD,
>   to the house of the God of Jacob.
> He will teach us his ways,
>   so that we may walk in his paths."
> The law will go out from Zion,
>   the word of the LORD from Jerusalem.
> He will judge between the nations
>   and will settle disputes for many peoples.
> They will beat their swords into plowshares
>   and their spears into pruning hooks.
> Nation will not take up sword against nation,
>   nor will they train for war anymore.
>   (Isa. 2:1–4)

When God's kingdom comes in its fullness, his name will be exalted, all nations will turn to him, his righteousness will be established throughout the world, and nations will no longer make war against each other. From an Old Testament perspective, this is the hope of God's future kingdom.

The book of Daniel also refers repeatedly to the coming of God's kingdom. The writer uses the word *kingdom* thirty-two times in the book, often in relation to God's kingdom coming to overthrow earthly kingdoms. Daniel 7, in particular, concerns four kingdoms of the earth that are overthrown by the kingdom of God.[21]

King Belshazzar of Babylon has a dream in which he sees four great beasts emerging from the sea. The first is a lion, the second a bear, and the third a leopard. All are mighty beasts. But then a fourth and more terrifying animal appears, a beast with ten horns that crushes and devours its victims.

At this point, the scene changes, and the Ancient of Days enters the picture. His appearance is arresting. His clothing and his hair are as white as wool and fire flows from his throne. Thousands upon thousands attend him while he takes his seat for judgment. The beasts are stripped of their authority to rule, even though they are allowed to remain present before the Ancient of Days.

Then the Son of Man enters the scene, and the Ancient of Days gives him all power, authority, and glory.[22] All peoples and nations bow down and worship him, and his kingdom is said to be a lasting kingdom that will not pass away.

An interpretation of this dream is given in Daniel 7:15–28. The first three beasts represent three earthly kingdoms. The fourth beast is an even stronger kingdom that will devour the whole earth and trample down all other kingdoms. The ten horns are symbolic of ten kings, three of whom will be defeated. God's people will be oppressed by this kingdom for a certain time before God comes and judges the kingdom and takes its power away. God's everlasting kingdom will then be over his people, and everyone will worship him.

In this passage, we find several important ideas about God's kingdom:

1. The coming of God's kingdom is greatly anticipated.
2. When God's kingdom appears, the righteous will be rewarded and the unfaithful will suffer loss.
3. The presence of a messianic figure can be seen in the description of the Son of Man.[23] (Although the nature of this person has been debated in recent days, at the time of Christ, the Jews understood the Son-of-Man figure as messianic.)[24]

These points summarize what comprised Jewish hopes, during the time of the Old Testament, for the coming of the kingdom.[25]

Throughout human history, many people have hoped for a kingdom in which peace and righteousness reign. One such example can be seen in the garden at the United Nations, which contains several sculptures and statues donated by member nations. One of these statues, presented by the Soviet Union in 1959, is called "Let Us Beat Swords into Plowshares." The bronze sculpture depicts a man holding a hammer in one hand and a sword in the other, which he is making into a plowshare. The statue symbolizes humanity's desire to put an end to war and convert the means of destruction into creative tools for the benefit of all mankind. Despite these human aspirations for peace and righteousness in our time, the Old Testament teaches that God alone will bring peace and righteousness when he establishes his future kingdom.

THE NEW TESTAMENT AND THE KINGDOM

Teaching about the kingdom of God is more prevalent in the New Testament than in the Old Testament. New Testament understanding of the kingdom is nonetheless based firmly on Old Testament ideas about the kingdom.[26]

The Gospels use three terms to express the idea of the kingdom of God: "the kingdom of God," "the kingdom of [the] heaven[s]," and simply "the kingdom." These are used interchangeably throughout the Gospels.[27]

Jesus Is King over All Creation

When Jesus refers to the kingdom of God in many of his parables, he has in mind a global perspective. In the parable of the weeds (Matt. 13:24–30), for example, Jesus equates the kingdom of God with a field, which represents the entire world. In the parable, the farmer sows good seed in the field, but someone else comes at night and sows weeds (called tares, in some translations) among the good seed. When the wheat sprouts, so do the weeds. Upon seeing the weeds, the servants of the master ask the owner of the field how it happened. The owner explains that an enemy came in the middle of the night and sowed the weeds. The servants then ask the master if they should uproot the weeds, but the master tells them not to do so for fear that the wheat would be uprooted as well. He encourages them instead to allow both wheat and tares to grow together until harvest time. At that time, the weeds will be bound and burned, but the wheat will be gathered and placed in the owner's barn.

In Matthew 13:36–43, Jesus interprets this parable for the disciples, giving them private insight into the kingdom of God. Jesus, as the Son of Man, is the planter of the good seed (which represents the sons of the kingdom). The evil one plants the weeds. The entire field is the world. At the end of the growing season, the entire world will be subject to the judgment of Jesus. At that time the Son of Man and his angels will uproot all those belonging to the evil one. Thus, this parable displays the global nature of the kingdom of God, according to Jesus. He will rule and judge the entire world.

In Matthew 13:47–50, the parable of the net, Jesus again states in parable form that his kingdom will eventually be global in extent.[28] In this parable, the kingdom is likened to a net that is put down in the water, representing the whole world. The net catches every kind of fish. When it is full, the fisherman hauls it in, and he and his helpers sort all of the fish, placing the good fish in baskets but throwing out the bad.

Jesus interprets this parable in a similar way to the parable of the weeds.[29] At the end of the age, the angels will come and separate the wicked from the righteous. Once again, the kingdom will extend across the globe.

Yet another parable that shows the global extent of God's kingdom is that of the sheep and the goats (Matt. 25:31–46). Jesus introduces this teaching by noting that the events it refers to will occur when he, the Son of Man, comes in his glory. When he returns, he will judge all nations, separating the sheep from the goats.[30] As king of the entire world, he will then invite one group into his eternal kingdom, but he will send the others to eternal punishment.

Other places, too, in the New Testament envision the kingdom of Christ stretching over the entire earth. John's Gospel, for example, makes the point that Jesus knew that all things had been put into his hands by the Father (John 13:3). In 1 Corinthians 15:24–28, Paul states that Jesus must reign as king until he has put everything under his feet. This includes every rule, dominion, power, and authority. Philippians 2:9–10 indicates that Jesus has been exalted to the highest place and given the name that is above every name so that at his name every knee should bow, in heaven and on earth and under the earth. Revelation 5:9–10 pictures Jesus as the Lion of the Tribe of Judah, who reigns over people from every tongue, tribe, and nation.[31]

The New Testament also repeatedly presents Jesus as seated, or to be seated, at the right hand of God, a position of honor, significance, and power.[32] In the ancient world, being seated at the right hand of a king indicated being invested with great power. In Jesus' time, the right hand of God was known as the place of highest power, meaning that the one sitting there was sharing the throne of glory with God himself.[33] Because God's authority is over the entire world, Jesus' being seated at God's right hand indicates that his rule and authority extends worldwide as well.[34]

Jesus Is King of His People

From a New Testament perspective, God's kingdom is envisioned as eventually encompassing the entire world, but its present extent is already realized among God's people.[35] This present and future reality is also in agreement with the Old Testament understanding of the kingdom.

From the earliest presentation of Jesus in the gospel of Matthew, it is evident that he is to be king over God's people. Matthew 1 begins, in fact, with Christ's royal lineage, linking him with King David, Israel's righteous king (vv. 6, 17, 20).

In the narrative of Christ's birth, Matthew again emphasizes that Jesus is to be king of God's people. To the Magi who traveled from the east, Jesus is known to be born "king of the Jews" (Matt. 2:2). His birthplace in Bethlehem again aligns him with King David, and his birth in that city also establishes him through fulfillment of messianic prophecy as ruler of God's people (v. 6; cf. Mic. 5:2). Jesus' first public message recorded in Matthew is "the good news of the kingdom" (Matt. 4:23),[36] and his miracles are signs that the kingdom has come near (9:35; 12:28).[37]

Some of Jesus' parables also reveal that his kingdom is already present among God's people. The parable of the sower in Matthew 13:1–9, for example, indicates that the kingdom has already taken root in the hearts of people who receive Jesus' words. In the parable, a man spreads seed over different types of soil. Some falls on the road, where it does not take root, and the birds come and devour these seeds. Other seeds fall on rocky soil, and although the seeds germinate, the shoots wither because the roots are not deep enough. Yet other seeds fall among the weeds and thistles. Once again, the seeds sprout, but this time they are choked out by the weeds. Finally, some seed falls on fertile soil, and this seed produces fruit—a hundred-, sixty-, or thirtyfold.

Jesus connects the parable to the kingdom of God when he interprets it for his followers (Matt. 13:18–23). The seed is the message of the kingdom, which goes out into the field. Some refuse it outright, others respond briefly but without commitment, and others have the word of the kingdom choked out by concerns of this world. Those whose hearts are ready, however, will produce abundant fruit, thereby realizing the kingdom of God in their midst.

One other element of the parable of the sower indicates that the kingdom is most fully realized among Jesus' disciples. In Matthew 13:16–17, Jesus says, "Blessed are your eyes because they see, and your ears because they hear. For I tell you the truth, many prophets and righteous men longed to see what you see but did not see it, and to hear what you hear but did not hear it." The kingdom of God in the presence of Christ the King can only be fully appreciated by God's people.

In parallel gospel accounts of the same parable (Mark 4:1–23; Luke 8:5–15), the writers emphasize the same point: God's people are able to grasp the message of the kingdom, but those outside the kingdom cannot perceive it. Mark 4:10–12 is particularly noteworthy, because it highlights the inability of outsiders to grasp the essence of the kingdom:

When he was alone, the Twelve and the others around him asked him about the parables. He told them, "The secret of the kingdom of God has been given to you. But to those on the outside everything is said in parables so that,

"'they may be ever seeing but never perceiving,
and ever hearing but never understanding;
otherwise they might turn and be forgiven!'"

In the Sermon on the Mount (Matt. 5–7), and particularly in the Beatitudes (5:3–12), Jesus associates the kingdom of God with those who are pursuing his will. In verse 3, those who are poor in spirit are promised the kingdom of heaven. In verse 10, those who are persecuted on account of their righteousness are also promised the kingdom. In verses 19–20, Jesus promises that those who practice and teach his commandments will be great in the kingdom of heaven. In the Lord's Prayer, recorded in Matthew 6:10, Jesus encourages his disciples to pray for God's kingdom to come and God's will to be done. In 6:33, he encourages his followers to seek first the kingdom and his righteousness, promising that all other necessary things will be added to them as well. Lastly, in 7:21, Jesus declares that his disciples who actually follow his words will be like a man who built his house on a rock. They will enter the kingdom of heaven, because those who follow God's will are part of God's kingdom.

The kingdom of God is also especially evident among the followers of God in the book of Acts and in the Pauline epistles. In Acts, Philip is seen preaching to the Samaritans about the good news of the kingdom of God, and many respond to his message (8:12). In chapter 14, Paul warns the citizens of Lystra, Iconium, and Antioch that they must endure many trials in order to enter the kingdom of God. In Acts 19, Paul enters the synagogue in Ephesus and preaches about the kingdom of God (v. 8). Later, in his farewell speech to the Ephesian elders, he reminds them of how he has gone about preaching the kingdom of God (20:25). Luke's final picture of Paul is that of his being in Rome, preaching the kingdom to all who will hear (28:23, 31).

Paul's letters, too, indicate that the kingdom of God is realized among God's people.[38] In 1 Corinthians 6:9–10; Galatians 5:21; and Ephesians 5:5, he writes that a person's behavior will indicate whether he or she will enter the kingdom of God. One's behavior will not determine whether one is in the kingdom, but it does provide a sign of being a part of it.

Great Anticipation of God's Kingdom

As in the Old Testament, the New Testament looks forward with great anticipation to the coming kingdom.[39] This eager expectancy is referred to in many places in Jesus' teaching.[40] In Jesus' parables, he speaks of a future time when the kingdom of God will come. Then, the righteous and the wise will be rewarded, and the unrighteous and foolish will suffer loss. The parable of the wise and foolish virgins is an example (Matt. 25:1–13). In this parable, ten virgins are preparing for the lighted processional that would usher the bride to the bridegroom's home when he comes for her. This was an important processional in Jewish culture, even causing religious leaders to suspend lectures and ritual obligations.[41] To be without oil for this lighted procession would be shameful.

In the parable, five of the virgins act wisely, finding ways to have enough oil in their lamps. The other five are foolish and neglect to maintain enough oil. When the bridegroom comes, the five with oil rise up and go with him to celebrate the wedding feast, but those without oil are unable to accompany the bridegroom. Jesus concludes the parable by urging his followers to remain vigilant for the coming kingdom of God (Matt. 25:1–13).

The eager anticipation of the kingdom is seen not only in the Gospels but also in other portions of the New Testament. In some of Jesus' last words before his ascension, he speaks of the future sense of the kingdom. In Acts 1:6, the disciples ask him if he is going to restore the kingdom to Israel immediately. This would have been the opportunity for Jesus to point to the present aspect of the kingdom, but he instead points to the future. The kingdom will come at a time that the Father has set by his own authority. Jesus then promises that the disciples will receive power when the Holy Spirit comes upon them so that they can be witnesses of the kingdom to the ends of the earth (vv. 7–8).

Paul's letters also speak of the future prospects of the kingdom. In 1 Corinthians 6:9–10, he writes, "Do you not know that the wicked will not inherit the kingdom of God? Do not be deceived: Neither the sexually immoral nor idolaters nor adulterers nor male prostitutes nor homosexual offenders nor thieves nor the greedy nor drunkards nor slanderers nor swindlers will inherit the kingdom of God." Similar sentiments are found in Galatians 5:21 and Ephesians 5:5, in which the future aspect of the kingdom is anticipated.

The book of Revelation provides the best picture of the future orientation of the kingdom. The book records the apostle John's vision of the future, in which he is shown how the people of God have been made into a kingdom of priests (Rev. 1:5; 5:10). He sees the Son of Man amid the churches of his day and seated on a cloud for the purpose of judgment (Rev. 1:13; 14:14). John also sees Jesus as the Lamb of God on a throne, with people from every tongue, tribe, and nation bowing down before him (Rev. 4–5).

As in Daniel, the Old Testament book that speaks the most plainly concerning the coming kingdom, the Messiah is often present as the Son of Man in New Testament considerations of God's future kingdom. In the parable of the sheep and the goats (Matt. 25:31–46), for example, Jesus declares that the separation of the sheep and the goats will occur "when the Son of Man comes in his glory, and all the angels with him" (v. 31). In the parable of the weeds, it is the Son of Man who sows the good seed and who will send his angels to weed out the tares and judge everything that causes sin as well as all who do evil. And although Jesus does not refer explicitly to the kingdom of God in the Olivet Discourse (Mark 13), he envisions his own return in all power and glory when the Son of Man comes to gather his elect from the four corners of the earth.[42]

FIGURE 7.1: THE KINGDOM OF GOD AND THE WORLD

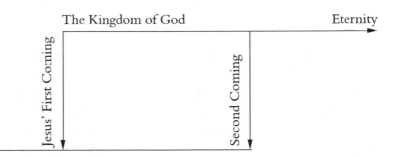

During the nineteenth century, a group of Christians known as the Clapham Sect, in Victorian England, were particularly influenced by their anticipation of the kingdom of God. William Wilberforce, who was devoted to the abolition of slavery and the reformation of morals in Britain, was a member of this group.[43] For forty-five years, he struggled against the evils of slavery in British society, finally achieving the passage of the Abolition of Slavery Bill in 1833.

John Venn, who was the rector of the Clapham Sect, laid much emphasis on a person's moral accountability to God. His sermons prompted journalist R. C. K. Ensor to make the following observations about evangelical Christianity in nineteenth-century Britain:

> [They were certain] about the existence of an after-life of rewards and punishments. If one asks how nineteenth-century English merchants earned the reputation of being the most honest in the world . . . the answer is: because hell and heaven seemed as certain to them as tomorrow's sunrise, and the Last Judgment as real as the week's balance-sheet.[44]

This viewpoint radically affected the members of the Clapham Sect. Henry Thornton, a member of Parliament, once explained the reason for his vote, "I voted today so that if my Master had come again at that moment I might have been able to give an account of my stewardship."[45] William Wilberforce and other Clapham members could have said the same thing. An awareness of the kingdom that will come at the end of time was a driving motivation for these influential Christians of the nineteenth century.

God's great kingdom is what his people are to seek and anticipate. David Livingstone, the famous Scottish missionary, philanthropist, traveler, and doctor, was another man who sought the kingdom with enthusiasm. Motivated at a young age by his love for God and the quest for the kingdom of God, Livingstone studied medicine. He planned for a missionary career to China, but when circumstances changed, he set his mind on Southern Africa, setting off with great enthusiasm. He traveled thousands of miles, opening up new territory for Western exploration, and discovering marvelous landmarks such as Lake Ngami, Victoria Falls, and the Zambezi River. His medical and missionary efforts brought the benefits of Western medicine to many Africans, and led to the conversion of many to the Christian faith.

Because of his motivation to seek God's kingdom, Livingstone made enormous sacrifices. He was away from home for many years, was once mauled by a lion, and never fully recovered from recurrent bouts with malaria. Yet despite the sacrifices, he never lost his desire to seek God's kingdom first. At one point he said, "I will place no value on anything I have or possess unless it is in relationship to the kingdom of God." Livingstone's motivation to seek first the kingdom of God led to countless benefits for Africans as well as Westerners.

The Christian's anticipation of the coming kingdom of God is captured well in the lyrics from Isaac Watts's classic hymn "Jesus Shall Reign."

> Jesus shall reign where'er the sun
> Does His successive journeys run,
> His kingdom spread from shore to shore,
> 'Til moons shall wax and wane no more.

> To Him shall endless prayer be made,
> And endless praises crown His head;
> His name like sweet perfume shall rise
> With every morning sacrifice.

> People and realms of every tongue
> Dwell on His love with sweetest song;
> And infant voices shall proclaim
> Their early blessing on His name.

> Let every creature rise and bring
> His grateful honors to our King;
> Angels descend with songs again,
> And earth repeat the loud "Amen!"[46]

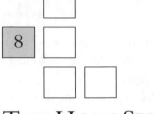

THE HOLY SPIRIT

The Comforter Has Come!

The Holy Spirit of grace desires to disturb your sleep. Blessed are you if you awaken.

—Lars Linderot

The Spirit of God is given to the true saints to dwell in them, as his proper lasting abode; and to influence their hearts, as a principle of new nature or as a divine supernatural spring of life and action.

—Jonathan Edwards

Many Christians today yearn for a richer experience of the Holy Spirit. The growth of movements, revival groups, and churches devoted to the experience of the Spirit is evidence of such a craving. Many yearn for the Holy Spirit to touch and minister to their churches, their countries, and themselves. Many, in their quest to experience the Spirit, are willing to go to great extremes for a deeper spiritual enthusiasm and a richer sense of God's presence.

Such was also the case in the early decades of the church. At that time, the followers of Montanus, a charismatic individual who drew many to himself but also caused division in the church, devoted themselves to fresh experiences of the Holy Spirit. Some Montanists who were designated as prophets made bold claims about their connection to God and to the Holy Spirit. Montanus himself was chief among the prophets making such claims. Indeed, in one of his prophecies, uttered in a trancelike state, he claimed that he was the Lord Almighty dwelling in a man. By this he meant not that he was divine, but rather that God spoke through him. Montanus was convinced that he was an embodiment of the Holy Spirit.

Because the group was so convinced that it was influenced by the Holy Spirit, they often behaved abnormally. In their meetings, people would fall into states of possession, or abnormal ecstasy, becoming frenzied and babbling and uttering strange sounds. The Montanists followed a strict rule of life, including severe fasting that went well beyond normal Christian practice. When they did eat, it was often a strange diet, such as meals of parched foods or feasts of radishes. Other evidence of their abnormal way of life can be seen in their celebration of Lent three times per year rather than once. They also condemned the remarriage of widows, believed that some sins were unforgivable, and disapproved of Christians who evaded martyrdom.

Church history, for the most part, remembers the Montanists as intensely interested in the Holy Spirit but decidedly heretical. A minority view sees the group as merely fanatical rather than heretical. Yet both viewpoints reveal that the Montanists' radical quest for spiritual experiences was not in accordance with the Scripture, and any quest that takes a follower outside of Scripture can lead to heresy, fanaticism, or both.[1]

In our current day, a greater appreciation of the Holy Spirit is naturally to be encouraged. Yet this enthusiasm should not be misplaced, like that of the Montanists. Rather than relying on the prophecy of charismatic individuals, the testimony of Scripture should guide the way for understanding the Spirit. The balanced testimony of the Holy Spirit from Old and New Testaments provides grounding for true experiences of the Spirit. This chapter, then, traces some functions of the Holy Spirit as found in the Old Testament and considers how they provide a foundation for our understanding of the Holy Spirit in the New Testament.[2]

THE HOLY SPIRIT IN THE OLD TESTAMENT

The Holy Spirit Creates Life

In the Old Testament, the Holy Spirit creates and sustains life. From the beginning, in fact, the Spirit is depicted as being involved in the creation of life. Genesis 1:2 states, "In the beginning God created the heavens and the earth. Now the earth was formless and empty, darkness was over the surface of the deep, and the Spirit of God was hovering over the waters."[3] Here the Spirit brings order and beauty out of the primeval chaos and conducts the cosmic forces toward the goal of an ordered universe.[4]

Many sources that date from a time close to the composition of the New Testament also viewed the Spirit involved with creation. Intertestamental Jewish references to creation, for example, speak of the Spirit as a part of creation.[5] Many of these early Jewish sources are quite attentive to the Old Testament documents.[6] Recent studies that consider intertestamental literature have noted how these documents are greatly interested in the proper interpretation of the Old Testament.[7]

The early Christians also saw the Spirit as involved in the creation accounts. A number of early Christian fathers, in fact, saw the Holy Spirit as explicitly present in the Genesis 1 narrative.[8] Thus, both Jewish and Christian sources near the time of the writing of the New Testament recognize the Spirit as being involved in the creation account of Genesis 1.

Other passages from the Old Testament certainly indicate that the Holy Spirit is present in creating and sustaining the creatures. Psalm 104:29–30, for example, says, "When you hide your face, they are terrified; when you take away their breath, they die and return to the dust. When you send your Spirit, they are created, and you renew the face of the earth." Other passages suggest that the Holy Spirit makes the skies beautiful (Job 26:13), creates stars by the breath of his mouth (Ps. 33:6), and makes fields fruitful (Isa. 32:15).

The book of Job also connects the Holy Spirit with the giving of life. Elihu, one of Job's counselors, testifies of the life-sustaining nature of the Spirit: "The Spirit of God has made me; the breath of the Almighty gives me life" (33:4). Later in his discourse, Elihu again testifies to the creative and life-giving nature of the Holy Spirit: "If it were his intention and he withdrew his spirit [*ruah*] and breath, all mankind would perish together and man would return to the dust" (34:14–15).[9] Thus, the Holy Spirit creates and sustains life, but his absence leads to death (cf. Gen. 6:3).

The Holy Spirit Works Among God's People

In addition to his work in creation, the Holy Spirit has been active among God's people from the time of the Old Testament. His presence is particularly evident in the lives of certain individuals,[10] coming upon the earliest leaders of the nation of Israel. Moses was endowed with the Holy Spirit so that he could serve and lead God's people (Num. 11:17, 29). The seventy elders whom Moses appointed to help him were also endowed with the Spirit (vv. 25–29). Joshua, who succeeded Moses as leader of the people, is said, too, to have had the Holy Spirit residing upon him. In 27:18, for instance, the Lord tells Moses, "Take Joshua son of Nun, a man in whom is the spirit, and lay your hand on him."[11]

God's Spirit continues to be found in certain people at the time of the Judges. The Spirit of the Lord came upon Othniel, the judge, and gave him the power to defeat the King of Aram (Judg. 3:10). The Holy Spirit strengthened Gideon, assisting him in calling together the forces of Israel to defeat the Midianites (Judg. 6–7). In 11:29, the Spirit of the Lord comes upon Jephthah so that he is able to advance against the Ammonites. The Spirit also enabled Samson to tear apart a lion with his bare hands (14:6), strike down thirty men from Ashkelon (v. 19), and strike down a thousand men with the jawbone of a donkey (15:14–15).

The Spirit of God also came upon kings. When King Saul, for example, was anointed with the Holy Spirit, he was able to prophesy (1 Sam. 10:6, 10). King David, too, from the time that he was anointed as king, was resided upon by the Spirit (16:13). When he sinned with Bathsheeba, he, in fact, feared the removal of the Spirit (Ps. 51:10–12). The Holy Spirit was also found to be with King Solomon, particularly when he was planning to build the temple of the Lord (1 Chron. 28:12).

The Holy Spirit was also found among the prophets. From the times of Elijah and Elisha, the Spirit was seen to be among those who prophesied. Elijah was said to have been compelled and driven by the Spirit (1 Kings 18:12). Elisha, the prophet who succeeded Elijah, recognized the greatness of the Spirit that was on Elijah and asked for a double portion for himself (2 Kings 2:9).

In the books of the prophets, the Holy Spirit is closely associated with prophecy in multiple places. Hosea 9:7 says, "Because your sins are so many and your hostility so great, the prophet is considered a fool, the inspired man a maniac." Other translations of the Bible render "inspired man" as "man of the spirit," thereby more explicitly drawing this connection.[12] A similar connection between a prophet and the Holy Spirit can also be found in other passages in the Prophets. Ezekiel, Isaiah, and Zechariah are all seen to be influenced by the Spirit.[13] Daniel, the great prophetic interpreter of dreams, was also noted to have "the spirit of the holy gods" upon him (Dan. 5:11). It is especially noteworthy that the pagan Babylonians recognized Daniel as influenced by the Spirit.

The Holy Spirit was also found to be present with those who performed special tasks. He was present with the seventy elders who resolved Israel's disputes (Num. 11:25–29), as well as among the craftsmen who built the tabernacle (Exod. 28:3; 31:3; 35:31). He was present, too, with those who rebuilt the temple following the time of exile (Zech. 4:5–7).

The Old Testament also anticipates a day when, with the Messiah, the Holy Spirit will be more fully present:

> A shoot will come up from the stump of Jesse;
>   from his roots a Branch will bear fruit.
> The Spirit of the LORD will rest on him—
>   the Spirit of wisdom and of understanding,
>   the Spirit of counsel and of power,
>   the Spirit of knowledge and of the fear of the LORD—
> and he will delight in the fear of the LORD.
>
> He will not judge by what he sees with his eyes,
>   or decide by what he hears with his ears;
> but with righteousness he will judge the needy,
>   with justice he will give decisions for the poor of the earth.
> He will strike the earth with the rod of his mouth;
>   with the breath of his lips he will slay the wicked.[14]
>
>   (Isa. 11:1–4)

Other texts from Isaiah also indicate that in the future the Holy Spirit is to be present upon the Messiah (cf. Isa. 42:1; 61:1).[15]

It is true that in the Old Testament the Holy Spirit for the most part resides upon particular leaders who had responsibility for directing God's people. Expressed, too, though is a future hope that all of God's people would someday be blessed with the presence of the Spirit. The coming of the Spirit to rest on all of God's people was a significant mark of the new age,[16] and was, in fact, a fervent hope for the nation of Israel, as Joel 2:28–29 prophesies:

> And afterward,
> > I will pour out my Spirit on all people.
> Your sons and daughters will prophesy,
> > your old men will dream dreams,
> > your young men will see visions.
> Even on my servants, both men and women,
> > I will pour out my Spirit in those days.

Indeed, Israel was looking forward to a day when the Spirit would be poured out from on high, making the desert into a field, and a field into a forest (Isa. 32:15). God was expected to pour out his Spirit on his people as water is poured out on the thirsty land, and streams on the dry ground (44:3; cf. Ezek. 39:29). At the time when his Spirit is poured out, the people would be led to obey God and they would be restored (Jer. 31:31–34; Ezek. 36:24–29).

The Holy Spirit Reveals God's Will

The Holy Spirit is also depicted in the Old Testament as the channel of communication between God and his people. In this role, the Holy Spirit is seen as the Spirit of prophecy and revelation.

Many of the prophets connected the Spirit with their prophecies. Micah 3:8 states so succinctly: "But as for me, I am filled with power, with the Spirit of the LORD, and with justice and might, to declare to Jacob his transgression, to Israel his sin." Isaiah testified that the Holy Spirit was with him when he prophesied: "Come near me and listen to this: 'From the first announcement I have not spoken in secret; at the time it happens, I am there.' And now the Sovereign LORD has sent me, with his

Spirit" (Isa. 48:16). Zechariah looked back upon earlier prophets and says that the Holy Spirit had come with them (Zech. 7:12). The prophet Ezekiel began his prophecies with the phrase, "Thus says the Lord," or its equivalent, and then ascribed his messages directly to the Spirit of God.[17]

Even more striking, however, is that the Spirit caused to prophecy many people who were not called to be prophets. When, for example, the Spirit descended upon some of the elders who were helping Moses in the leadership of the nation, they prophesied (Num. 11:25–29). When the Spirit came upon King Saul at Gibeah, he prophesied (1 Sam. 10:10). When Saul's men were chasing after David, they had an experience in which the Holy Spirit fell upon them, diverting them from their mission and causing them to prophesy. When Saul sent more men after David to seize him, they too encountered the Holy Spirit and prophesied (19:20–21).[18]

A good summary of the Holy Spirit's ability both to cause people to prophesy and to enliven all of God's people, can be seen in Ezekiel 37. As the chapter begins, the prophet is led into a valley wherein he sees nothing but dry human bones. The entire valley is filled with bones—hips, femurs, toes, arms, ribs, skulls, and so on. Nobody is there to bury them or to respect the memory of the people who had perished. Perhaps these bones had been left unburied due to a battle in which thousands of warriors had been slain, and perhaps their flesh had been eaten by scavengers. How discouraging this must have been for the prophet to walk amid the unburied remains of God's people.

The Lord leads Ezekiel back and forth through the valley in order to reinforce the number of bones that are present and how brittle and dry they are. After impressing this upon him, God then asks Ezekiel if these dry bones can ever live. Ezekiel concedes, "O Sovereign LORD, you alone know" (Ezek. 37:3).

Although the vision of these bones seems depressing and hopeless, the Lord commands Ezekiel to prophesy, promising him that he will breathe life into Ezekiel who will then breathe life into the bones. Amazingly, as Ezekiel follows God's instruction, his prophesying results in a rattling sound as the bones come together. The dry and lifeless bones are invigorated, and as the bones connect to each other, God clothes them with tissue and skin. As Ezekiel continues to prophesy, the bones come to life and stand on their feet as a vast army, representing the nation of Israel that will come out from exile. What a dramatic change from lifelessness, and what a tremendous hope this would have provided for God's people in exile.[19]

Ezekiel's vision well summarizes the Old Testament perspective of the Holy Spirit. It shows once again the special anointing of the Holy Spirit upon select individuals in the Old Testament. It also reveals how the Spirit can invigorate anything that seems dry and dead. That life-giving energy is given through prophecy, which is God's revelation. Ezekiel's life-giving prophecy resulted in the nation of Israel being touched by the Holy Spirit (Ezek. 37:10-14).

THE HOLY SPIRIT IN THE NEW TESTAMENT

The Holy Spirit's role increases dramatically in the New Testament. He is spoken of more frequently and his presence is more visible. Even though he is more prominent in the New Testament, the ideas that were present in the Old Testament can still be seen as foundation stones for understanding the Spirit in the New Testament.[20]

The Holy Spirit Creates Life

In the Old Testament, the Holy Spirit was seen as a life-giver, and from the earliest chapters of the Gospels this emphasis can also be seen in the New Testament. In Matthew 1:18, Mary is found to be with child through the Holy Spirit. Regarding Mary, an angel tells Joseph that "what is conceived in her is from the Holy Spirit" (v. 20). The same emphasis on the creation of life by the Holy Spirit can also be seen in Luke's account of Mary's pregnancy (Luke 1:35, 47). From the beginning of the New Testament, then, the Spirit is involved in giving life to Jesus Christ, the most central person of the Bible.

The life-giving nature of the Holy Spirit was also visible in the miracles that attended Jesus' ministry.[21] By the power of the Spirit, Jesus cast out demons and healed the sick. Matthew 12:15–18 draws a direct connection between Jesus' miracles and the Holy Spirit:

Many followed him, and he healed all their sick, warning them not to tell who he was. This was to fulfill what was spoken through the prophet Isaiah: "Here is my servant whom I have chosen, the one I love, in whom I delight; I will put my Spirit on him, and he will proclaim justice to the nations."

By quoting Isaiah 42:1–2, Matthew offered an explanation of Jesus' healings and identified the Holy Spirit as the source of healing power.[22] Jesus himself attributed his miracle-working power to the Spirit when in the gospel of Matthew he asserts that he drives out demons by the Spirit of God and not by Beelzebub (Matt. 12:28). These miracles were life-giving, bringing a restoration of life into situations of death and misery.

Jesus also affirmed the life-giving essence of the Spirit in his teaching. Jesus proclaimed, "The Spirit gives life; the flesh counts for nothing. The words I have spoken to you are spirit and they are life" (John 6:63). In a later discourse, he prophesied about the life to be found in the Spirit:

On the last and greatest day of the Feast, Jesus stood and said in a loud voice, "If anyone is thirsty, let him come to me and drink. Whoever believes in me, as the Scripture has said, streams of living water will flow from within him." By this he meant the Spirit, whom those who believed in him were later to receive. Up to that time the Spirit had not been given, since Jesus had not yet been glorified. (John 7:37–39)

The apostle Paul also taught that the Holy Spirit brings invigorating life to God's people. The Spirit brings Christians out of their former way of life into one in which they can be made pure in God's sight (Rom. 10:11; 1 Cor. 6:11). Christians who were formerly alienated from God become indwelled with the Holy Spirit and are then empowered to live a life that is pleasing to God, a life that is pure, free, and powerful.[23] The Holy Spirit also brings life to the church, providing it with diverse gifts to strengthen it (1 Cor. 12–14). Indeed, the "Spirit gives life" to Christians rather than bringing death (cf. 2 Cor. 3:6).

The Holy Spirit grants life in the daily struggle to overcome the flesh, which is a constant battle for God's people: "For if you live according to the sinful nature, you will die; but if by the Spirit you put to death the misdeeds of the body, you will live" (Rom. 8:13; cf. Gal. 6:8). The flesh can actually be the undoing of some, as Paul relates in Romans 7.[24] The Spirit, however, is the antithesis of the flesh and is able to give God's people power in their struggle with the flesh.[25] Those who walk in the Spirit will find the life they need to overcome the flesh (Gal. 5:15–25).

A. J. Gordon, influential pastor in the Boston area in the late nineteenth century, provides a good example of the invigorating essence of the Spirit. He once told a story of his walking and looking across a field at a house. Beside the house was a man who appeared to be pumping a hand pump. As Gordon watched, the man continued to pump at a furious rate. He seemed absolutely tireless, pumping up and down, without ever slowing down or stopping.

It was truly a remarkable sight, so Gordon went to take a closer look. As he drew near, he saw that it was not a man at the pump, but rather it was a wooden figure painted to look like a man. The arm that appeared to be pumping so fast was attached to the pump handle with a wire. The water was pouring forth because the pump was connected to an artesian well. In actuality, the water was pumping the man.[26] This is a good illustration of the Holy Spirit's work; he invigorates people, making people who were lifeless spiritually vibrant. What was formerly dead becomes alive when the Holy Spirit is at work.

The Holy Spirit Works Among God's People

In the New Testament, the Holy Spirit not only creates life, but he also, as in the Old Testament, is uniquely present on specific individuals. This presence is particularly true with the person of Jesus Christ who is uniquely associated with the Spirit.[27]

The gospel of Luke most directly expresses this association, beginning with its opening verses in which the Holy Spirit is shown to be closely associated with the birth narratives. John the Baptist, for example, is expected to have the presence of the Spirit upon him so that he can herald the presence of the Christ in the world (Luke 1:17).[28] John grows strong in the Spirit as a child in preparation for the time when he will herald the coming of Jesus (v. 80).

Luke's gospel, too, points to the involvement of the Spirit in the life of Jesus. The Spirit comes upon Mary so that Jesus is conceived (1:35, 47).

At Jesus' baptism, the Holy Spirit descends upon him in the Jordan River (3:22). At the time of his temptation, Jesus is led by the Spirit to enter the wilderness (4:1), and following his temptation, he returns to his hometown, led by the Spirit (v. 14).

Luke also draws attention to the Spirit's presence when Jesus visits the synagogue in his hometown. Jesus reads Isaiah 61:1–2, a text that speaks of the Spirit's anointing of God's messenger:

> "The Spirit of the Lord is on me,
>   because he has anointed me
>   to preach good news to the poor.
> He has sent me to proclaim freedom for the prisoners
>   and recovery of sight for the blind,
> to release the oppressed,
>   to proclaim the year of the Lord's favor."

> Then he rolled up the scroll, gave it back to the attendant and sat down. The eyes of everyone in the synagogue were fastened on him, and he began by saying to them, "Today this scripture is fulfilled in your hearing." (Luke 4:18–21)

In the words of one theologian, "Jesus himself, all that he says and does, is God's presence. . . . His life and proclamation is the event of God's presence, fulfilling all prophetic expectations."[29] Jesus' life, then, is the life of the Holy Spirit.

As in the Old Testament, these special manifestations of the Spirit show that he is present with specific individuals who minister to God's people. The apostles are said to have had the Holy Spirit working on them to a special degree. The mystery of Christ, for example, was revealed to the apostles through the Holy Spirit (John 14:26; Eph. 3:5). Stephen, the first Christian martyr, displayed a special sense of the Spirit immediately before he was killed (Acts 6:10), and Paul carried on a new covenant ministry of the Spirit (2 Cor. 3). John the apostle received his revelation of Jesus Christ when he was in the Spirit (Rev. 1:10).

In the New Testament, the Holy Spirit not only rests upon Jesus and the apostles, but also upon all of God's people.[30] This is a significant development from the Old Testament.[31] On the Day of Pentecost, Acts 2 testifies that the Spirit comes first upon the apostles, causing them to speak in a variety of different languages. People in the crowd accuse them of being drunk, but Peter announces to all of Jerusalem that the proliferation of languages reveals that the Holy Spirit has now come upon all of God's people. In his explanation, he refers to the Old Testament prophecy of Joel:

> This is what was spoken by the prophet Joel: "In the last days, God says, I will pour out my Spirit on all people. Your sons and daughters will prophesy, your young men will see visions, your old men will dream dreams. Even on my servants, both men and women, I will pour out my Spirit in those days, and they will prophesy." (Acts 2:16–18; cf. Joel 2:28–29)

Later in that same speech, Peter declares that the Spirit is available to all who will place their faith in Jesus Christ: "Repent and be baptized, every one of you, in the name of Jesus Christ for the forgiveness of your sins. And you will receive the gift of the Holy Spirit" (Acts 2:38).

Many other passages in the New Testament indicate that the Spirit promised in the Old Testament is now present for those who trust in Jesus Christ.[32] Paul wrote to many different churches, sharing that the Spirit had come upon them. Christians in Thessalonica received the Spirit, even though Paul had ministered there for less than a month (1 Thess. 1:6). In the affluent, pagan city of Corinth, the Spirit was poured out there on all who professed Jesus Christ (1 Cor. 12:3). Indeed, Christians should consider themselves corporately as the temple of the Holy Spirit (3:16–17). To the churches in the province of Galatia, Paul declared that those who hear the message and simply believe, have the Spirit (Gal. 3:1–5; 4:1–7), and to the Romans, Paul said that if they do not have the Spirit, they do not belong to Jesus (Rom. 8:9). The understanding that the Holy Spirit has been given to all Christians is, in fact, a basis of Paul's teaching.[33]

The Holy Spirit Reveals God's Will

In the New Testament, the Holy Spirit is identified with prophecy and revelation. Harking back to the time of the Old Testament, the New Testament writers repeatedly indicate that Old Testament prophecies were delivered by means of the Holy Spirit.

Hebrews 10:15–16, which quotes Jeremiah 31:33, offers a striking example:

> The Holy Spirit also testifies to us about this. First he says: "This is the covenant I will make with them after that time, says the Lord. I will put my laws in their hearts, and I will write them on their minds."[34]

By introducing an Old Testament prophecy in this way, the writer of Hebrews declares that the Old Testament text has been delivered through the Holy Spirit.[35] First Peter 1:10–12 makes a similar point:

> Concerning this salvation, the prophets, who spoke of the grace that was to come to you, searched intently and with the greatest care, trying to find out the time and circumstances to which the Spirit of Christ in them was pointing when he predicted the sufferings of Christ and the glories that would follow. It was revealed to them that they were not serving themselves but you, when they spoke of the things that have now been told you by those who have preached the gospel to you by the Holy Spirit sent from heaven. Even angels long to look into these things.

The New Testament writers also see the Holy Spirit as revealing new things in the New Testament. The book of Revelation is quite explicit about the prophetic nature of the Holy Spirit. That book begins with John's declaration that he was in the Spirit at the time of the vision (1:10). After he sees an image of the glorified Christ, John is instructed to write to seven churches, prophesying to each of them. At the end of each of the prophecies, he closes with the same statement: "He who has an ear, let him hear what the Spirit says to the churches."[36] It is clear, then, that in the New Testament, the Holy Spirit reveals God's will, just as he did in the Old Testament.[37]

The role of the Spirit in the New Testament community indicates his prophetic nature. The gifts associated with the Spirit in the book of Acts are similar to prophetic gifts given in the Old Testament, namely, the Spirit is the author of revelatory visions and dreams,[38] as well as revelatory words, guidance, or instruction.[39] He also provides wisdom,[40] invasive praise,[41] and teaching or witness.[42] All of these prophetic practices are similar to those in the Old Testament.[43]

First Corinthians 12–14 specifically connects the Holy Spirit with prophecy and the revealed will of God. The Corinthians are to "eagerly desire spiritual gifts, especially the gift of prophecy" (14:1). Although some people would debate the definition of "prophecy" as Paul uses it in 1 Corinthians, it apparently involves revelation of some sort and is clearly associated with the Holy Spirit.[44] Prophecy was not to be stifled lest one quench the Spirit (1 Thess. 5:18–20).

Jonathan Edwards, the great eighteenth-century American theologian and pastor, held a view of the Holy Spirit that was firmly grounded in both the Old and New Testaments. In his day, the time of the First Great Awakening, spiritual enthusiasm was at a high point as the American colonies experienced a fresh outpouring of the Holy Spirit. At that time, Edwards commented on this spiritual enthusiasm in a number of his writings, attempting to isolate the good marks of God's Spirit from those that might be counterfeit. In a treatise titled "The Distinguishing Marks of a Work of the Spirit of God," he writes:

> We are to take the Scriptures as our guide in such cases. This is the great and standing rule which God has given to his church, in order to guide them in things relating to the great concerns of their souls; and it is an infallible and sufficient rule. . . . Doubtless that Spirit who indited the Scriptures knew how to give us good rules by which to distinguish his operations from all that is falsely pretended to be from him.[45]

It is likely that the exuberance of the Montanists as well as other spiritually enthusiastic groups could be regulated by appealing to the Bible. By considering both the Old and New Testaments, an understanding of the Holy Spirit would focus spiritual enthusiasm on the creative life that the Spirit brings, his presence on leaders in the Old Testament, his special manifestation on Jesus Christ, his involvement in every Christian's life, and the prophetic and revelatory words of Scripture.

A hymn composed by Cecil Frances Alexander in the nineteenth century encompasses many of these themes from the Old and New Testaments:

> Spirit of God, that moved of old
> Upon the waters' darkened face,
> Come when our faithless hearts are cold,
> And stir them with an inward grace.
>
> Thou that art power and peace combined,
> All highest strength, all purest love,
> The rushing of the mighty wind,
> The brooding of the gentle dove,
>
> Come give us still Thy powerful aid,
> And urge us on, and keep us Thine;
> Nor leave the hearts that once were made
> Fit temples for Thy grace divine;
>
> Nor let us quench Thy sevenfold light;
> But still with softest breathings stir
> Our wayward souls and lead us right,
> O Holy Ghost, the Comforter.[46]

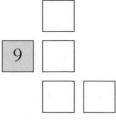

THE PEOPLE OF GOD

A Kingdom of Priests and a Holy Nation

> Just as God's will is creation and is called "the world," so his intention is the salvation of men, and it is called "the Church."
> —Clement of Alexandria

> The church is the only institution supernaturally endowed by God. It is the one institution of which Jesus promised that the gates of hell will not prevail against it.
> —Chuck Colson

> Let him who wants a true church cling to the word by which everything is upheld.
> —Martin Luther

At times, in our busy modern world, we forget how dependent we are upon others. Oftentimes, the intense focus that must be placed on work, finances, or family leads to tunnel vision. But at moments, too, we realize that we are connected to each other as part of a larger whole.

On August 14, 2003, many North Americans realized that they were part of a bigger picture—one that transcended national borders—when the electricity went off along the eastern power grid, which supplies the East Coast of the United States and southeast Canada. Dozens of cities such as Cleveland, Detroit, Toronto, and New York City were without power for many hours. Trains and elevators stopped, traffic came to a halt, and water supplies were impeded.

In New York City, the absence of electrical power was particularly

157

noticeable. Thousands emerged from stalled subway lines and began walking toward their destinations. With no electricity to run computers, other office equipment, and even air conditioners, businesses shut down. Entertainment was canceled throughout the city. Travel was disrupted as airlines canceled flights into LaGuardia and John F. Kennedy airports. Many travelers couldn't even get into their hotel rooms because the electronic locks wouldn't work. The Big Apple was largely brought to a standstill by the failure of the power network.

When power was restored the next day, most people were able to return to their normal activities. They were, however, more appreciative of others who had helped to provide electric power so that daily activities could resume. They realized that their lives were connected to others and that they were part of a bigger picture.

A parallel can be drawn to the way that many Christians perceive church life. Many have tunnel vision, focusing on their own particular Christian experiences, their own small group of Christian friends, their particular Sunday school class, their own church building, and their own pastor. Many are so involved in their own Christian experiences that they forget that they are part of a larger picture. Occasionally, perhaps, something happens, causing Christians to appreciate that they are a part of something bigger.

In the words of Dr. Martin Lloyd-Jones, the well-known, twentieth-century English preacher, "We must cease to think of the church as a gathering of institutions and organizations, and we must get back the notion that we are the people of God."[1] Certainly, for many Christians, the appreciation of the church has been diminished by its bureaucracy, committees, boards, and the other layers that govern institutions. Viewing God's people from the perspective of both Old and New Testaments together, though, can help to broaden appreciation for the church in our day.[2]

While "the church" is not identified as such in the Old Testament, God has been seeking a people to follow him from earliest times.[3] When the Old Testament is considered, it reveals key characteristics of God's people that have been present from generations past. Such a consideration can also provide a fresh focus to those whose faith has been short-circuited by tunnel vision.

GOD'S PEOPLE IN THE OLD TESTAMENT

A Special People

From a very early point within the Old Testament, God has been gathering a people to himself and treating them as special. One of the earliest attestations of God's interest in gathering a people to him can be seen in the calling of Abraham:

> The LORD had said to Abram, "Leave your country, your people and your father's household and go to the land I will show you.

> "I will make you into a great nation
> and I will bless you;
> I will make your name great,
> and you will be a blessing.
> I will bless those who bless you,
> and whoever curses you I will curse;
> and all peoples on earth
> will be blessed through you."[4]
> (Gen. 12:1–3)

From this early chapter in Genesis, God singles out a person for himself, namely, Abraham. He does so in order to give him special blessings—a land, a seed, and a blessing. He also promises that Abraham will become a great nation and eventually bless all peoples on the earth.

In Genesis 17, God reaffirms that he is gathering a special people to himself through Abraham. There he promises that Abraham will be the father of many nations and Sarah, his wife, will be the mother of many nations. Not only will many generations of people come from them, but kings as well (vv. 4–7, 15–16).

The importance of this promise is underscored by God's changing both of their names. The changing of a name in ancient Near East society indicates a change in a person's character, destiny, reputation, or fame.[5] For God to change Abram's name to Abraham and Sarai's name to Sarah would have been a highly significant event for them and an indication of their destiny (Gen. 17:5, 15–16). Thus, the people descending from Abraham will be not only Abraham's people, more importantly they will be special and a people belonging to God. They are to be devoted to God and to keep his covenant (vv. 9–14).

Throughout the Old Testament, God is repeatedly kind to the people of Abraham because they are special to him. In the rest of Genesis, God appears to Abraham's descendants such as Isaac, Jacob, and Joseph. Because these people are special to God, he promises to bless them—despite the difficulties they face, some of which result from their own wrongdoing.[6]

In the book of Exodus, God promises to rescue Abraham's descendants from the rule of Pharaoh because he is committed to his people.[7] In Deuteronomy, God promises to lead his people into the Promised Land because of the promises previously made to Abraham.[8] In 1 Kings, Elijah, in order to triumph over the priests of Baal on Mount Carmel, even claims the special status of God's people (18:36). The nation of Israel had a special relationship with God as a result of God's special relationship with their physical father, Abraham.[9]

In Exodus 19:10–11, the children of Israel are singled out by God from among the nations of the world, and he declares that his people will be a kingdom of priests and a holy nation. In Deuteronomy 7:6–8, Moses declares the uniqueness of the people of Israel:

> For you are a people holy to the LORD your God. The LORD your God has chosen you out of all the peoples on the face of the earth to be his people, his treasured possession. The LORD did not set his affection on you and choose you because you were more numerous than other peoples, for you were the fewest of all peoples. But it was because the LORD loved you and kept the oath he swore to your forefathers that he brought you out with a mighty hand and redeemed you from the land of slavery, from the power of Pharaoh king of Egypt.

Other Old Testament passages, too, describe how God views his people as special. In some instances, the people of Israel are even called the "people of God," indicating their unique status (Judg. 20:2; 2 Sam. 14:13). The prophet Isaiah declares that God looks after his chosen people in the desert (Isa. 43:20) and will give these special people an inheritance (63:9; 65:22).

The promise that God will gather a people to himself so that they will proclaim him as their God can be found throughout the Old Testament. This promise is prominently displayed in Jeremiah 31:33: "I will put my law in their minds and write it on their hearts. I will be their God."[10] Similar promises appear in other texts in Jeremiah (24:7; 31:1; 32:38), but they are also found in other prophetical books, such as Ezekiel (11:20; 14:11; 34:30; 37:23, 27), Hosea (2:23), and Zechariah (8:8; 13:9). Indeed, God's choosing a people for himself is a major theme of the Old Testament,[11] and he, in fact, did so from the very beginning.

A Worshipping People

God also called his people to worship him. They were not simply to be a social organization or a group of people joined together by location or by blood relationship. Worship was the purpose for which God called his people and was a prominent idea from the very first time that the nation of Israel is mentioned in the Old Testament.

The patriarchs of the nation of Israel—Abraham, Isaac, and Jacob—worshipped the Lord (Gen. 22:5; 47:31), and such worship became a defining aspect of the nation of Israel from the time of the Exodus. The motive of worship is the original reason that Moses appealed to Pharaoh for the release of God's people.[12] Through Moses, God demanded of Pharaoh, "Let my people go, *so that* they may *worship* me in the desert"[13] (Exod. 7:16, emphasis added). Moses repeated this motive numerous times before Pharaoh—that is, God's people must not only leave the land of Egypt but they must also go and worship the Lord.[14] The requirement of worship was, in fact, so firmly engrained in Pharaoh's mind that when he ordered Moses and the people to leave Egypt, he told them to go and worship the Lord (Exod. 12:31). Thus, from early in the history of God's people, worship was a defining characteristic.

The importance of worship for God's people can also be seen from the number of times that it is commanded in the Old Testament.[15] In the

Pentateuch, God commands that his people worship him (Exod. 23:25), and worship is, indeed, assumed in the many passages in which God prohibits his people from the worship of false gods.[16] Many times in the Psalms—the hymnbook for the nation of Israel—the people are exhorted to worship, as in Psalm 95:6: "Come, let us bow down in worship, let us kneel before the LORD our Maker."[17]

That worship is a defining characteristic of God's people in the Old Testament can be seen, too, in the book of Jonah. Notice how succinctly Jonah describes himself to those of other nationalities who are on board the ship that he takes, bound for Joppa. When he is discovered as the reason for their calamity, he introduces himself by saying, "I am a Hebrew and I *worship* the LORD, the God of heaven, who made the sea and the land'" (Jonah 1:9, emphasis added).

God deemed worship to be so important that he set aside one of the tribes of Israel, the descendants of Levi, to lead the nation in worship. They offered sacrifices,[18] practiced divination,[19] instructed God's people through the Torah,[20] and tended to the house of worship.[21]

The most significant building in the land of Israel, the temple built by King Solomon, was also devoted to worship. It was decorated extravagantly with stone, gold, and the finest woods. Most important, it was the place where God's presence was noted to dwell (cf. 1 Kings 8:1–11). Annual pilgrimages to the temple were highly important occasions, imbued with spiritual value and joy for God's people.[22]

Special days also were set aside for worship of the Lord. The most notable day of worship was the Sabbath day, the seventh day of the week, when all of Israel was to lay aside their work and devote themselves wholly to the Lord (Exod. 20:8–11). Other special days included the Day of Atonement, an annual event devoted to the cleansing of sin from the community, and the festival of the Passover and Feast of Unleavened Bread, both weeklong commemorations of the Exodus. Other feasts, such as the Feasts of Firstfruits, Trumpets, and Tabernacles encouraged thanksgiving to God for deliverance or provision or confession of sin.[23] All of these special days emphasized that God's people, the Israelites, were a people devoted to the worship of God.

A Blessing to Others

One purpose for God's calling his people to worship him is so they would become a blessing to others. This purpose can be seen from as early as Genesis 12:3, in which God promises that he will bless Abraham so that the entire world "will be blessed through you." The idea that God's people will bless the entire world through Abraham's lineage is repeated in later portions of Genesis (18:18; 22:18; 26:4; 28:14). Many of these texts were referred to in the previous section, in which God is described as drawing a people to himself.

At the end of Genesis, this promise to bless the world through Abraham's lineage is realized in the life of Joseph, Abraham's great grandson. Joseph was sold into slavery in Egypt because of his brothers' envy of him, but his life ultimately became a blessing to many. God used him as an advisor to Pharaoh to prepare for a coming famine and thus save the lives of his brothers and their families, as well as the nation of Egypt and many people from surrounding nations (cf. Gen. 41:38–57).

When much later Israel became established in the Promised Land, the nation also became a means for blessing others. During King Solomon's prosperous reign, he built the temple of the Lord. Certainly, it would function as a place for God's people to come and worship, but it was also to be a place where all nations would come and worship God. Part of Solomon's dedication prayer for the temple, recorded in 1 Kings 8:41–43, is particularly revealing in this regard:

> As for the foreigner who does not belong to your people Israel but has come from a distant land because of your name—for men will hear of your great name and your mighty hand and your outstretched arm—when he comes and prays toward this temple, then hear from heaven, your dwelling place, and do whatever the foreigner asks of you, so that all the peoples of the earth may know your name and fear you, as do your own people Israel, and may know that this house I have built bears your Name.

The book of Isaiah, too, speaks of the temple as a place to which all nations could come: the temple of the Lord is to be a "house of prayer for all nations" (56:7). Further, the final words of the book of Isaiah speak of the promise that God will "come and gather all nations and tongues, and they will come and see my glory" (66:18).

The witness to other nations can be seen not only in the initial calling of God's people and in the establishment of the temple, but it can also be seen in the prayers of God's people from generations past. Psalm 67, for example, records a song of God's people that shows they are to be a blessing to all people:

> May God be gracious to us and bless us and make his face shine upon us, that your ways may be known on earth, your salvation among all nations. May the peoples praise you, O God; may all the peoples praise you. May the nations be glad and sing for joy, for you rule the peoples justly and guide the nations of the earth. May the peoples praise you, O God; may all the peoples praise you. Then the land will yield its harvest, and God, our God, will bless us. God will bless us, and all the ends of the earth will fear him.[24]

In the midst of this psalm that speaks of God's blessing on his people, the psalmist also tells how God will bless the entire earth. Psalm 67 was probably sung at the Feast of Pentecost, the feast where God's people considered how the Holy Spirit was to be poured out on all people, further emphasizing that the whole world might come to be God's people.[25]

Other prophetic sections of the Old Testament indicate that the nation of Israel is to be a light to the world. Isaiah is quite noteworthy in this regard, Isaiah 2 providing a picture of the mountain of the Lord that will be raised up high:

> In the last days
> the mountain of the LORD's temple
>   will be established
>   as chief among the mountains;
> it will be raised above the hills,
>   and all nations will stream to it.
> Many peoples will come and say,

"Come, let us go up to the mountain
   of the LORD,
   to the house of the God of Jacob.
He will teach us his ways,
   so that we may walk in his paths."
The law will go out from Zion,
   the word of the LORD from Jerusalem.
                                    (Isa. 2:2–3)

The sense of this text is that all nations will come to the mountain of the Lord, the very place where the "house of the God of Jacob" is.[26]

Isaiah 2 is one of several places where the prophet mentions the mission of God's people.[27] The servant figure mentioned in the latter portions of Isaiah will also draw the nations to God. He will "bring justice among the nations" (42:1), and he is to be a "light for the Gentiles" that he "may bring my salvation to the ends of the earth" (49:6).

At points in the Old Testament, the Israelites become a blessing to people outside their nation. When Israel marches into the Promised Land, for example, they save Rahab the harlot and her family (Josh. 6:17–25). When God withholds rain from Israel, the prophet Elijah becomes a blessing to the widow in Zaraphath (1 Kings 17), and Elisha heals Naaman, a Syrian general (2 Kings 5). Jonah is perhaps the most striking example. He is commissioned to preach to the Ninevites but acts disobediently by choosing to run away from God. Nonetheless, he is used by God to turn the wicked city of Nineveh to God.

Images of God's People

The Old Testament portrays God's relationship with his people through a variety of colorful images. In the books of the Prophets, for example, God is said to be the husband to Israel, his bride.[28] At times, Israel is pictured as a holy bride, lovingly devoted to God as her husband (Jer. 2:2); at other times, God's people are pictured as a wayward wife playing the harlot (Ezek. 16:13; Hos. 2:1–3:1). God is the great protector and nurturer of Israel as a loving husband is for his wife (Isa. 54:4–6).

God's people are also pictured as his children (Deut. 14:1; Isa. 1:4;

45:11). Jerusalem, for example, is spoken of as a virgin daughter,[29] and God's people refer to each other as brothers. The Psalms in particular refer to people within God's household as brothers (22:22; 122:8; 133:1). In addition, Israel is designated as a "firstborn" son (Exod. 4:22).[30]

The Old Testament also presents God's people as sheep and the Lord as the great shepherd. Psalm 95:7 declares, "He is our God and we are the people of his pasture, the flock under his care." Psalm 100:3 says, "Know that the LORD is God. It is he who made us, and we are his; we are his people, the sheep of his pasture." These are representative of a number of passages in the Old Testament where God's people are called sheep.[31]

This image is not a complimentary one, however. Sheep oftentimes go their own way (Isa. 53:6). They can, in fact, wander so far that they do not remember where their home is (Jer. 50:6). Rather than moving to a fresh field to find fresh pasture, they will oftentimes eat the one pasture to oblivion. When a predator arrives, instead of running they may even roll over and offer themselves to that predator.[32]

Despite the waywardness of his people, God acts as their good shepherd. He leads them to green pastures and still waters, and is present even in the shadow of death (Psalm 23). He will rescue his people from inattentive shepherds and take care of them (cf. Ezek. 34; Zech. 11). He will also provide good human shepherds to look after his people (Num. 26:16–17; Jer. 3:15).

The Old Testament also uses the image of a vineyard to refer to God's people. Psalm 80:8–18 compares Israel to a vine planted by God and describes Israel's history in relation to what happened to the vine. In other places in the Old Testament, Israel is referred to as a vineyard that had many difficulties (Isa. 5:1–7) and as a fruitful vineyard that the Lord watches over (27:2–6). In each case, God is pictured as the one who plants, looks after, and cares for his people, the vineyard.

Another image of God's people in the Old Testament is as a remnant. This image refers to a leftover group of faithful Israelites who remain loyal to God despite the waywardness of the rest of the nation. That the future of Israel is bound up with this group is an idea that is especially prevalent in the Prophets. In the prophecies of Isaiah in particular, the remnant is seen as "a holy seed," or spiritual kernel, which should survive impending judgment and become the kernel of God's people, being

Sheep grazing near Wadi Makkuk. Sheep were common in the Ancient Near East, and the picture of God's people as sheep is common throughout Scripture. (Photograph courtesy of Todd Bolen and BiblePlaces.com.)

blessed of God and being made a blessing.[33] Isaiah 40–66 develops the theme of this holy group, which will have a bright future following the judgment that has come upon the rest of the nation.[34]

THE NEW TESTAMENT AND GOD'S PEOPLE

A Special People

Like Israel in the Old Testament, the church is described in the New Testament as a people special to God.[35] Beginning with Jesus' selection of his disciples, it is evident that God is calling out a people to be his own. As it says in John 15:16, "You did not choose me, but I chose you and appointed you to go and bear fruit—fruit that will last." Jesus selected Simon and Andrew while they were mending their fishing nets, and then called them to become fishers of men (Mark 1:14–19). He chose Matthew the tax collector while he was counting his money (Matt. 9:9). Other disciples were called after Jesus spent a night in prayer (cf. Luke 6:12–16).

God also selected his people from among the Gentiles, even though at the time the Gentiles were seen as strangers and intruders among the Jews. Nevertheless, God selected them.

He sent the apostle Philip to the Ethiopian eunuch in Acts 8:26–40, and he selected Saul of Tarsus (later Paul) to be his apostle to the Gentiles, declaring him to be his "chosen instrument" for the task (9:15). In 10:1–11:18, God sends Peter to reach out to Cornelius, a Gentile centurion. Then, in Acts 15, the Jerusalem Council of the church decides that God is calling Gentiles to himself.

God's selection of a people for himself also extends to the letters in the New Testament. One of Peter's letters describes how God selects his people:

> But you are a chosen people, a royal priesthood, a holy nation, a people belonging to God, that you may declare the praises of him who called you out of darkness into his wonderful light. Once you were not a people, but now you are the people of God; once you had not received mercy, but now you have received mercy. (1 Peter 2:9–10)

Several of Paul letters also declare that Christians are selected by God (cf. Rom. 8:28–29; Eph. 1:3–10; 1 Thess. 1:2–5; Titus 2:14).[36] When God grafted Gentiles into the "olive tree," an image Paul used to represent the nation of Israel (Rom. 11:17), the Gentiles became associated with heroes of the faith such as Abraham, Joseph, Moses, Samuel, Gideon, David, and Daniel. As contemporary children of God, how good it is to be numbered among his people down through the ages, as well as with those who are enduring persecution and temptation in our world today.[37]

As God's people, Christians take on a role similar to that of Israel in the Old Testament. Christians are a selected people who are to conform themselves to the will of God and thereby draw people from all nations to worship Christ.

A Worshipping People

As God's people were drawn together to worship him in ages past, so too in the New Testament are they drawn together to worship him in the person of Jesus Christ.

From the earliest chapters of the Gospels, God's people are seen as people of worship. When Mary is told that she would bear the Messiah, for example, she breaks into worship (Luke 2:46–55). When the angels announce Jesus' birth, they burst forth into songs of worship (v. 14), leading the shepherds to worship (v. 20). The wise men who came from the east seek Jesus so that they might worship him (Matt. 2:2). And when Jesus is first presented at the temple, the righteous and devout Simeon lifts his arms in praise to God (Luke 2:25).

The first appearances of Jesus following his resurrection also elicited worship. The women who saw Jesus immediately after his resurrection worshipped him (Matt. 28:9), and when the disciples saw him, they, too, worshipped him (v. 17; Luke 24:52). Even Thomas overcame his initial doubts and worshipped Jesus, after realizing that the Lord had indeed risen (John 20:24–31). Worship of Jesus Christ was thus a defining characteristic of those who met him.

As the church takes root in the book of Acts, their gatherings center on acts of worship. Their earliest meetings indicate that they devoted themselves to worship, seen in devotion to the apostles' teaching, as well as fellowship, the breaking of bread, prayer, and fasting (Acts 2:42; 13:1–3).[38]

The importance of worship can be seen, too, throughout the letters of the New Testament. These letters begin many times with declarations of worship and praise. Ephesians begins with a chapter devoted to praising God. Likewise, 1 Peter opens with a chapter ascribing praise to God. Other books, such as Romans, Colossians, 1 Thessalonians and 2 Thessalonians, begin with statements of thanksgiving to God for his faithful work among his people. The book of Hebrews begins by ascribing worship to Jesus, who is above angels and whose way of prophecy is superior to that of Moses.

Although the New Testament does not include a book like Leviticus, which specifically regulates worship, many of the New Testament letters offer guidance for Christian worship. First Corinthians 11–14, for example, describes how Christians should partake of the Lord's Supper, exercise their spiritual gifts, and speak within the gathered assembly. Things are to be done in order when someone has something to contribute to a worship service (1 Cor. 14:40). Ephesians and Colossians instruct Christians on how to conduct themselves in worship, speaking and singing psalms, hymns, and spiritual songs to each other (cf. Eph. 5:18–21; Col. 3:16–17). Books such as 1 Timothy, 2 Timothy, and Titus describe character qualities that should typify leaders within the worshipping community (1 Tim. 2:8–3:16; 2 Tim. 2:1–4:7; Titus 1:3–9).

Worship is as much a part of being a Christian as it was a defining aspect of God's people in the Old Testament.[39] In his letter to the Philippians, Paul specifically identifies Christians according to the distinguishing marks of God's people in the Old Testament.[40] He writes, "For it is we who are the circumcision, we who *worship* by the Spirit of God, who glory in Christ Jesus, and who put no confidence in the flesh" (Phil. 3:3, emphasis added). In Romans 12:1, Paul speaks of worship as incumbent upon all Christians: "Therefore, I urge you, brothers, in view of God's mercy, to offer your bodies as living sacrifices, holy and pleasing to God— this is your spiritual act of worship."

First Peter also declares the importance of worship, describing Christians as a spiritual house, a holy priesthood, offering spiritual sacrifices acceptable to God through Jesus Christ (1 Peter 2:5). The apostle expands on this image in verse 9: "But you are a chosen people, a royal priesthood, a holy nation, a people belonging to God, that you may declare the praises of him who called you out of darkness into his wonderful light."

The importance of worship is summed up in the last book of the New Testament. In Revelation, God's people—again depicted as a kingdom of priests—are found around the throne of God, worshipping Jesus:

> And they sang a new song: "You are worthy to take the scroll and to open its seals, because you were slain, and with your blood you purchased men for God from every tribe and language and people and nation. You have made them to be a kingdom and priests to serve our God, and they will reign on the earth" (Rev. 5:9–10).

It is clear, then, that from the beginning of time until the final chapter, God calls his people to worship.[41]

A Blessing to Others

As in the Old Testament, the people of God in the New Testament are blessed so that they may become a blessing to others and draw others to God. In calling his disciples to become "fishers of men," Jesus indicates that they are to be a blessing to others.

Immediately after he calls the disciples, he, in fact, sends them to bless others (Matt. 10:1–42). At other noteworthy times in his ministry, too, Jesus teaches that his followers are to be a blessing to others. In 5:14–16, for example, he tells them,

> You are the light of the world. A city on a hill cannot be hidden. Neither do people light a lamp and put it under a bowl. Instead they put it on its stand, and it gives light to everyone in the house. In the same way, let your light shine before men, that they may see your good deeds and praise your Father in heaven.

Christian history is, in fact, replete with missions that have been considered lighthouses. The monastery of Iona, for example, which was established on the west coast of Scotland by Columba in the sixth century A.D., was considered a place of worship but also a place of mission. On this bleak and foggy island, a mere three miles long and a mile-and-a-half wide, Columba and twelve of his companions constructed a place for God's people to come and worship the Lord. Yet it was also a base from which to send people out into the world for mission activity. Columba himself made many forays into Scotland, converting large numbers. His missionary endeavors were used by the Lord to convert an entire tribe of pagans, the Picts. He confronted Druids, contesting with them over their alleged magical arts. Legend also has it that Columba performed miracles to counter the works of the Druids. Thus, from this tiny monastery, a place devoted to worship, mission efforts emerged to bless many with the Christian faith.[42]

Columba took seriously, then, Jesus' final words to his disciples at the end of the Gospels, indicating the importance of being a blessing to others.

His encouragement for them to spread the good news of salvation can be seen in the final chapter of each of the Gospels (cf. Matt. 28:18–20; Mark 16:15–16; Luke 24:46–49).[43]

Again, at the beginning of Acts, in his final words to the disciples before his ascension, Jesus encourages them to be a blessing to others: "But you will receive power when the Holy Spirit comes on you; and you will be my witnesses in Jerusalem, and in all Judea and Samaria, and to the ends of the earth" (Acts 1:8). After speaking these words, Jesus was taken up into heaven, leaving his disciples with a distinct and memorable mandate: Witness to what you have seen, and in so doing, bless others.

The blessing of others is a constant theme, too, in the book of Acts, which describes the early days of the Christian church. On the Day of Pentecost, blessing resulted when the Holy Spirit came upon the disciples and three thousand people came to faith in Jesus Christ (2:41). In chapters 3–4, Peter and John insist that they are unable to stop teaching about Jesus to all who will listen. In chapter 8, the disciples spread the good news in Samaria, a region they would have avoided at all costs in years past. In chapters 10–11, Peter reaches out to the Roman centurion Cornelius.

It is in the context of worship and fasting that the church at Antioch commissions Paul and Silas to be sent out as a blessing to other people (Acts 13:2–3). From this point forward, Paul's missionary journeys dominate the book of Acts. In the final chapters (Acts 22–28), Paul is seen witnessing his faith to kings such as Agrippa, Festus, and Felix.[44] In the New Testament, as in the Old Testament, worship leads to blessing others.

In the book of Revelation, the result of the gospel message being spread around the world will be that God's people from every nation, tribe, people, and language will gather around the throne to worship him (Rev. 5:9; 7:9). As previously noted, God's people are blessed in order that they might be a blessing to others. "The church is a conspiracy of love for a dying world," writes theologian Peter Kreeft "a spy mission into enemy occupied territory ruled by the powers of evil, a prophet from God with the greatest news the world has ever heard, the most life changing and most revolutionary institution that has existed on earth."[45]

Images

Many of the images associated with the people of God in the Old Testament are carried forward into the New Testament. As God's people were likened to a family in the Old Testament, the church in the New Testament is called the family or household of God (1 Peter 4:17). Jesus indicates in the Gospels that he has formed a new family. In one instance, his natural family arrives at the home where Jesus is teaching. When the people tell Jesus that his mother and his brothers have arrived, Jesus responds by saying, "Here are my mother and my brothers! Whoever does God's will is my brother and sister and mother" (Mark 3:34–35). Likewise, in Matthew 23:8, Jesus speaks of the disciples as brothers (cf. 28:10; John 20:17; 21:23).

Paul, Peter, James, John, and the writer of Hebrews have included this same imagery in their letters, referring to their hearers as "brothers."[46] Paul, Peter, and the writer of Hebrews have called the church a family,[47] and Paul has encouraged special attention to the care of this spiritual family: "Therefore, as we have opportunity, let us do good to all people, especially to those who belong to the family of believers" (Gal. 6:10).

The image of God's people as sheep is also carried forward into the New Testament, especially in the Gospel of John.[48] In John 10, Jesus identifies himself as the good shepherd of God's people. He is the gate into the sheepfold; the shepherd who leads his sheep and knows them by name. He will lay down his life for the sheep and protect them. Only by following the good shepherd will God's people find protection and nourishment.

The agricultural imagery used to represent God's people in the Old Testament also occurs in the New Testament. In John 15, Jesus refers to himself as the true vine and his people as the branches. God's people become fruitful when they remain in him (vv. 1–8). In 1 Corinthians 3, Paul notes that God's people are like a planting of the Lord.[49]

The image of God's people as a remnant appears, too, in the New Testament as it does in the Old Testament. The apostle Paul refers to the remnant imagery in Romans 9:6: "For not all who are descended from Israel are Israel," and in verse 27 and 11:5, Paul declares that only a remnant of Israel will be saved.

As we have seen in both the Old and New Testaments, God has drawn a people to himself from generations past. As God's people worship him, they become a blessing to others. In his hymn "We Are God's People," Bryan Jeffrey Leach captures these characteristics of God's people:

> We are God's people, the chosen of the Lord
> Born of His Spirit, established by His Word;
> Our cornerstone is Christ alone,
> And strong in Him we stand:
> O let us live transparently,
> And walk heart to heart and hand in hand.
>
> We are God's loved ones,
> The Bride of Christ our Lord,
> For we have known it,
> The love of God outpoured;
> Now let us learn how to return
> The gift of love once given:
> O let us share each joy and care,
> And live with a zeal that pleases Heaven.
>
> We are the Body of which the Lord is Head,
> Called to obey Him, now risen from the dead;
> He wills us be a family,
> Diverse yet truly one;
> O let us give our gifts to God,
> And so shall His work on earth be done.
>
> We are a Temple, the Spirit's dwelling place,
> Formed in great weakness, a cup to hold God's grace;
> We die alone, for on its own
> Each ember loses fire:
> Yet joined in one the fame burns on
> To give warmth and light, and to inspire.[50]

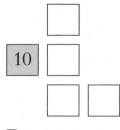

PROPHECY AND FULFILLMENT

Making Good on Promises

God's lips know not how to lie, but he will accomplish all his promises.

—Aeschylus

There is a living God; he has spoken in the Bible. He means what he says and will do all he has promised.

—Hudson Taylor

Every promise God has ever made finds its fulfillment in Jesus.

—Joni Eareckson Tada

At the end of October 1991, a monster storm developed. Stronger than any in recorded history, it built off the coast of Gloucester, Massachusetts, a fishing town on Cape Anne, north of Boston. The storm reached enormous proportions over the Atlantic Ocean when three storm systems collided and then merged into what became known as "the perfect storm." The massive storm front created waves up to one hundred feet high, the equivalent of a ten-story building, and winds reached 120 miles per hour (193 kilometers).

Out to sea in the midst of this gathering storm, the six-man fishing crew of the *Andrea Gail* was hoping to reverse their fortunes after a string of poor outings. They had heard the warnings of bad weather but had chosen not to heed them. Instead, their poor catch, a result of fishing by the Grand Banks, lured them farther out into the Atlantic Ocean, all the way to the Flemish Cap. As they motored east, they continued to ignore the warnings of a massive storm forming behind them.

After a successful time of fishing near the Flemish Cap, the crew of the *Andrea Gail* steamed westward toward their home port at Gloucester, and into the teeth of the massive storm. The boat ultimately was lost five hundred miles from port beneath the rolling seas and high waves. Because they had ignored the warnings, they suffered the unfortunate consequences.

Other fishermen from Gloucester paid attention to the warnings and chose to stay in port. Still other boats that were out, but close to shore, were able to find safety and shelter. Forecasting helped many who heeded the warning, yet when the forecasting was ignored, great peril resulted.

God's people have been fortunate throughout history to have had the benefit of prophetic forecasts of future events. By some estimates, more than twenty-five percent of the Bible involves prediction.[1] The nation of Israel had many notable prophets, some of whose prophecies are recorded in the Old Testament. God's people in the New Testament also had prophets operating in their midst.[2]

While Old Testament prophecies present tremendous expectation of the Messiah's coming[3], the Old Testament also provides specific information regarding the Messiah's birth and death. Thus, this chapter considers four specific prophecies: two that helped God's people look forward to the coming of the Messiah and two that speak about the Messiah's death. To round out this chapter, comments on the nature of prophecy will be offered as well as a consideration of biblical prophecies yet to be fulfilled.

OLD TESTAMENT PROPHECY OF THE MESSIAH

The Nature of Old Testament Prophecy

The writings of the prophets are well known in the Old Testament.[4] They are usually divided into the Major Prophets (Isaiah, Jeremiah, Ezekiel, and Daniel) and the Minor Prophets (Hosea, Joel, Amos, Obadiah, Jonah, Micah, Nahum, Habakkuk, Zephaniah, Haggai, Zechariah, and Malachi). In addition to these prophets, after whom books of the Bible are named, many other prophets were active in Israel during the time of the Old Testament. Moses, for example, was regarded as a prophet without equal (Deut. 34:10–12). Samuel was also recognized as being a prophet of the Lord (1 Sam. 3:19–20), although the books that bear his name are included in the historical narrative section of the Old Testament. Prophetic voices also were raised in the time of the judges (Judg. 2:1–5; 3:9–11; 4:4; 6:8; 1 Sam. 3:1). After the separation of the northern and southern kingdoms, Ahijah, Elijah, and Elisha also prophesied (1 Kings 14–15, 18–19; 2 Kings 5ff.). The veracity of these prophets was attested to by miracles, the fulfillment of their predictions, and their loyalty to God.[5] Other lesser known prophets are also found in the Old Testament.[6]

Prophets were not magicians but rather messengers of God.[7] They were not people who forced God's hand but who served God under divine constraint, proclaiming God's divinely inspired words and not their own. Multiple times throughout the Old Testament, prophets communicate the words of God using the phrase "thus says the Lord."[8]

This information about prophets provides a significant backdrop to the prophecies about Jesus. These prophesies were given by God to prophets in the Old Testament, and their fulfillment was anticipated down through the ages.[9]

Old Testament Prophecies About Jesus' Birth

Multiple passages could be examined to consider how Old Testament prophecies about the Messiah were fulfilled in the New Testament. Four prophecies, though, are noteworthy—two concerning Jesus' birth, and two concerning his death.[10]

The Virgin Birth (Isa. 7:1–16)

The first prophetic passage that will be considered about the Messiah's birth is Isaiah 7:1–16. Much debate surrounds this prophecy, particularly considering the virgin birth. Thus it deserves special attention when considering the birth of Jesus.[11]

The occasion of the prophecy was an imminent threat against the kingdom of Judah, circa 735 B.C. Judah had refused to join an alliance against the nation of Assyria, and in response, Rezin, the king of Aram, and Pekah, the king of Samaria, combined forces and marched against Judah to over-throw King Ahaz.[12] The two kings hoped to overthrow Jerusalem and the house of David and set up their own king, the son of Tabeel (Isa. 7:6). Because the combined forces of Aram and Samaria were threatening Judah, God's people were quite shaken (v. 2).

Amid the general alarm, Isaiah was called upon to turn public opinion. In chapter 7, he appeals to King Ahaz and the people, trying to buoy their spirits. By divine direction, Isaiah meets Ahaz at the end of the upper pool, where he tells him to have no fear of "these two smoldering stubs of firewood," Rezin and Pekah. Like dying torches, they would speedily be extinguished (vv. 3–9). After failing to win the young king's confidence, Isaiah goes a second time, this time with an offer from God to do anything from the deepest depths or the highest heights to prove that these other nations will not harm him. Ahaz, however, refuses to ask for a sign for frivolous reasons.

It is then that Isaiah prophesies about the Messiah, Immanuel, who is to be born to God's people: "Hear now, you house of David! Is it not enough to try the patience of men? Will you try the patience of my God also? Therefore the Lord himself will give you a sign: The virgin will be with child and will give birth to a son, and will call him Immanuel" (Isa. 7:13–14). It is an incredible prediction, uttered in dire circumstances during which not even the king of Israel would accept hope.

The debate over this passage centers on two issues, both of which are important in considering whether this prophecy refers to the Messiah. The first concerns the meaning of the word *'almah,* which can be trans-lated either as "virgin" or "young woman."[13] The second issue concerns whether the prophecy refers to the near future—to Hezekiah, Ahaz's son—or later, to the coming Messiah.

Although the meaning of *'almah* is not as precise as the word *bitulah,* which specifically means virgin, *'almah* is never used of a married woman in the Old Testament.[14] In one place, it is clearly used to describe the virgin Rebekah, who was to be married to Isaac.

Old Testament scholars differ about whether enough evidence is present to determine that *'almah* refers to a virgin, but many early inter-preters of Isaiah 7:14 believe that the prophet is referring to a virgin.[15] In the Septuagint—the Greek version of the Old Testament, which dates from the third century B.C., and thus before Jesus' birth[16]—the word '*almah* is translated using the Greek word *parthenos,* which specifically means "the virgin."[17]

Although some scholars doubt that Jewish readers would have understood Isaiah 7:14 as referring to conception by a virgin, early Christians were unanimous in their understanding of the verse as referring to "the virgin."[18] Several writers such as Jerome, Justin Martyr, and Eusebius of Caesarea also dealt in detail with the question of whether in Isaiah's day this prophecy referred to a son like Hezekiah or to the Messiah. They were convinced the passage referred to the Messiah because no other child could be called Immanuel, which means "God with us."[19]

It might well be alleged that the early church interpreted this text in a way that would reinforce the divinity of Jesus and thus bolster support for Christianity. There is little evidence to suggest, however, that the early Christians would have wanted to do anything to discredit Jesus' family by issuing a controversial interpretation. Due to the church's high regard for the Old Testament and the opposition they were facing from adversaries who were strongly influenced by Judaism, it seems unlikely they would have made a case for the virgin birth based on a questionable interpretation of Isaiah 7:14. There are good reasons, then, to consider this text as a prophecy of the Messiah and that it is fulfilled in Jesus Christ.

Messiah's Birthplace (Mic. 5)

The Old Testament also forecasts the place where the Messiah will be born: "But you, Bethlehem Ephrathah, though you are small among the clans of Judah, out of you will come for me one who will be ruler over Israel, whose origins are from of old, from ancient times" (Mic. 5:2). The reference to the Messiah is clear in the phrase "one who will be ruler over Israel whose origins are from of old, from ancient times," which is better translated, "His goings forth are from long ago, from the days of eternity."[20] In other words, this prophesy speaks of the birthplace of the eternal one, who other Old Testament texts acknowledge to be the Messiah.[21]

This prophesy of Messiah's birth and coming was issued, as was that of Isaiah, in the midst of trial and suffering. Micah's prophecy speaks of devastation among God's people. Jerusalem is seen to be crying aloud. At the time of the prophecy, exile is predicted for Israel as she is expected to be taken to Babylon (Mic. 4:9–10), and calamities such as hard labor and a siege are predicted as well in verse 13 and 5:1.

Yet, as with the prophecy of the virgin birth, there will be hope amid tragedy; a new day will dawn for God's people. When the Messiah comes, God's people will no longer be abandoned. Instead, they will be shepherded by the great shepherd. Peace and security will reign among God's people and eventually over the entire earth (Mic. 5:3–5).

A representation of the sign that guided the Magi from the east to Bethlehem. Some have said that the star was a comet, a nova, or a special constellation. All the Magi say is that they have seen the Messiah's star "in the East." (Photograph courtesy of Todd Bolen and BiblePlaces.com.)

Old Testament Prophecy About Jesus' Death

In addition to the many Old Testament prophecies about Jesus' birth that are fulfilled in the New Testament, many Old Testament prophecies about Jesus' death are also fulfilled in the New Testament. As previously stated, two of the these passages are prominent.[22]

The Righteous Sufferer (Ps. 22)

Psalm 22 contains many ideas that prefigure the death of Jesus Christ. That this should be so may seem odd because the Psalms are not written by a prophet, and thus may not seem like prophecy. Prophetic material, however, can be found in the Psalms. According to theologian J. Barton Payne, the Psalms are "the greatest single block of predictive matter concerning the Savior to be found anywhere in the Old Testament."[23]

Psalm 22, a psalm of lament, is also a passional psalm (i.e., a psalm referring to the death of Jesus), containing many points of sadness and suffering.[24] The opening words illustrate well the suffering that the Messiah would endure: "My God, my God, why have you forsaken me? Why are you so far from saving me, so far from the words of my groaning? O my God, I cry out by day, but you do not answer, by night, and am not silent." The psalm also predicts that the Messiah will be forsaken, his body will be decimated, his strength will dry up, his enemies will overpower him, and his enemies will divide his clothing among them.

The psalm is divided into two distinct parts. The first describes the gloom of suffering and death (Ps. 22:1–21), and the second depicts the jubilation of having overcome such suffering. Thus, the psalm begins in despair but brightens by its conclusion.

Although Psalm 22 is attributed to King David, its prophetic nature is seen in the magnitude of suffering it depicts, far greater adversity than David himself experienced. J. E. Smith notes,

No Old Testament person could have imagined that his personal deliverance from death could be the occasion for the world's conversion. Such a hope must be restricted to the future Redeemer. Under inspiration of the Holy Spirit, David in Psalm 22 saw his descendant resembling but far surpassing himself in suffering. Furthermore, the deliverance of this descendant would have meaning for all mankind.[25]

Although David did experience suffering, it seems unlikely that he is referring only to himself in this psalm. Moreover, the worldwide acclaim in reaction to this suffering suggests an event related to something greater than the person of David (Ps. 22:27–31).

This lament psalm reveals many feelings that the righteous sufferer would have felt. The scholar S. Tostengard concurs: "The depth of the forsakenness of the psalmist serves as a proper background for the depth of the experience of the cross."[26] The vicious enemies that Jesus encounters, the emaciation of his body, and the agony of a broken heart are all found in Psalm 22.

Mel Gibson's film, *The Passion of the Christ,* brought to many people's minds the horrors of crucifixion. Gibson's movie rightly showed it as a horrendous act of violence. In our day, when crosses are worn as jewelry, it is easy to forget the violence associated with crucifixion. The emotional agony of that event, however, has been recorded for us in the words of King David.

The Suffering Servant (Isa. 52:13–53:12)

A second influential passage that predicts the Messiah's death is Isaiah 52:13–53:12. Many observers throughout church history have noted its importance in forecasting the Messiah's death. Polycarp, the church father who lived in the second century A.D., called these verses the "golden *passional* of the Old Testament." Old Testament scholar Franz Delitzsch notes the depth of suffering and the importance of this passage: "In how many an Israelite has [Isaiah 52:13–53:12] melted the crust of his heart! It looks as if it had been written beneath the cross upon Golgotha. . . . It is the unraveling of Psalm [22] . . . and Psalm [100]. It . . . is the most central, the deepest, and the loftiest thing that the Old Testament prophecy, outstripping itself, has ever achieved."[27] Walter Kaiser writes, "Undoubtedly, this is the summit of Old Testament prophetic literature. Few passages can rival it for clarity on the suffering, death, burial, and resurrection of the Messiah."[28]

The passage begins by declaring that the servant will prosper and be exalted. Although his appearance may seem marred to many, he will cause kings to shut their mouths when he accomplishes his task (Isa. 52:13–15). Indeed, the servant song ends by showing the servant highly exalted.[29]

Thus, victory and exaltation bracket the suffering displayed in the rest of the servant song.

The second section (Isa. 53:1–3) portrays the rejection of the servant, describing how the servant's works and words have been discarded. He is despised, forsaken by men, thought to be an offense, and counted as little value to anyone. He is a man of sorrows before whom people hide their eyes.

The third section (Isa. 53:4–6) speaks of the servant's great sacrifice. He is the one who bears grief and sorrows. He is pierced for transgressions and crushed on account of human iniquities, but his penalty pays the price for all of God's people, referred to here as sheep. Like sheep, we all go astray, but the servant by his sacrifice pays for everyone's sin (v. 6).

The fourth section (Isa. 53:7–9) considers the servant's submission. When oppressed and afflicted, he does not open his mouth. Instead, he is silent before his killer, like a sheep taken to the slaughter. He is oppressed and delivered to a death about which it seems nobody cares. His grave is to be with wicked men.

The final part of the servant song describes victory once again. He is exalted to prosperity, his life will be prolonged, and he will see his offspring. Furthermore, he will see the plan of God accomplished, for he will not remain dead but will be resurrected. He will ultimately be rewarded, having "a portion among the great" and "spoils among the strong," because he will bear the sin of many (Isa. 53:12).

The primary question about this passage in Isaiah concerns the identity of the servant. It has been proposed that he is an ordinary individual; that he is a representation, symbolizing the nation of Israel; that he is the representation of an ideal; that he is messianic. When all four of the servant songs in Isaiah are considered, it may initially seem as if the nation of Israel is to be called the servant of the Lord. Isaiah 49:3, for example, says, "He [God] said to me, 'You are my servant, Israel, in whom I will display my splendor.'" Yet when other verses in the servant songs are considered, however, it seems as if Israel is ruled out, because the servant's mission is to Israel:

And now the LORD says—
   he who formed me in the womb to
      be his servant
to bring *Jacob* back to him
   and gather *Israel* to himself,
for I am honored in the eyes of the LORD
   and my God has been my strength—
he says:
"It is too small a thing for you to
      be *my servant*
   to restore the tribes of Jacob
   and bring back those of Israel I have kept.
I will also make you a light for the Gentiles,
   that you may bring my salvation to the
      ends of the earth."
                    (Isa. 49:5–6, emphasis added)

The dilemma of the servant's identity can be resolved in a number of ways. C. H. Scobie suggests seeing the servant songs as a "job description." Although Israel was called on to be a servant to the nations, the Old Testament reveals how repeatedly they failed. Only a remnant (namely, outstanding individuals within Israel) have risen to the occasion. The only hope for God's people will eventually emerge at the coming of the Messiah, the true servant of God.[30]

G. P. Hugenberger suggests that the servant is predominantly a second Moses (cf. Deut. 18:14ff.; 34:10ff.). The servant leads his people out of bondage and through a second Exodus experience. Isaiah 40–66 contains a large amount of Exodus imagery (see box below). Such an understanding of the servant dovetails well with the New Testament's messianic interpretation of this passage from Isaiah.[31] Jesus, then, is the prophesied new Moses from the servant songs.

Whatever rationale is used to identify the servant from the Old Testament, it is clear that the New Testament writers saw the Messiah as present in the servant songs and in Isaiah 52:13–53:12. They applied these words to Jesus in many writings in the New Testament.[32]

EXAMPLES OF EXODUS IMAGERY IN ISAIAH

- God as Redeemer: Exodus 15:13; Isaiah 43:14
- God's people liberated: Exodus 12:31–42; Isaiah 49:9
- God makes a way through the sea and all pursuers are drowned: Exodus 14:28–29; Isaiah 43:16–17; 50:2
- Making a way in the desert: Exodus 13:17–14:31; 15–19; Isaiah 42:16; 43:19
- Moses as deliverer: Exodus 14:21–22; Isaiah 63:11–13
- Prohibition of idols: Exodus 20:1–6; Isaiah 44:6–20

PROPHECY AND FULFILLMENT IN THE NEW TESTAMENT

Jesus' Birth

Although other Gospels allude to the four prophecies considered above, Matthew directly refers to the Old Testament texts that support these prophecies. In each case, the Old Testament predictions are attributed to the prophets, so that God is seen as the ultimate author of Jesus' birth story.[33]

In the description of the virgin birth, found in Matthew 1:18–25, Mary and Joseph are pledged to be married, but Mary becomes pregnant before they are wed. Naturally, Joseph is faced with a dilemma. He does not want to shame Mary, but the code of honor in his day would dictate that he look for another wife. Rather than shaming Mary through a public trial, he plans to quietly divorce her. Joseph's plans are interrupted, however, by a dream. An angel appears to him and instructs him to take Mary as his wife, because she has conceived "through the Holy Spirit" (v. 20).

At this point, Matthew offers an explanation of this event by referring directly to the prophecy in Isaiah 7:14: "All this took place to fulfill what the Lord had said through the prophet: 'The virgin will be with child and will give birth to a son, and they will call him Immanuel'—which means, 'God with us'" (Matt. 1:22–23). Matthew thus affirms that prophecy is being directly fulfilled according to Old Testament Scripture.[34] Jesus is the Immanuel prophesied by Isaiah.

In Matthew 2, the wise men appear. They have come from the east, following a star, and they are looking for the one who has been born "king of the Jews." Their desire is to worship this child and bring him gifts fit for a king—gold, frankincense, and myrrh. When they arrive from the East, however, they find that most everyone is unprepared to worship. King Herod is, in fact, disturbed by the report and all Jerusalem with him (v. 3). It is ironic that these wise men, Gentiles, were more prepared to worship Jesus than were the Jews in Judea.

Although Herod—as well as others—are not ready to receive the Christ child, they do know where Jesus is supposed to be born. In response to the wise men's questions, they reply, "'In Bethlehem in Judea, . . . for this is what the prophet has written: "But you, Bethlehem, in the land of Judah, are by no means least among the rulers of Judah; for out of you will come a ruler who will be the shepherd of my people Israel"'" (Matt. 2:5–6). In citing Micah 5:2, Matthew points directly to Old Testament prophecy that proclaims the birthplace of the Messiah.

Over the years, skeptics have challenged this reading of Matthew, suggesting that the early church twisted Micah 5:2 to fit the birthplace of Jesus. If, however, Jesus was not born in Bethlehem of Judea, it would have been easy to refute the church's claims during the first century. The real site of Jesus' birth could have been stated, thereby setting aside the connection to verse 2.[35] In the absence of any conflicting information, however, the fulfilled prophecy further supports the claim that Matthew makes throughout his Gospel about Jesus' divinity.

Something else is striking about this fulfilled prophecy. The Old Testament prophecies of Isaiah 7 and Micah 5 are issued amid calamity, and both appear in the New Testament at times of trouble. The prophecy from Isaiah is introduced by Matthew at the time when Joseph is about to give up on his marriage. The Micah 5 prophesy is fulfilled when God's people are being ruled by the Romans and not by their own king, a tragedy in the minds of the Jewish nation. Further, Micah's prophecy is present in Matthew 2, in which Herod sends his legions to slay the little children born at the time of Jesus. Yet, despite the tragedy, Jesus is the one who will be "Immanuel," and the great shepherd who will bring great hope to God's people.

Jesus' Death

The New Testament portrays Jesus as the servant who suffers and dies for others. Ideas from Psalm 22 and Isaiah 53 fill portions of the New Testament that speak of his death. Psalm 22 can be found in portions of the Gospel accounts, whereas Isaiah 53 significantly influences portions of the New Testament letters.

Psalm 22 permeates the accounts of the crucifixion in all four Gospels. It is echoed so often within the passion accounts that S. B. Frost calls the psalm "the fifth gospel."[36]

PSALM 22 IN THE GOSPELS

22:1:	"My God, My God, why have you forsaken me?"	(quoted in Matt. 27:46 and Mark 15:34)
22:7:	Mocked and insulted	(Matt. 27:39; Mark 15:29; Luke 23:35)
22:8:	"Let the LORD rescue him"	(Matt. 27:43)
22:14:	"I am poured out like water"	(John 19:34)
22:15:	Mouth is dried up	(John 19:28)
22:16:	"They have pierced my hands and feet"	(John 19:23, 37; 20:25, 27)
22:18:	Divide garments and cast lots	(Matt. 27:35; Mark 15:24; Luke 23:34; quoted in John 19:23–24)

The passion narratives are, then, infused by Psalm 22.

Particularly striking is Jesus' quotation of Psalm 22:1 in the "Cry of Dereliction" (Matt. 27:46; Mark 15:34). His recitation of this verse describes the singularly terrifying situation of being forsaken by God.[37] Although Jesus may have recited the entire psalm (which he would have known by heart), the presence of simply the first verse in Matthew's and Mark's accounts emphasizes the sense of abandonment that Jesus, the righteous sufferer, experienced. H. J. Kraus writes, "He alone is able to take upon himself the indescribable totality of what it means to be forsaken by God and to be far from his presence."[38]

The prophecies of Isaiah 52:13–53:12 can also be heard in the Gospel accounts.[39] Jesus is called by God and is obedient from the earliest sections of the Gospel narratives. He predicts his own suffering and death in at least three places, all of which can be seen as allusions to 52:13–53:12.[40]

During the Last Supper, echoes of Isaiah 52:13–53:12 can be heard in Jesus' speaking of the Passover wine as the symbol of his impending death, his life blood poured out for the many (cf. 53:12 in Matt. 20:28 and Mark 14:24). In the accounts of the crucifixion, Jesus was despised and forsaken by men, he was a man of sorrows, acquainted with grief (cf. Isa. 53:3). On the cross, Jesus was pierced for iniquities and crushed for transgressions (v. 5). His death was among the lawless, which Jesus himself speaks about before his death, directly referring to verse 9 (cf. Luke 22:37). Although he was crucified between two thieves, a rich man, Joseph of Arimathea, was involved in his death (Isa. 53:9). All of these allusions to 52:13–53:12 in the Gospel accounts affirm that Jesus' death fulfilled Isaiah's prophecy.

Apart from the Gospel accounts, the fulfillment of Isaiah 53 is clearly seen in Acts and the letters of the New Testament. In several places it is plain that what has been predicted of the Messiah's death in the Old Testament has now been fulfilled through Jesus' death in the New Testament.

In Acts 8:26–40, which refers to Isaiah 53:7–8, the apostle Philip is traveling from Samaria to Gaza. He had left Jerusalem following the death of Stephen. Along the way to Gaza, Philip encounters an Ethiopian eunuch who is eagerly reading the Old Testament and trying to decipher verses 7–8:

The eunuch was reading this passage of Scripture: "He was led like a sheep to the slaughter, and as a lamb before the shearer is silent, so he did not open his mouth. In his humiliation he was deprived of justice. Who can speak of his descendants? For his life was taken from the earth." The eunuch asked Philip, "Tell me, please, who is the prophet talking about, himself or someone else?" (Acts 8:32–34).

Peter also alludes to Isaiah 53 when, referring to Christ's death on the cross, he writes about being willing to suffer for doing what is right:

To this you were called, because Christ suffered for you, leaving you an example, that you should follow in his steps. "He committed no sin, and no deceit was found in his mouth." When they hurled their insults at him, he did not retaliate; when he suffered, he made no threats. Instead, he entrusted himself to him who judges justly. He himself bore our sins in his body on the tree, so that we might die to sins and live for righteousness; by his wounds you have been healed. For you were like sheep going astray, but now you have returned to the Shepherd and Overseer of your souls. (1 Peter 2:21–25)

Other passages in the New Testament find their origins in Isaiah 52:13–53:12. In each case, the New Testament writers refer to Jesus or the message of Jesus' death.[41] What was predicted in the Old Testament regarding the death of Jesus is now seen as fulfilled by multiple authors in the New Testament.

This chapter has considered only a few examples of divine prophecies from the Old Testament that are fulfilled in the New Testament. Many other examples could have been explored.[42] Furthermore, other biblical prophecies have yet to be fulfilled. Just as the promises in the Old Testament regarding the coming of the Messiah were fulfilled hundreds of years later in the New Testament, other prophecies—such as those concerning the return of Jesus Christ and the resurrection of all flesh—can also be expected to be fulfilled.[43] Heeding these prophecies will result in divine blessing, whereas ignoring them will lead to great peril.

Finally, prophecy and its fulfillment reveals one other important aspect about the Bible: the divine hand at work behind the Scriptures. Only by divine imprint could the Bible so accurately forecast the future. "Only the supernatural mind can have prior knowledge to the natural mind," writes G. B. Hardy. "If then the Bible has foreknowledge, historical and scientific, beyond the permutation of chance, it truly then bears the fingerprint of God."[44] Fulfillment of prophecy clearly exhibits God's divine artistry.

Henry W. Baker's hymn "Lord, Thy Word Abideth" illustrates well the certainty of God's predictions and the blessings that result from listening to his word:

> Lord, Thy word abideth
> And our footsteps guideth;
> Who its truth believeth
> Light and joy receiveth.
>
> When our foes are near us,
> Then Thy word doth cheer us,
> Word of consolation,
> Message of salvation.
>
> When the storms are o'er us,
> And dark clouds before us,
> Then its light directeth,
> And our way protecteth.
>
> Who can tell the pleasure,
> Who recount the treasure,
> By Thy word imparted
> To the simple hearted?
>
> Word of mercy, giving
> Succour to the living;
> Word of life, supplying
> Comfort to the dying!

O that we, discerning
Its most holy learning,
Lord, may love and fear Thee,
Evermore be near Thee![45]

CONCLUSION

The Old Testament provides significant information for understanding the New Testament. Ten major Old Testament themes, in particular, have significant influence on the New Testament. Grasping how each of the ten themes is developed in the Old Testament provides significant insight into the New Testament.

Old Testament ideas about creation, for example, shed light on Jesus Christ as the Creator, how Christians are new creations, and the ultimate destiny of the new heavens and new earth. The dire warnings about idolatry in the Old Testament add gravity to the warnings about idolatry in the New Testament.

Furthermore, Old Testament anticipation of the Messiah enlightens the understanding of portions of the New Testament, particularly the Gospels. The Messiah, Jesus, is the great hope of God's people. His role and titles are defined in the Old Testament and realized in the New Testament. Significant specific prophecies about his birth and death are given in the Old Testament and fulfilled in the New Testament. Without the Old Testament, our understanding of the uniqueness of Jesus Christ, the Desire of Nations, would be significantly reduced.

The Old Testament also defines significant terms in the New Testament. The meaning of words like *redemption, atonement,* and *justification* become more profound by an Old Testament understanding of these terms. The meanings of other words, too, such as *covenant,* are obscure in the New Testament unless the importance of the idea is considered in the Old Testament.

The significance of the Law in New Testament writings would be lost without an Old Testament perspective on the value of the Law. Moreover, the influence of the Law continues to regulate Christian behavior, thus illustrating a unified ethic between the Old and New Testaments. Further, the value of the Law elevates Jesus Christ, the one person who is greater than the Law.

The Old Testament also establishes a basis for certain ideas that are largely developed in the New Testament. Consideration, for example, of the role of the Spirit of God in the Old Testament provides a basis for understanding the Holy Spirit as the creator of life, the Spirit of revelation, and the one who works among God's people. The Spirit, too, upon being received by regenerate Christians, initiates those Christians into the kingdom of God. The Old Testament also provides a basis for understanding Jesus' proclamation of the kingdom of God. His much anticipated kingdom is one in which Jesus rules over all.

The Old Testament provides the basis for understanding the nature of the New Testament church in relation to the Old Testament people of God. Now, as then, God's people are a chosen people, called to worship, and called to be a blessing to others.

For these reasons, and others, the Old and New Testaments deserve to be considered together as parts of one great divine masterpiece, the Holy Scripture. Individual verses and books of the Bible should not be seen as individual jewels, as beautiful and as compelling as they may be on their own. They need to be read in light of the greater, inspired whole message of the Bible. Making sense of the Bible, then, requires the reading of both Testaments—together in unity.

ENDNOTES

PREFACE

1. Other examples of Rembrandt's ability to compose masterful individual elements into a transcendent work of art include *The Anatomy Lecture of Dr. Nicolaes Tulp* and *The Syndics of the Clothmaker's Guild (The Stallmeesters)*.
2. Consider also D. Fuller, *The Unity of the Bible* (Grand Rapids: Zondervan, 1992).
3. See further, V. Poythress, "Divine Meaning of Scripture," *WTJ* 48 (1986): 241–79.
4. In stark contrast to contemporary attitudes toward the Bible, many notable Western statesmen perceived the Bible to be a literary masterpiece. Patrick Henry, for example, said, "The Bible is worth all other books which have ever been printed." Abraham Lincoln also declared the Bible's value when he said, "I believe that the Bible is the best gift God has given to man." Woodrow Wilson, echoed these sentiments: "A man has deprived himself of the best there is in the world who has deprived himself of the Bible." Quotations taken from M. Water, comp., *The New Encyclopedia of Christian Quotations* (Grand Rapids: Baker, 2000), 111–17.
5. http://www.gallup.com/poll/content/default.aspx?ci=2416.
6. C. Hardiman, "Final Answer: Bible Literacy Slipping," *Amarillo Globe News,* April 2001.

CHAPTER 1: CREATION: A WHOLE NEW WORLD

1. For a discussion of creation as an overarching theme of the Bible, see S. J. Hafemann, ed., *Biblical Theology: Retrospect and Prospect* (Downers Grove,

Ill.: InterVarsity; Leicester: Apollos, 2002). See especially the chapters by B. G. Toews, "Genesis 1–4: The Genesis of Old Testament Instruction," 38–52; W. Dumbrell, "Genesis 2:1–17: A Foreshadowing of the New Creation," 53–65; and G. K. Beale, "The New Testament and New Creation," 159–73.

2. For a discussion of how Old Testament ideas of creation have made their way into other sections of the Old Testament, see M. Fishbane, *Biblical Interpretation in Israel* (Oxford: Clarendon Press, 1985).

3. For a good survey of the current debate about creation, time, and manner, see H. Blocher, *In the Beginning: The Opening Chapters of Genesis*, trans. D. G. Preston (Downers Grove, Ill.; Leicester, England: InterVarsity, 1984), 39–59.

4. For parallels between the *Enuma Elish* and the Genesis account see A. Heidel, *The Gilgamesh Epic and Old Testament Parallels* (Chicago: University of Chicago Press, 1963).

5. For a rebuttal of current scientific approaches to creation see J. P. Moreland, *Scaling the Secular City: A Defense of Christianity* (Grand Rapids: Baker, 1987) and L. Strobel, *The Case for a Creator: A Journalist Investigates Scientific Evidence That Points to God* (Grand Rapids: Zondervan, 2004).

6. For further description of how God created the universe out of nothing see H. Blocher, *In the Beginning*, 63–66 and G. Wenham, *Genesis 1–15*, Word Biblical Commentary 1 (Waco: Word, 1987), 11–17.

7. For a discussion on views of the days in Genesis, whether they were literal, figurative, or a literary construction, see H. Blocher, *In the Beginning*, 39–59.

8. G. R. Bergman, "The Wonders of the Natural World: God's Design," *Decision* (April 1981), 7.

9. Exodus 31:7; Deuteronomy 1:6; 1 Samuel 7:2; Proverbs 20:3; Isaiah 14:4; 24:8; Lamentations 5:15; Amos 6:3.

10. P. K. Jewett, *The Lord's Day* (Grand Rapids: Eerdmans, 1971), 157.

11. M. Water, ed., *The New Encyclopedia of Christian Quotations* (Grand Rapids: Baker, 2000).

12. C. Swindoll, *The Tale of the Tardy Oxcart and 1,501 Other Stories* (Nashville: Word, 1998), 265.

13. M. P. Green, ed., *Illustrations for Biblical Preaching* (Grand Rapids: Baker, 1989), 184.

14. "When this Passing World is Done," from *The Scottish Psalter and Church Hymnary* (Oxford: Oxford University Press, 1929).

CHAPTER 2: COVENANT: GOD'S PROMISES ARE FOREVER

1. For a further account of the revival see D. Campbell, *The Lewis Awakening* (Edinburgh: Faith Mission, 1954).

2. Scholars who see the idea of covenant as a key concept in understanding God and the Bible would include L. Berkhof, *Systematic Theology* (Grand Rapids: Eerdmans, 1941); R. L. Dabney, *Systematic Theology* (Edinburgh/ Carlisle, Pa.: Banner of Truth, 1985); C. Hodge, *Systematic Theology,* abridged ed.; Edward N. Gross, ed. (Grand Rapids: Baker, 1992); M. G. Kline, *The Structure of Biblical Authority* (South Hamilton, Mass.: M. G. Kline, 1989); O. P. Robertson, *The Christ of the Covenants* (Phillipsburg: Presbyterian and Reformed, 1981); G. Vos, *Biblical Theology* (Edinburgh/Carlisle, Pa.: Banner of Truth, 1996); W. J. Dumbrell, *Covenant and Creation: An Old Testament Covenantal Theology* (Grand Rapids: Baker, 1993); T. E. McComiskey, *The Covenants of Promise: A Theology of the Old Testament Covenants* (Grand Rapids: Baker, 1985); N. T. Wright, *The Climax of the Covenant: Christ and the Law in Pauline Theology* (Edinburgh: T. and T. Clark, 1991).

3. Some scholars prefer to divide biblical covenants into covenants of works and covenants of grace, a discussion too detailed for this current volume. For further development of this idea, see L. Berkhof, *Systematic Theology,* 265–83 and C. Hodge, *Systematic Theology,* 265–70, 337–50.

4. For example, see the following covenants between people. Jonathan and David make a covenant of an intensely personal nature (1 Sam. 18:3; 20:8; 22:8; 23:18). David and Abner make a covenant with political ends (2 Sam. 3:12f.). Abraham and Abimelech (Gen. 21:22–32), Isaac and Abimelech (26:26–31), and Jacob and Laban (31:44–54) make covenants as heads of their respective tribes. Rahab and the Israelite spies make a covenant before the invasion of Jericho (Josh. 2:8–21). Kings can covenant with individuals, such as King Solomon does with Shimei (1 Kings 2:42–46). Kings can also covenant with nations, such as King David does with Israel (2 Sam. 5:1; 1 Chron. 11:3), King Joash with Judah (2 Kings 11:17), and King Zedekiah with Judah (Jer. 34:8). Covenants can occur between states (Josh. 9:6, 11, 15f.; 1 Sam. 11:1f.; 1 Kings 20:34; Ezek. 17:13; and Hos. 12:1). Covenants can also be seen in the marital alliance (Mal. 2:14).

5. Some scholars identify a covenant between God and Adam in the opening chapters of Genesis (e.g., L. Berkhof, *Systematic Theology,* 211–18), but this is not as clear as the reference to covenant found in Genesis 6.

6. Rainfall in these countries averages eighty-four inches per year in some places.

7. Some scholars see two covenants between God and Abraham. For a discussion of this view, see P. R. Williamson, "Covenant," in *The New Dictionary of Biblical Theology,* T. D. Alexander and B. S. Rosner, eds. (Leicester: InterVarsity, 1998), 419–29.

8. Note that Abraham's name changes in Genesis 17:5.

9. For a further discussion of the Abrahamic covenant, see G. Wenham, *Genesis,* 331–35. Cf. Jeremiah 34:18. Note also that the way Abraham arranges the animals is reminiscent of other sacrifices presented in Old Testament times (cf. Lev. 1:6, 17).

10. For a further explanation of ancient covenantal structures, see J. A. Thompson, "Covenant (OT)" in the *International Standard Bible Encyclopedia,* G. W. Bromiley, ed., 4 vols. (Grand Rapids: Eerdmans, 1979–1988), 1:790–791.

11. Cf. P. R. Williamson, "Covenant," 426.

12. Although the idea of a new covenant is mentioned by other prophets, such as Ezekiel (34; 36–37) and Isaiah (40–66), the passage most clearly associated with the new covenant is Jeremiah 31:31–34.

13. For other sadness in Jeremiah's life due to the disobedience of God's people, see Jeremiah 11:18–23; 12:6; 18:18; 20:1–3; 26:1–24; 37:11–38:28.

14. O. P. Robertson, *The Christ of the Covenants,* 281.

15. Cf. Matthew 3:15; 5:17–48; 9:16–17; 11:28–30.

16. Cf. Matthew 8:12; 13:12–14; 23:37–39; Luke 16:19–31.

17. Matthew 2:15; 12:18–21; 25:31–34; 28:19.

18. Matthew 1:21; 8:1–4, 17; Mark 2:1–12; Luke 5:12–26; 15:1–32; John 8:1–11.

19. Introducing the new covenant with his blood relates his words to Jeremiah's prophecy.

20. For a more detailed look at the role of Jeremiah 31:31–34 in 2 Corinthians 3:3, 6 see S. J. Hafemann, *Paul, Moses, and the History of Israel,* Wissenchaftliche Untersuchungen zum Neuen Testament 81 (Tübingen, Germany: J. C. B. Mohr [Paul Siebeck], 1995), 119–40. Cf. Ezekiel 36:25.

21. For a further look at Paul's new covenant ministry in 2 Corinthians, see S. J. Hafemann, *Suffering and the Spirit: An Exegetical Study,* Wissenchaftliche Untersuchungen zum Neuen Testament 2.19 (Tübingen, Germany: J. C. B. Mohr [Paul Siebeck], 1986) and T. Savage, *Power Through Weakness: Paul's Understanding of the Christian Ministry in 2 Corinthians,* Society for New Testament Studies Monograph Series 86 (Cambridge: Cambridge University Press, 1996).

22. "There Is a Green Hill Far Away," from *The Scottish Psalter and Church Hymnary* (Oxford: Oxford University Press, 1929).

CHAPTER 3: IDOLATRY: NO GODS BUT GOD

1. M. Halbertal and A. Margalit, *Idolatry,* trans. N. Goldblum (Boston: Harvard University Press, 1992), 10.

2. For further reading see W. S. LaSor, "Religions of the Biblical World: Egypt," in the *International Standard Bible Encyclopedia,* 4:101–7; E. M. Yamauchi, "Religions: Persia," in the *International Standard Bible Encyclopedia,* 4:123–29; G. H. Wilson, "Religions of the Biblical World: Canaanite (Syria and Palestine)," in the *International Standard Bible Encyclopedia,* 4:95–101; A. Terian, "Idolatry," in the *International Standard Bible Encyclopedia,* 2:796–800.

3. M. R. Wilson, "The Shema," in the *International Standard Bible Encyclopedia,* 4:469–470.

4. J. Calvin, *The Institutes of the Christian Religion,* Library of Christian Classics, J. T. McNeill, ed., F. L. Battles, trans., 2 vols. (London: SCM, 1961), 2:8.385.

5. For a good devotional reading on the jealousy of God see J. I. Packer, *Knowing God* (Downers Grove, Ill.: InterVarsity, 1993), 151–58.

6. Although the Epistle of Jeremiah is part of the Old Testament Apocrypha and is not a canonical book, it also regards idols as worthless no matter how much is invested in their making. Even when God's people are exiled in Babylon, they are to beware of following idols.

7. Cf. Genesis 26:6–11; 39:6–20. J. I. Durham, *Exodus,* Word Biblical Commentary 3 (Waco: Word, 1987), 422.

8. Note that Cecil B. DeMille's classic movie, *The Ten Commandments,* depicts other sins found at the time of the golden calf: sexual immorality, violence, and human sacrifice.

9. Kings are often assessed as being either good or bad in response to their dealings with idols. A good king like Josiah rid the land of false gods and idols. He burned the idols in his kingdom. Because of his enthusiasm for destroying idols, he is remembered as a good king who turned to the Lord with all of his heart, soul, and strength (2 Kings 23:4–30).

10. B. S. Rosner, "The Concept of Idolatry," *Themelios* 24, no. 3 (1999): 21.

11. Following King Solomon's reign, the nation of Israel was divided into two kingdoms—the northern kingdom of Israel and the southern kingdom of Judah.

12. For further reading see H. F. Vos, "Religions of the Biblical World: Greco-Roman," in the *International Standard Bible Encyclopedia*, 4:107–17.

13. For further reading see R. Oster, "Ephesus as a Religious Center Under the Principate, I. Paganism Before Constantine," *Aufsteig und Niedergang der römischen Welt: Geschichte und Kultur Roms im Spiegel der neueren Forschung*, H. Temporini and W. Haase, eds. (Berlin: Walter de Gruyter, 1990), 2.7.2, 1661–1728.

14. The apostle Peter affirms the same idea in 1 Peter 4:3.

15. M. Water, ed., *The New Encyclopedia of Christian Quotations* (Grand Rapids: Baker, 2000), 522.

16. With this as a charge, it is no wonder that the apostle John would conclude 1 John with these words, "Little children, keep yourselves from idols" (1 John 5:21).

17. See also B. S. Rosner, "Idolatry," in *The New Dictionary of Biblical Theology*, 560–75.

18. D. Rowe, *The Real Meaning of Money* (London: HarperCollins, 1997), 148.

19. For further developments of this idea see R. Keyes, "The Idol Factory," in *No God but God: Breaking with the Idols of Our Age*, O. Guinness and J. Seel, eds. (Chicago: Moody, 1992), 29–48; D. Wells, *God in the Wasteland: The Reality of Truth in a World of Fading Dreams* (Grand Rapids/Leicester: Eerdmans/InterVarsity, 1994), 50–59; H. Schlossberg, *Idols for Destruction: Christian Faith and Its Confrontation with American Society* (Nashville: Nelson, 1983); and B. Goudzwaard, *Idols of Our Time*, M. Vander Vennen, trans. (Downers Grove, Ill.: InterVarsity, 1984).

20. Note Martin Luther's answer as he reflected on the first commandment in his larger catechism: "Whatever your heart clings to and relies upon, that is your God; trust and faith of the heart alone make both God and idol."

See B. S. Rosner, "Idolatry" in *The New Dictionary of Biblical Theology,* 575.

21. "Sing Praise to God Who Reigns Above," from *The Pilgrim Hymnal* (Boston: Pilgrim Press, 1968).

CHAPTER 4: THE MESSIAH: UNTO US A CHILD IS BORN

1. From what can be seen in first-century Jewish literature, messianic expectation was great. See G. W. Nickelsburg and J. J. Collins, eds., *Ideal Figures in Ancient Judaism,* Septuagint and Cognate Studies 12 (Chico, Calif.: Scholars Press, 1980); J. Neusner, W. S. Green, and E. Frerichs, *Judaism and their Messiahs at the Turn of the Christian Era* (Cambridge: Cambridge University Press, 1987).

2. Prophecies pertaining to the birth and death of the Messiah will be considered within the chapter on prophecy and fulfillment.

3. Cf. Genesis 49:7; Job 20:14, 16; Psalm 140:3; Isaiah 59:5; Micah 7:17. See W. Kaiser, *Toward an Old Testament Theology* (Grand Rapids: Zondervan, 1978), 77–79.

4. For further consideration of the Jewish view of Genesis 3, see L. W. Hurtado, *One God, One Lord: Early Christian Devotion and Ancient Jewish Monotheism,* 2nd ed. (Edinburgh: T. and T. Clark, 1998).

5. See Romans 16:20; Hebrews 2:14; Revelation 12:4–5, 17.

6. J. E. Smith, *What the Bible Teaches About the Promised Messiah* (Nashville: Nelson, 1993), 38.

7. C. A. Briggs, *Messianic Prophecy* (New York: Scribner's, 1886), 73.

8. Cf. Genesis 9:25–27; 12:1–3; 49:8–12; Numbers 24:15–19; 2 Samuel 2:1–10, 35.

9. Note how the original language of 2 Samuel 7:19 can be translated, "And as if this were not enough in your sight, O Adonai Yahweh, you have spoken about the future of the house of your servant. This is the charter for humanity, O Adonai Yahweh." W. Kaiser, *The Messiah in the Old Testament* (Grand Rapids: Zondervan, 1995), 79–80.

10. Besides the verses addressed in this section, see also Jeremiah 23:5–6; 30:9, 21; 33:14–26; Ezekiel 17:22–24; 21:25–27; 34:23–31; 37:15–28; Daniel 9:24–27; Hosea 3:4–5; Amos 9:11–15; Micah 2:12–13; 5:1–4; Haggai 2:6–9, 21–23.

11. See Isaiah 7:10–15; 11:1–16; 14:28–32; 24:21–25; 32:1–8; 33:17–24; 55:3–

5; 61:1–6; 63:1–6. See also J. Alec Motyer, *The Prophecy of Isaiah: An Intro-duction and Commentary* (Downers Grove, Ill.: InterVarsity, 1993), 3–16.

12. The literal translation of the Hebrew of this verse is "a wonder of a counse-lor." See E. J. Young, *The Book of Isaiah*, 3 vols. (Grand Rapids: Eerdmans, 1965), 1:334.

13. See W. Kaiser, *The Messiah in the Old Testament*, 57–61.

14. See Deuteronomy 17:8–13 for "judges," vv. 14–20 for "kings," 18:1–8 for "priests," and vv. 9–14 for "false prophets."

15. E.g., Psalms 18:50; 84:9; 89:22–37; 132:1, 17.

16. B. W. Anderson, *Out of the Depths: The Psalms Speak for Us Today* (Phila-delphia: Westminster, 1983), 188–92.

17. See also Genesis 49:8–12; Numbers 24:15–19; 1 Samuel 2:10; Isaiah 24:21–25; 63:1–6; Jeremiah 23:5–6; 30:9, 21; Ezekiel 21:25–27; Daniel 9:24–27; Micah 5:1–4; Zechariah 9:9–10.

18. See also Zechariah 3:8–10.

19. See the larger description of Isaiah 52:13–53:12 in chapter 10. For a fur-ther treatment of the Messiah as Servant, and the various opinions sur-rounding this depiction, see R. T. France, "Servant of Yahweh," in *Dictionary of Jesus and the Gospels*, J. B. Green and S. McKnight, eds. (Downers Grove, Ill.: InterVarsity, 1992), 744–747.

20. For a further treatment of the Messiah as Son of Man, and the various opinions surrounding this depiction, see I. H. Marshall, "Son of Man," in *Dictionary of Jesus and the Gospels*, 775–81.

21. See other images of how the Messiah is pictured in the Old Testament that also set forward characteristics of the Messiah. Although these are less prevalent in the Old Testament, they nonetheless present characteristics of the Lord. In Isaiah 7:14 and 8:8, the Messiah is called *Immanuel*, which means "God with us." Ezekiel 34:23–31 calls the Messiah "the shepherd of God's people." In Haggai, he is "the desire of nations" (2:6–9) and "God's signet ring" (vv. 21–23), a sign of uniqueness and relation to God. In Zechariah 10:4, the Messiah is described as "the cornerstone," "the tent peg," and "the battle bow." Malachi 4:2 describes him as the "sun of righ-teousness." Zechariah 12:10 calls him "the one they have pierced." He is also called the "branch, shoot, or sprout of the Lord" (Isa. 4:2; 11:1; Jer. 23:5–6; Ezek. 17:22–24; Zech. 3:8; 6:12).

22. For a larger development of these ideas, see I. H. Marshall, "Jesus Christ,"

in *The New Dictionary of Biblical Theology.* For an examination of early Judaism as a cradle for belief in Jesus Christ, see L. W. Hurtado, *One God, One Lord: Early Christian Devotion and Ancient Jewish Monotheism* (New York: Continuum, 1998).

23. Matthew's gospel also suggests the anticipation of Christ's birth, and his account will be treated more fully in chapter 10, in a discussion of prophecy and its fulfillment.

24. Note that Gabriel is only mentioned in the New Testament in the opening chapters of Luke (Luke 1:19, 26). He dwells in the presence of God but appears in order to announce the births of two important people—John the Baptist and Jesus.

25. See also Acts 3:6, 16; 10:34–43; 16:18; Romans 5:1–10; 8:32; Hebrews 1:1–3.

26. P. N. Findlay, "Handel's *Messiah* Through the Centuries" in *Early Music News,* vol. 24, no. 4 (December 1999).

27. E.g., Matthew 11:21–24; 23:13–19; Mark 2:5, 8; 3:10–11; Luke 9:47; John 2:24–25.

28. Luke 24:19; John 4:19; 6:14; 9:17.

29. For further discussion of Jesus' prophetic self-understanding, see G. F. Hawthorne, "Prophets, Prophecy," in Green and McKnight, *Dictionary of Jesus and the Gospels,* 636–43.

30. E.g., Matthew 5:18, 26; 6:2, 5, 16, 8:10; 10:15, 23, etc. G. F. Hawthorne, "Amen," in *Dictionary of Jesus and the Gospels,* 7–8.

31. Cf. 2 Kings 9:12f.; 1 Maccabees 13:51.

32. For further discussion, see the chapter on the kingdom of God.

33. See I. H. Marshall, *The Origins of New Testament Christology,* 2nd ed. (Downers Grove, Ill.: InterVarsity, 1990); R. T. France, *Jesus and the Old Testament: His Application of Old Testament Passages to Himself and His Mission* (Downers Grove, Ill.: InterVarsity, 1971); C. Caragounis, *The Son of Man: Vision and Interpretation,* Wissenchaftliche Untersuchungen zum Neuen Testament 38 (Tübingen: J. C. B. Mohr [Paul Siebeck], 1986).

34. Acts 3:13, 26; 4:27, 30.

35. See also Mark 1:11; 9:7, which can be seen as an allusion to Isaiah 42:1; Mark 14:24, which can be seen as an allusion to Isaiah 53:11–12; John 1:29, 36, which can be seen as an allusion to Isaiah 53:7; Matthew 27:57, which can be seen as an allusion to Isaiah 53:9. R. T. France, "Servant of Yahweh," in *Dictionary of Jesus and the Gospels,* 744–47.

36. Other possible allusions in the Epistles to Jesus as the stone include 1 Corinthians 3:10 and 2 Timothy 2:19.

37. E.g., Mark 8:31; 9:9, 12, 31; 10:33, 45.

38. See Mark 8:38; 13:26; 14:62. Son of Man is also used in similar ways in the gospels of Matthew and Luke. In John, the sense of "lifting up" is more apparent (cf. John 3:14; 8:28; 12:34). See I. H. Marshall, "Son of Man," in *Dictionary of Jesus and the Gospels*, 775–81.

39. The phrase also occurs in Hebrews 2:6; quoting Psalm 8:5.

40. See also Revelation 14:14, where Christ's spiritual authority is set forth.

41. For the many inspiring ways that New Testament writers and the church have seen Jesus, see also J. Stott, *The Incomparable Christ* (Downers Grove, Ill.: InterVarsity, 2001).

42. For other studies that consider themes from the Old Testament for messianic expectation see E. P. Clowney, *The Unfolding Mystery: Discovering Christ in the Old Testament* (Colorado Springs: NavPress, 1988) and C. D. Drew, *The Ancient Love Song: Finding Christ in the Old Testament* (Phillipsburg, N.J.: Presbyterian and Reformed, 1996).

43. "Lo, How a Rose E'er Blooming" from *The Pilgrim Hymnal* (Boston: Pilgrim Press, 1968).

CHAPTER 5: LAW: REGULATING THE GOOD LIFE

1. T. Cahill sees the Law as one of the "gifts of the Jews." See T. Cahill, *The Gifts of the Jews* (New York: Doubleday, 1998).

2. For summaries of current discussion on Jesus and his view of the Law, see the lengthy bibliography found in F. Thielman, "Law," in *Dictionary of Jesus and the Gospels*, 529–42. For current discussion on Paul and his view of the Law, see the lengthy bibliography in D. J. Moo, "Law," in *Dictionary of Paul and His Letters: A Compendium of Contemporary Biblical Scholarship*, G. F. Hawthorne and R. P. Martin, eds. (Downers Grove, Ill.: InterVarsity, 1993), 450–61. S. J. Hafemann has written, "Paul's understanding of the Law is currently the most debated topic among Pauline scholars" (S. J. Hafemann, "Paul and His Interpreters," in *Dictionary of Paul and His Letters*, 671. See also T. R. Schreiner, "Law," in *New Dictionary of Biblical Theology*, 629–36).

3. For a discussion of the Law as a key component of the first five books of the Old Testament, see T. D. Alexander, *From Paradise to the Promised Land:*

An Introduction to the Main Themes of the Pentateuch (Grand Rapids: Baker, 1995), 82–142.

4. Law and wisdom become connected to each other in the time between the Old and New Testaments. See Sirach 15:1; 19:20; 21:11; 34:8; 39:8. For a detailed study of this connection in the Dead Sea Scrolls and other literature contemporary with the New Testament, see E. J. Schnabel, *Law and Wisdom from Ben Sira to Paul: A Tradition-Historical Enquiry into the Relation of Law, Wisdom, and Ethics,* Wissenchaftliche Untersuchungen zum Neuen Testament 2.16 (Tübingen: J. C. B. Mohr [Paul Siebeck], 1985).

5. For a classification of the Law into five separate sections see R. K. Harrison, "Law," in the *International Standard Bible Encyclopedia,* 3:76–85.

6. Much of the book of Leviticus emphasizes the holiness of the Lord and the holiness demanded from his people. Holiness is referred to directly more than sixty times in this book. According to Wenham, "'Be holy, for I am holy' (Lev. 11:44–45; 19:2; 20:26) could be termed the motto of Leviticus." See G. Wenham, *Leviticus,* New International Greek Testament Commentary (Grand Rapids: Eerdmans, 1979), 18–25 (quotation is from p. 18).

7. The ceremonial law details the elaborate clothing that priests were required to wear when they served in holy places (Exod. 39:41). Religious purity was especially necessary for the high priests, who would enter the holy place and atone for the nation (Lev. 16, 20). Ceremonial law also governed annual festivals of Passover (Exod. 12:3–34), Pentecost (Lev. 23:15), Tabernacles (Exod. 23:16f.; Lev. 23:33–43), communal feasts (Exod. 5:1; Deut. 16:14), the Sabbath (Lev. 23:1), the New Moon festival (Num. 28:11–15), circumcision (Lev. 12), cleansing of lepers (Lev. 14:1–23), and bodily discharges (Lev. 15:13–30).

8. See Leviticus 10 and the sacrilege that Nadab and Abihu performed, which led to their deaths.

9. See other leaders in the Old Testament who honored and followed the Law of the Lord and were blessed (Cf. 2 Chron. 13:3–5; 17:1–19; 23:18–21; 31:20–21; Neh. 8).

10. Note that Manasseh does repent. See 2 Chronicles 33:12–16. The apocryphal book Prayer of Manasseh provides what some believe is Manasseh's great prayer of repentance following his breaking of the Law.

11. 1 Kings 16:29–30; 2 Kings 13:1–2; 15:17–18; 17:1–2; 21:19–20; 23:36–37; 24:8–9.

12. See also the discussion of the new covenant in chapter 2.

13. For a detailed study on Jesus' view of the Law see D. Macleod, "Jesus and Scripture," in *The Trustworthiness of God: Perspectives on the Nature of Scripture*, P. Helm and C. Trueman, eds. (Leicester: InterVarsity, 2002), 69–95.

14. C. Kruse, "Law," in *The New Dictionary of Biblical Theology*, 635.

15. See also the trouble caused by Peter's adherence to the restrictions of the Law and his avoidance of association with Gentile believers (Gal. 2:11–16).

16. The understanding of works of the Law in the first century as observance of Jewish boundary markers (i.e., food restrictions, Sabbath observance, and circumcision) has been promoted by J. D. G. Dunn and others. For a brief synopsis of this view see J. D. G. Dunn, "The New Perspective on Paul: Paul and the Law," in *The Romans Debate*, K. P. Donfied, ed. (Peabody, Mass.: Hendrickson, 1991), 299–308. For the traditional understanding, see P. Stuhlmacher, *A Challenge to the New Perspective: Revisiting Paul's Doctrine of Justification with an Essay by Donald A. Hagner* (Downers Grove, Ill.: InterVarsity, 2001).

17. For further explanation of Paul's view that the Old Testament Law is faithful see H. H. D. Williams, "'Let God Be Proved True': Paul's View of Scripture and the Faithfulness of God," in *The Trustworthiness of God: Perspectives on the Nature of Scripture*, 96–117.

18. Other places in the New Testament exhibit the high regard of Christian leaders for the Law. Stephen, the first Christian martyr, declares that the Law was "put into effect by angels" (Acts 7:53). James calls the law "royal" (James 2:8). James 4:11–12 warns believers not to speak against the Law and calls those who do such a thing "evil." While the Law is subservient to Christ in the New Testament, it still is of great value.

19. Note that Jesus also heals people and then encourages the ones who have been healed to keep the Law (Matt. 8:1–4; Mark 1:43–44; Luke 5:13–14). See D. J. Moo, "Law," in *Dictionary of Jesus and the Gospels*, 450–61.

20. E.g., Leviticus 19:18 in Romans 12:19; Leviticus 26:11 in 2 Corinthians 6:16; Deuteronomy 9:4 in Romans 10:6; Deuteronomy 25:4 in 1 Corinthians 9:9. Another study that sees allusions and echoes from the Old Testament as formative for Paul's ethics is B. S. Rosner, *Paul, Scripture, and Ethics: A Study of 1 Corinthians 5–7*, Arbeiten zur Geschichte des antiken Judentums und des Urchristentums 22 (Leiden; New York: Brill, 1994).

21. See P. J. Tomson, *Paul and the Jewish Law: Halakha in the Letters of the Apostle to the Gentiles,* Compendia rerum iudaicarum ad Novum Testamentum 3.1 (Assen: Van Gorcum, 1990).

22. See the close resemblance between these verses: Leviticus 19:12 and James 5:12; Leviticus 19:13 and James 5:4; Leviticus 19:15 and James 2:1, 9; Leviticus 19:16 and James 4:11; Leviticus 19:17b and James 5:20; Leviticus 19:18c and James 2:8. L. T. Johnson, *The Letter of James: A New Translation with Introduction and Commentary,* AB 37A (New York: Doubleday, 1995), 30–32.

23. See also Matthew 11:11–19.

24. For a detailed study of Christ as the end of the law see R. Badenas, *Christ the End of the Law: Romans 10:4 in Pauline Perspective,* Journal for the Study of the New Testament Supplement Series 10 (Sheffield: JSOT Press, 1985).

25. In the NIV the verses read, "So the law was put in charge to lead us to Christ that we might be justified by faith. Now that faith has come, we are no longer under the supervision of the law."

26. The King James Version uses "schoolmaster." Other versions, such as the NRSV, use the word "disciplinarian." The Greek word is *paidagōgos.* Note that Galatians 3:8 states how the Law functions as a teacher for the gospel. "The Scripture foresaw that God would justify the Gentiles by faith, and announced the gospel in advance to Abraham: 'All nations will be blessed through you.'"

27. Cf. Hebrews 2:1–4; 3:1–3; 5:1–7; 7:18–28; 9:11–22.

28. See also Colossians 2:16–17, where the Law is described as a shadow until Christ, who is the true substance, comes.

29. Cf. Ezekiel 11:19–20; 36:26–27; Jeremiah 31:31–33.

30. See also Hebrews 10:16–18.

31. See also chapter 8 on the Spirit.

32. See also Galatians 5:16–25, which indicates that life now in the Spirit is greater than being bound to any law. See also Galatians 5:1.

33. William Wallace How, "O Word of God Incarnate" from *The Scottish Psalter and Church Hymnary* (Oxford: Oxford University Press, 1929).

CHAPTER 6: SALVATION: AMAZING GRACE!

1. B. B. Warfield, "Redeemer and Redemption," in *The Person and Work of*

Christ, S. G. Craig, ed. (Philadelphia: Presbyterian and Reformed, 1950), 345–48.

2. J. Murray, "Redemption," in the *International Standard Bible Encyclopedia,* 4:61–63.

3. For further discussion of the concept of covenant, see chapter 2.

4. See R. L. Hubbard, "Redemption," in *The New Dictionary of Biblical Theology,* T. D. Alexander and B. S. Rosner, eds. (Leicester: InterVarsity, 1998), 716–20.

5. Cf. Isaiah 41:14; 43:14; 44:6, 24; 47:4; 48:17; 49:7, 26; 54:5, 8; 59:20; 60:16; 63:16.

6. T. E. Corts, "Blessed Bliss," www.gospelcom.net/chi/morestories/ppbliss.shtml.

7. "I Will Sing of My Redeemer" from *The Pilgrim Hymnal* (Boston: Pilgrim Press, 1968).

8. For a further development of the roots of redemption see L. Morris, *The Apostolic Preaching of the Cross,* 3d ed. (Grand Rapids: Eerdmans, 1992), 11–64.

9. The sheer volume of passages dealing with atonement within the Old Testament suggests that this is a very important idea. In the Old Testament, the NIV refers to some form of "atone" or "atonement" 114 times in 100 verses. It occurs in eighty-four verses in the Pentateuch, ten verses in the Prophets, and six verses in the Writings.

10. R. W. Yarborough, "Atonement," in *New Dictionary of Biblical Theology,* 389.

11. Exodus 30:10; Leviticus 6:30; 8:15, 35; 9:7; 12:7; 16:14f., 18, 27; 17:11; Numbers 35:33; Deuteronomy 21:8; 32:43; 2 Chronicles 29:24; Ezekiel 43:20.

12. For a further explanation of this day and how it is even revered in the modern world, see W. Moller, "Atonement, Day of," in the *International Standard Bible Encyclopedia,* 1:360–62.

13. Cf. Leviticus 16:16, 21, 30, 33.

14. "It is the blood that makes atonement for one's life" as Leviticus 17:11 says.

15. Cf. Leviticus 16:7 ff.,15–22, 24, 25, 27, 28, 32, 33.

16. Note how these other specific directions can be seen in other places in the Old Testament. Cf. Exodus 30:10; Leviticus 23:26–32; 25:9; Numbers 18; 29:7–11; Ezekiel 45:18f. For further detail on this important day see

W. Moller and J. B. Payne, "Day of Atonement," in the *International Standard Bible Encyclopedia*, 1:360–62.

17. Some view the Hebrew sacrificial system as substitutionary. The sacrificial victim endures the divine punishment due the sinner. Others, however, see the main significance of the sacrifice as the life of the animal being poured out. For further comments on these views, see Yarborough, "Atonement," and B. S. Childs, *Biblical Theology of the Old and New Testaments: theological reflection on the Christian Bible* (London: SCM, 1992), 507.

18. See M. A. Seifrid, "Righteousness, Justice, and Justification" in *The New Dictionary of Biblical Theology*, 740–45 and S. J. Hafemann, "The 'Righteousness of God,'" in *How to Do Biblical Theology*, P. Stuhlmacher, ed., Pittsburgh Theological Monograph Series 38 (Allison Park, Pa.: Pickwick, 1995), xv–xli.

19. See also Exodus 9:27; 2 Chronicles 12:1–6; Nehemiah 9:33; Isaiah 24–27; Lamentations 1:18; Daniel 7, 9:7; 12:1–4; Joel 3; Zechariah 14 where God's people are seen as guilty and in need of God's righteousness.

20. E.g., Genesis 12:1–3; 15:1–6; Exodus 34; Isaiah 43:25; 44:21–22; 45:17; 54:7–8; Hosea 11:8–9; Amos 7:1–3.

21. See M. A. Seifrid, "Righteousness, Justice, and Justification," in *The New Dictionary of Biblical Theology*, 741–42.

22. See Isaiah 51:6–11; 54:8–13. C. Stuhlmueller, *Creative Redemption in Deutero-Isaiah*, Analecta biblica 43 (Rome: Biblical Institute, 1970).

23. At other times in the Old Testament, God's righteousness is connected to the right ordering of creation (Pss. 71:19; 96:10–13; 98:7–9; 111:3; Isa. 45:8, 23–24; 51:6–8).

24. For further descriptions of the death upon the cross, see M. Hengel, *Crucifixion in the Ancient World and the Folly of the Message of the Cross* (London: SCM Press, 1977).

25. While at times more gruesome than an actual crucifixion, Mel Gibson's movie *The Passion of the Christ* displays the brutal nature of Christ's death.

26. For a further discussion on atonement as appeasing God's wrath rather than as expiation (i.e., the wiping away of sin), see L. Morris, *Apostolic Preaching of the Cross*, 208–13.

27. For a summary of the most recent discussions on justification in Paul's thinking see A. E. McGrath, "Justification," in the *Dictionary of Paul and His Letters*, 517–23.

28. Cf. Romans 3:28; 4:3–6, 8–11, 22–24; 9:8.
29. For this emphasis, see T. R. Schreiner, *Paul: Apostle of God's Glory in Christ* (Downers Grove, Ill.: InterVarsity, 2001), 201–5.
30. Cf. Romans 1:17; 3:22, 26; 4:3, 5, 9, 13; 9:30; 10:4, 6, 10: Galatians 3:6; 5:5; Philippians 3:9.
31. M. Water, comp., *The New Encyclopedia of Christian Quotations* (Grand Rapids: Baker, 2000), 84.
32. To a lesser extent, reconciliation also can be found in both Testaments. See L. Morris, *Apostolic Preaching of the Cross,* 214–50.
33. Philip P. Bliss, "Hallelujah, What a Savior!" from *Trinity Hymnal* (Philadelphia: Great Commission Publications, 1961).

CHAPTER 7: KINGDOM: JESUS RULES OVER ALL

1. Taken from Robert J. Morgan, *From This Verse* (Nashville: Nelson, 1998).
2. The references are largely found in the synoptic Gospels. Only three references are in John's Gospel: John 3:3, 5; 18:36.
3. Often it is said that John's concept of eternal life is his equivalent for the kingdom of God, to make the idea more intelligible to a Greek audience. L. Goppelt, *Theology of the New Testament,* Jürgen Roloff, ed.; J. E. Alsup, trans. (Grand Rapids: Eerdmans, 1981), 1:45.
4. The kingdom of God is mentioned eight times in Acts, sixteen times in Paul's letters, twice in Hebrews, once in James, once in 2 Peter, and seven times in Revelation.
5. See the discussion in N. Perrin, *Jesus and the Language of the Kingdom* (Philadelphia: Fortress, 1976), 16–32, 127–31, 197–99.
6. The validity of such an approach is suggested by D. Bock, *Jesus According to Scripture: Restoring the Portrait from the Gospels* (Grand Rapids: Baker, 2002), 568–69.
7. The expression does occur in the Septuagint version of the Old Testament Apocrypha in Wisdom 10:10.
8. Note how one Old Testament scholar takes the idea of kingdom as a unifying theme for all of biblical theology, in J. Bright, *The Kingdom of God* (New York: Abingdon, 1953).
9. See other passages in the first five books of the Bible in which God is considered Lord as well as Creator. Abraham calls God Creator and Lord in the same breath when he is before the King of Sodom (Gen. 14:22).

Moses asks the people in Deuteronomy 32:6, "Is this the way you repay the LORD, O foolish and unwise people? Is he not your Father, your Creator, who made you and formed you?"

10. Cf. Psalm 8; 93:1; 104:1–35; 136:1–9.

11. Cf. Job 38:1–42:6; Isaiah 37:16; 40:12–28; 42:5; 43:15; 45:5–18. G. Goldsworthy, "Kingdom of God," in *The New Dictionary of Biblical Theology*, 618.

12. For some scholars, this is considered the redemptive kingdom or theocracy. Cf. G. Vos, *Biblical Theology* (Grand Rapids: Eerdmans, 1948), 372–73.

13. Psalms 24:10; 29:10–11; 114:2; Isaiah 6:5; 33:22; Zephaniah 3:15; Zechariah 14:16–17.

14. This interchange takes place in the following verses: Exodus 5:1; 7:16; 8:1; 9:1, 13.

15. Cf. Joshua 1:1–9; 4:1f.; 5:13–15; 6:1–2; 8:1–2.

16. See chapter 5.

17. Isaiah 9:2–7; 60:4–16; Amos 9:11f.; Micah 4:13; 7:8–17.

18. Isaiah 1:25–26; 4:3–4; 26:2; 28:5–6; 52:13–53:12; Jeremiah 31:31–32; Ezekiel 36:25–26.

19. Isaiah 2:2–3; 9:5–6; 11:6–7; 35:9; Micah 5:4; Zechariah 9:9–10.

20. Isaiah 12; 21:17–24; 33:17ff.; 41:21–22; Jeremiah 31:1–14; Hosea 2:14–15; 14:4–5; Zephaniah 3:14–20. G. R. Beasley-Murray, *Jesus and the Kingdom of God* (Grand Rapids: Eerdmans, 1986), 20.

21. See also Nebuchadnezzar's dream of a statue made of many metals in Daniel 2. Each metal represents a human kingdom that is destroyed by a messianic stone that grows into a great kingdom.

22. For more on "Son of Man" see chapter 4.

23. For a discussion of a variety of options regarding Daniel 7, see G. R. Beasley-Murray, *Jesus and the Kingdom of God*, 26–35.

24. For a discussion of first-century texts, see C. Caragounis, *Son of Man: Vision and Interpretation*, Wissenchaftliche Untersuchungen zum Neuen Testament 38 (Tübingen: J. C. B. Mohr [Paul Siebeck], 1986), 104–12, 136–43 and W. Horbury, "The Messianic Associations of 'The Son of Man,'" *Journal of Theological Studies*, 36 (1985): 44–47. For a dissenting view, see M. Casey, *Son of Man: The Interpretation and Influence of Daniel 7* (London: SPCK, 1979).

25. Jewish hopes in God's kingdom and in the Messiah as a significant part of that kingdom are found in between the Old and New Testament. God's

comprehensive rule of all humanity is expressed in books like *1 Enoch* 9:4–5; 12:3; 25; 27:3; 81:3. The destruction of God's enemies and the freedom of God's people are found in *Psalms of Solomon* 17–18 and *2 Baruch* 36–40. The text of *Psalms of Solomon* 17–18 provides the lengthiest expression of messianic hope in that kingdom. The cry of the prayer of 2 Maccabees 1:24–29 summarizes well the hope of deliverance expected with God's kingdom. M. Lattke, "On the Jewish Background of the Synoptic Concept 'The Kingdom of God,'" in *The Kingdom of God*, B. Chilton, ed. (Philadelphia: Fortress, 1984), 72–91. For a summary of Jewish hopes for God's kingdom to come, see C. Caragounis, "Kingdom of God/Kingdom of Heaven," in *Dictionary of Jesus and the Gospels*, 418–20.

26. G. Goldsworthy, "Kingdom of God," in *The New Dictionary of Biblical Theology*, 615–20; D. Bock, *Jesus According to Scripture*, 566–69; C. Caragounis, "Kingdom of God/Heaven," in *Dictionary of Jesus and the Gospels*, 417–20; and G. R. Beasley-Murray, *Jesus and the Kingdom of God*, 3–38, take a similar approach.

27. Matthew uses "kingdom of heaven" in the same context that Luke uses "kingdom of God." Matthew 5:3 and Luke 6:20; Matthew 8:11 and Luke 13:29; Matthew 10:7 and Luke 10:9; Matthew 11:11 and Luke 7:28 and Matthew 13:33 and Luke 13:20. Matthew 4:17 and 13:11 use "kingdom of heaven" while Mark 1:15 and 4:11 use "kingdom of God." Note how Matthew 6:33 uses "kingdom of God" while Luke 12:31 uses "kingdom."

28. The parable of the mustard seed and the parable of the leaven also indicate that the kingdom of God will be large and may imply a global extent to the kingdom of God (Matt. 13:31–33; cf. Mark 4:30–32; Luke 13:18–21). The parable of the great feast in Matthew 22:1–14 (cf. Luke 14:16–24) implies that the whole world is invited.

29. D. Bock, *Jesus According to Scripture*, 208–9.

30. In Matthew 8:11, Jesus envisions all nations coming to the kingdom: "I say to you that many will come from the east and the west, and will take their places at the feast with Abraham, Isaac and Jacob in the kingdom of heaven."

31. Cf. Revelation 11:15 and 12:10, which envision a global kingdom.

32. Matthew 22:44; 26:64; Mark 12:36; 14:62; 16:19; Luke 20:42f.; 22:69; Acts 2:33–34; 5:31; 7:55f.; Romans 8:34; 1 Corinthians 15:25; Ephesians 1:20; Colossians 3:1; Hebrews 1:3, 13; 8:1; 10:12f.; 12:2; 1 Peter 3:22.

33. M. Hengel, *Studies in Early Christology* (Edinburgh: T. and T. Clark, 1995), 216.

34. That this idea can be traced to Psalm 110:1 further suggests that Jesus as king and his rule over the entire world can be seen from the Old Testament. See M. Hengel, *Studies in Early Christology,* 119–225.

35. This is one of the large discussions about the kingdom: Is it present, future, or both present and future? For the emphasis that the kingdom of God is to be found in the present see C. H. Dodd, *The Parables of the Kingdom* (New York: Scribner, 1961). For the emphasis that the kingdom of God is to be found in the future see A. Schweitzer, *The Mystery of the Kingdom of God: The Secret of Jesus' Messiahship and Passion* (New York: Macmillan, 1954). For the view that it is to be seen in the present and future see A. Hoekema, *The Bible and the Future* (Grand Rapids: Eerdmans, 1979), 1–75. For a short summary on all viewpoints see C. Caragounis, "Kingdom of God/Heaven," in *Dictionary of Jesus and the Gospels,* 417–30.

36. See also Mark 1:15. Jesus' first discourse in Mark is about the kingdom of God.

37. G. Goldsworthy, "Kingdom of God," in *The New Dictionary of Biblical Theology,* 616.

38. For Paul's references to the kingdom of God see Romans 14:17; 1 Corinthians 4:20; 6:9f.; 15:24, 50; Galatians 5:21; Ephesians 2:2; 5:5; Colossians 1:12f.; 4:11; 1 Thessalonians 2:12; 2 Thessalonians 1:5; 2 Timothy 4:1, 18.

39. See also G. E. Ladd, who balances the idea of Jesus' kingdom coming in the present with the expectation of its ultimate presence in the future. In his book *Jesus and the Kingdom,* Ladd states, "The Kingdom of God was the dynamic rule of God which had invaded history in his own [Jesus'] person and mission to bring men in the present age the blessings of the messianic age, and which would manifest itself yet again at the end of the age to bring this same messianic salvation to its consummation." G. E. Ladd, *Jesus and the Kingdom: the Eschatology of Biblical Realism* (New York: Harper and Row, 1964), 303.

40. See parables, such as the parable of the talents (Matt. 25:14–30), the judge and the widow (Luke 18:1–8), the mustard and the leaven (Mark 4:30–32), the weeds (Matt. 13:24–30), the dragnet (vv. 47–50), the sheep and the goats (25:31–46), which also speak of the kingdom that is to come in the future. As Jesus tells these parables, he creates anticipation for his coming kingdom.

41. For a further description, see C. Keener, *A Commentary on the Gospel of Matthew* (Grand Rapids: Eerdmans, 1999), 356–58.

42. For a comprehensive study of Mark 13, see G. Beasley-Murray, *Jesus and the Last Days: The Interpretation of the Olivet Discourse* (Peabody, Mass.: Hendrickson, 1993).

43. For a presentation of his views on these see W. Wilberforce, *A Practical View of Christianity: Personal Faith As a Call to Political Responsibility,* K. Belmonte, ed. (Peabody, Mass.: Hendrickson, 1996).

44. R. C. K. Ensor, *England 1870–1914* (Oxford: Oxford University Press, 1936), 137–38.

45. M. Hennell, *John Venn and the Clapham Sect* (London: Lutterworth Press, 1958), 207.

46. "Jesus Shall Reign," from *The Pilgrim Hymnal* (Boston: Pilgrim Press, 1968).

CHAPTER 8: HOLY SPIRIT: THE COMFORTER HAS COME!

1. Consider the writings of Eusebius on the heretical nature of the Montanists. Eusebius, *The History of the Christian Church,* G. A. Williamson and A. Louth, trans. (London: Penguin, 1998), 5:14–18. For a more favorable view of the Montanists, see D. F. Wright, "Why Were the Montanists Condemned?" *Themelios* 2, no. 1 (1976): 15–22.

2. The following books consider the Holy Spirit throughout the Bible and throughout history. A. Heron, *The Holy Spirit in the Bible, the History of Christian Thought, and Recent Theology* (Philadelphia: Westminster, 1983); E. Schweizer, *The Holy Spirit,* R. H. and I. Fuller, trans. (Philadelphia: Fortress, 1980); G. T. Montague, *The Holy Spirit: Growth of a Biblical Tradition* (New York; Paramus; Toronto: Paulist, 1976).

3. The NRSV and NAB use the word *wind* instead of *Spirit* in their translation, but they cross-refer to "the Spirit of God." For a more detailed look at this verse see G. Wenham, *Genesis 1–15* (Waco, Tex.: Word, 1987), 16–17.

4. Consider the following studies that see the Spirit involved with creation. E.g., W. Hildebrandt, *An Old Testament Theology of the Spirit of God* (Peabody, Mass.: Hendrickson, 1995), 30–35; M. G. Kline, *Images of the Spirit* (Grand Rapids: Baker, 1980), 15; L. Wood, *The Holy Spirit in the Old Testament* (Grand Rapids: Zondervan, 1976), 30–31.

5. Cf. Judith 16:14; Wisdom 1:7; Apocalypse of Moses 43:4; 2 Esdras 6:38–41;

2 Baruch 21:4; 23:5. M. Turner, "Holy Spirit," in *The New Dictionary of Biblical Theology,* 551.

6. See D. Instone-Brewer, *Techniques and Assumptions of Jewish Exegesis Before 70 CE,* Texte und Studien zum antiken Judentum 30 (Tübingen: J. C. B. Mohr [Paul Siebeck], 1992), 215–16.

7. See J. H. Charlesworth, "The Pseudepigrapha as Biblical Exegesis," in *Early Jewish and Christian Exegesis: Studies in Memory of William Hugh Brownlee,* C. A. Evans and W. F. Stinespring, eds. (Atlanta: Scholars, 1987), 139–52; A. Chester, "Citing the Old Testament," in *It Is Written: Scripture Citing Scripture: Essays in Honour of Barnabas Lindars,* D. A. Carson and H. G. M. Williamson, eds. (Cambridge: Cambridge University Press, 1988), 141–69. For the high regard for the Old Testament in early Jewish literature see *Mikra: Text and Translation, Reading and Interpretation of the Hebrew Bible in Ancient Judaism and Early Christianity,* Compendia rerum Iudaicarum ad Novum Testamentum 2.1 (Assen: Van Gorcum, 1988). See also the following studies that indicate that the Old Testament refracted through the lens of early Jewish writing influenced the apostle Paul. B. S. Rosner, *Paul, Scripture, and Ethics: A Study of 1 Corinthians 5–7,* Arbeiten zur Geschichte des antiken Judentums und des Urchristentums 22 (New York: Brill, 1994); H. H. D. Williams, *The Wisdom of the Wise: The Presence and Function in 1 Corinthians 1:18–3:23,* Arbeiten zur Geschichte des antiken Judentums und des Urchristentums 49 (Leiden; New York: Brill, 2001).

8. E.g., Ephrem the Syrian, Jerome, and Ambrose. See A. Louth, *Genesis 1–11,* Ancient Christian Commentary on Scripture 1 (Downers Grove, Ill.: InterVarsity, 2001), 5–6.

9. For another passage in the book of Job that testifies to the life-giving nature of the Holy Spirit, see Job's words in Job 27:3.

10. W. Hildebrandt also finds the Spirit at work in particular events within Israel's pilgrimage. He sees the Spirit present at the crossing of the Red Sea, as equivalent to the pillar of cloud and fire that leads Israel through the wilderness, as preservation for the nation, as aiding restoration, and for judgment on humanity. See W. Hildebrandt, *An Old Testament Theology of the Spirit of God,* 67–103.

11. See also Joseph, who is known to have a spirit of God upon him (Gen. 41:38).

12. Versions of the Bible such as the KJV, NAB, and NRSV use "man of the spirit" for "inspired man." This is the more literal translation.

13. Ezekiel 11:5–25; Isaiah 48:16; 61:1–3; Zechariah 7:12.

14. In these verses T. Maertens suggests, "This proliferation of names for the Spirit of God serves only to indicate the stupendous wealth of spiritual gifts which will proceed from that divine source." T. Maertens, *The Spirit of God in Scripture* (Montreal: Palm, 1966), 40.

15. This connection between the Spirit and the Messiah became even stronger in intertestamental Jewish literature. See texts such as *1 Enoch* 49:2–3; 62:1–2; *Psalms of Solomon* 17:37; 18:7; portions of the Dead Sea Scrolls such as 1QSb 5.25; 4Q215 iv.4, etc. Max Turner notes that a "major strand of Judaism anticipated a Messiah mightily endowed with the Spirit as *both* the Spirit of prophecy *and* of power" (italics his). M. Turner, *The Holy Spirit and Spiritual Gifts: Then and Now* (Carlisle: Paternoster, 1996), 19.

16. A. Heron, *The Holy Spirit in the Bible, the History of Christian Thought, and Recent Theology,* 17–20.

17. Ezekiel 2:2; 8:3; 11:1, 24; 13:3. See also Numbers 24:2; Isaiah 61:1–3; Ezekiel 11:5–25; Hosea 9:7.

18. By the time of the New Testament, prophecy and the Holy Spirit were decidedly connected. M. Turner concludes in his chapter on the Spirit in intertestamental Judaism, "The Spirit in intertestamental Jewish literature was above all the 'Spirit of prophecy.'" M. Turner, *The Holy Spirit and Spiritual Gifts,* 20.

19. This great hope has impressed many communities, particularly the African American community, which has many songs about this scene from Ezekiel 37, for example, the old spiritual "Dem Bones."

20. One aspect of the Holy Spirit is still to be anticipated, and will not be covered in the following discussion. He is the first installment, the first fruit of things to come (Rom. 8:23; 2 Cor. 1:22; 5:1–5; Eph. 1:13–14).

21. It is anticipated by the Holy Spirit alighting on Jesus as a dove at his baptism (Matt. 3:16–17; Mark 1:10; Luke 3:21–22).

22. See also Luke 7:21–22, where Luke recounts in language similar to Isaiah 61:1–2 Jesus' miracles. By connecting these miracles with the language of Isaiah 61:1–2, once again the work of the Holy Spirit is connected with Jesus' miracles. See M. Turner, *The Holy Spirit and Spiritual Gifts,* 32–36.

23. See Romans 8:1–4; 12:1; 2 Corinthians 5:9; Ephesians 5:10; 1 Thessalonians 4:1. T. Paige, "Holy Spirit," in the *Dictionary of Paul and His Letters,* 409.

24. The person discussed in Romans 7 has been seen to be Paul, Adam, Israel, or a representative of every man. For a fuller discussion on who the *I* is in Romans 7 see D. J. Moo, *Romans,* New International Greek Testament Commentary (Grand Rapids: Eerdmans, 1996), 424–31.

25. See Romans 8:3–14; 2 Corinthians 3:3–6; 5:1–5. For an insightful discussion on the contrast between flesh and Spirit and its Old Testament roots see F. F. Bruce, *Paul: Apostle of the Heart Set Free* (Grand Rapids: Eerdmans, 2000), 203–11.

26. M. Green, *Illustrations for Biblical Preaching,* 190.

27. "The Evangelists have no doubts that Jesus was the wholly unique man of the Spirit." E. Kamlah, J. D. G. Dunn, and C. Brown, "Spirit, Holy Spirit," in *The New International Dictionary of New Testament Theology* (Grand Rapids: Zondervan, 1978), 3:697.

28. For an explanation of how John the Baptist is filled with the Spirit, indicating that his presence signals a new order in which the Spirit will be outpoured, see J. D. G. Dunn, *Baptism in the Holy Spirit: A Re-examination of the New Testament Teaching on the Gift of the Spirit in Relation to Pentecostalism Today* (London: SCM, 1970), 8–22.

29. E. Schweitzer, *The Holy Spirit* (Philadelphia: Fortress, 1980), 57.

30. Note how the giving of the Holy Spirit is through Jesus Christ. John 14:16–17, 26; 15:26–27; 16:7–11, 13–15.

31. For a fuller development of this idea see C. H. Scobie, *The Ways of Our God: An Approach to Biblical Theology* (Grand Rapids: Eerdmans, 2003), 269–97.

32. See also John 3:5; Acts 11:17; Galatians 3:2; 1 Thessalonians 1:5–6; Titus 3:5; Hebrews 6:4; 1 Peter 1:2; 1 John 3:24; 4:13.

33. D. E. H. Whitely, *The Theology of St. Paul* (Oxford: Blackwell, 1964), 125.

34. In Hebrews 3:7, the Spirit introduces Old Testament Scripture from Psalm 95. Although this psalm is not prophetic, it introduces a prophetic warning and is introduced with the same formula, "As the Holy Spirit says."

35. See also Acts 1:16; 4:25; 7:51; 28:25.

36. Revelation 2:7, 11, 17, 29; 3:6, 13, 22.

37. See also Acts 21:11; 1 Timothy 4:1; James 4:5; Revelation 14:13.

38. Acts 2:17; 7:55–56.

39. Acts 1:2, 16; 4:25; 7:51; 8:29; 10:19; 11:12, 28; 13:2, 4; 15:28; 16:6, 7; 19:21; 20:22–23; 21:4, 11; 28:25.

40. Acts 5:3; 6:3, 5, 10; 9:31; 13:9; 16:18.

41. Acts 2:4; 10:46; 19:6.

42. Acts 1:4, 8; 4:8, 31; 5:32; 6:10; 9:17, 31; 13:52.

43. For a longer explanation on the similarity between the Spirit in the book of Acts and the Jewish view of the "Spirit of prophecy," particularly from Joel 2, see M. Turner, "The 'Spirit of Prophecy' as the Power of Israel's Restoration and Witness," in *Witness to the Gospel: The Theology of Acts*, I. H. Marshall and D. Peterson, eds. (Grand Rapids: Eerdmans, 1998), 333–37.

44. For a more extensive treatment of New Testament prophecy, see T. W. Gillespie, *The First Theologians: A Study in Early Christian Prophecy* (Grand Rapids: Eerdmans, 1994) and C. Forbes, *Prophecy and Inspired Speech in Early Christianity and its Hellenistic Environment*, Wissenchaftliche Untersuchungen zum Neuen Testament 75 (Tübingen: J. C. B. Mohr [Paul Siebeck], 1995). For an overview of issues in Paul's understanding of prophecy see C. M. Robeck, "Prophecy, Prophesying," in *Dictionary of Paul and His Letters*, 755–62.

45. Jonathan Edwards, *Jonathan Edwards on Revival* (Edinburgh: Banner of Truth, 1999), 87. Besides the treatise "The Distinguishing Marks of a Work of the Spirit of God," for Edwards's further comments on the Spirit in the First Great Awakening, see "A Narrative of Surprising Conversions" and "An Account of the Revival of Religion in Northampton 1740–1742."

46. "Spirit of God, that moved of old" from *The Scottish Psalter and Church Hymnary* (Oxford: Oxford University Press, 1929).

CHAPTER 9: THE PEOPLE OF GOD: A KINGDOM OF PRIESTS AND A HOLY NATION

1. M. Water, comp., *The New Encyclopedia of Christian Quotations* (Grand Rapids: Baker, 2000), 203.

2. Cf. G. Goldsworthy, "Biblical Theology as the Heartbeat of Effective Ministry," in *Biblical Theology: Retrospect and Prospect*, S. J. Hafemann, ed. (Downers Grove, Ill.: InterVarsity, 2002), 286.

3. The purpose of this chapter is not to become embroiled in the debate between dispensationalists and covenant theologians concerning the nation of Israel and the church. It is rather to draw broad parallels from the Old and New Testaments regarding God's people. For a viewpoint that sees Israel as distinct from the church, see R. L. Saucy, *The Church in*

God's Program (Chicago: Moody, 1972), 69–97; and C. C. Ryrie, *Dispensationalism Today* (Chicago: Moody, 1965), 132–55. For a viewpoint that sees Israel and the church as similar, see L. Berkhof, *Systematic Theology* (Grand Rapids: Eerdmans, 1978), 570f.; E. P. Clowney, *The Church* (Leicester; Downers Grove, Ill.: InterVarsity, 1995); K. Giles, *What on Earth Is the Church? An Exploration in New Testament Theology* (Downers Grove, Ill.: InterVarsity, 1995), 182–89, 230–40.

4. Abram's name is changed to Abraham in Genesis 17.
5. See G. F. Hawthorne, "Name," in the *International Standard Bible Encyclopedia*, 3:481–83.
6. E.g., Genesis 26:24; 28:13; 31:42; 50:24.
7. E.g., Exodus 2:23–25; 3:7; 22:23.
8. E.g., Deuteronomy 6:10; 29:10; 30:20.
9. Other texts in which the special relationship of Israel with God is based on their relationship to Abraham include 1 Chronicles 29:18; 2 Chronicles 20:7; 30:6; Nehemiah 9:7; and Psalm 47:9.
10. See chapter 2.
11. For a fine development of this theme, see W. Kaiser, *Toward an Old Testament Theology* (Grand Rapids: Zondervan, 1978).
12. E. P. Clowney, "The Biblical Theology of the Church," in *The Church in the Bible and the World*, D. A. Carson, ed. (Grand Rapids: Baker, 1987), 17.
13. Worship also is one of the intentions that God has for Moses at his calling at the burning bush (Exod. 3:12).
14. Exodus 8:1, 20; 9:1, 13; 10:3, 7.
15. For a discussion of the importance of worshipping the one true God rather than idols, see chapter 3.
16. Cf. Deuteronomy 5:9; 8:19; 12:4; 13:2, 6; 31:2.
17. See also Psalms 22:29; 29:2; 86:9; 96:9; 97:7; 99:5, 9; 100:2; 102:22; 132:7.
18. Leviticus 1:1–15; 4:10; 5:8–10; 14:9; 15:15, 30; 17:5; Deuteronomy 18:3.
19. Note that every time the Urim and Thummim of the Old Testament are used for direction for God's people, they are used by a priest. Cf. Exodus 28:30; Leviticus 8:8; Numbers 27:21; Deuteronomy 33:8; 1 Samuel 14:41; 28:6; Ezra 2:63; Nehemiah. 7:65. P. Ellingworth, "Priests," in *The New Dictionary of Biblical Theology*, 698.
20. E.g., Leviticus 10:10; Deuteronomy 24:8; 33:10; 2 Chronicles 15:3; Ezra 7:21; Jeremiah 18:18; Ezekiel 7:26.

21. E.g., 1 Samuel 7:1; 1 Kings 8:6–11; 2 Kings 12:4–10; 1 Chronicles 28:21; 2 Chronicles 23:6.

22. Cf. Isaiah 30:29; 35:10; Psalms 42:1–4; 43:3–4; 84:1–2; 122:1–9; 137:6. R. J. McKelvey, "Temple," in *The New Dictionary of Biblical Theology*, 807.

23. For a biblical theological view of these feasts see L. McFall, "Sacred Meals," in *The New Dictionary of Biblical Theology*, 750–53.

24. This psalm is fashioned after the Aaronic blessing, a blessing that many hear each Sunday in church. Numbers 6:24–26 says, "The LORD bless you and keep you; the LORD make his face shine upon you and be gracious to you; the LORD turn his face toward you and give you peace." See also Psalms 33:8; 68:32; 96:10–13; 98:2; 100:1–2.

25. W. Kaiser, "Israel's Missionary Call," in *Perspectives on the World Christian Movement*, R. D. Winter and S. C. Hawthorne, eds. (Pasadena, Calif.: William Carey, 1981), 31–33.

26. See also Micah 4:2; Zechariah 8:3.

27. Cf. Isaiah 11:10, 12; 12:4; 25:3; 43:9; 54:3; 55:5; 60:3, 5; 61:11; 62:10; 66:18–20.

28. E.g., Jeremiah 2:2; Ezekiel 16:8–14; Hosea 2:1–3:1.

29. E.g., 2 Kings 19:21; Isaiah 23:12; 37:22; Lamentations 2:13.

30. See E. Ferguson, *The Church of Christ: A Biblical Ecclesiology for Today* (Grand Rapids: Eerdmans, 1996), 121–33.

31. Cf. Psalms 74:1; 78:52; 79:13; 119:176; Isaiah 13:14; Jeremiah 23:1; Ezekiel 34; Zechariah 10:2.

32. For further discussion on God's people as sheep, see W. P. Keller, *A Shepherd Looks at Psalm 23* (Grand Rapids: Zondervan, 1997).

33. Cf. Isaiah 10:20–34; 11:11, 16; 17:3; 28:5; 37:4, 31f.; Jeremiah 6:9; 11:23; 23:3; 31:7; 40:11, 15; 42:2, 15, 19; 43:5; 44:7, 12, 14, 28; 47:4f.; 50:20, 26; Micah 2:12; 4:7; 5:7, 8; 7:18; also Joel 2:32; Zephaniah 2:7; 3:13; Haggai 1:12,14; Zechariah 8:6.

34. See M. W. Elliot, "Remnant," in *The New Dictionary of Biblical Theology*, 723–26.

35. Even the idea of God being his people's God and they being his people is repeated in the New Testament in 2 Corinthians 6:16 and Revelation 21:3. See how W. Kaiser sees this theme as being woven from the Old Testament into 2 Corinthians and Revelation, in W. Kaiser, *Toward an Old Testament Theology*, 32–35.

36. See also Romans 8:29.

37. Consider some of the stories collected by the organization *Voice of the Martyrs*, www.voiceofthemartyrs.org.

38. D. Peterson, "The Worship of the New Community," in *Witness to the Gospel*, 389–95.

39. "The gathering of the church community in the presence of the Holy Spirit was imbued with great importance among the first Christians. From descriptions of how they gathered, ate, prayed, and sang together, is learned more about them, perhaps, than from any other source. In early congregations, meetings were neither restrictively 'religious' nor agenda-driven, unlike so many of today's scheduled 'services.'

   "To the early Christians, the gathering of the Body was sustenance, life, and identity. At meetings, demons were expelled, confessions made, forgiveness requested and granted, gifts exercised, leadership recognized and affirmed, goods shared, and individual and corporate needs met. Most importantly, the name 'which is above all names' was exalted and glorified." Eberhard Arnold, ed., *The Early Christians in Their Own Words* (Farmington, Pa.: Plough, 1997), 198.

40. Note the comparison to Jonah when he shares that he is an Israelite and he worships God (Jonah 1:9).

41. See J. Piper, *Desiring God: Meditations of a Christian Hedonist* (Sisters, Ore.: Multnomah, 1996), 72–95, where worship is seen as a "feast" for God's people.

42. For further reading about monasteries that became training grounds for missionaries, see T. Cahill, *How the Irish Saved Civilization* (New York: Doubleday, 1991).

43. The implication to reach out to others is also suggested in Jesus' final talk with Peter in John 20.

44. Indeed, some have seen God's offering of salvation through Jesus Christ to Jews and Gentiles, thereby creating a new people, as the primary theme of the entire book of Acts. See *Witness to the Gospel*, 167–324. Note also B. S. Rosner, "The Progress of the Word," in *Witness to the Gospel*, 229–33, which asserts that unending progress is suggested by Paul's witness and imprisonment in the final verses of Acts (28:30–31).

45. See also Robert Short, the author of *The Gospel According to Peanuts* who said, "The church is the great lost and found department." Taken from *The New Encyclopedia of Christian Quotations*, 203.

46. Numerous references describe the church as "brothers." For a sampling from each writer of the Epistles, consider 1 Corinthians 1:10; Philippians 1:12; 2 Thessalonians 2:1; Hebrews 13:22; James 1:2; 1 Peter 1:22; 1 John 3:13.

47. See Galatians 6:10; Ephesians 3:15; Hebrews 2:11; 1 Peter 4:17.

48. Matthew 9:35; 10:6; 15:24; Mark 14:27; Luke 15:3–7; 1 Peter 2:25.

49. For a more detailed connection between Paul's writing in 1 Corinthians 3 and the vineyard of the Lord from Isaiah 5, see H. H. D. Williams, *The Wisdom of the Wise*, 49:237–55.

50. Bryan Jeffrey Leach, "We Are God's People," in *Worship His Majesty* (Alexandria, Ind.: Gaither Music Co., 1987).

CHAPTER 10: PROPHECY AND FULFILLMENT: MAKING GOOD ON PROMISES

1. E.g., W. Kaiser, *The Messiah in the Old Testament* (Grand Rapids: Zondervan, 1995), 235.

2. Cf. 1 Corinthians 14.

3. See chapter 4.

4. Much of the content from this section on the nature of Old Testament prophecy follows the excellent discussion found in W. A. Grudem, "Prophecy/Prophets," in *The New Dictionary of Biblical Theology*, 701–10.

5. See 1 Samuel 9–10; 1 Kings 14:18; 16:12; 18:24, 39; 2 Kings 5:8.

6. Besides the better known prophets, the Old Testament mentions a number of lesser-known or secondary prophets. Groups or schools of prophets often functioned under the auspices of other prophets, such as the one hundred prophets hidden by Obadiah (1 Kings 18:4), and the company of prophets in Bethel (2 Kings 2:3), Jericho (vv. 5, 7), and Gilgal (4:38). Women such as Miriam and Deborah (Exod. 15:20; Judg. 4) were also known as prophets. Cf. W. A. Grudem, "Prophecy," in *The New Dictionary of Biblical Theology*, 702–3.

7. False prophets were often a concern during Old Testament times. A false prophet presumes to speak in God's name and at times may encourage people to follow other gods (Deut. 13:1–5; 18:20). False prophets are recognized by their advocating other gods and their predictions' not coming true (13:2–5; 18:22).

8. In the NIV translation, the phrase is used 438 times in the Prophets.

9. W. Brueggemann, *Theology of the Old Testament: Testimony, Dispute,*

Advocacy (Minneapolis: Fortress, 1997), 164–73; cf. W. Kaiser, *Toward an Old Testament Theology*. For a detailed description of Old Testament prophecy, see E. J. Young, *My Servants the Prophets* (Grand Rapids: Eerdmans, 1955). See also D. B. Sandy, *Plowshares and Pruning Hooks: Rethinking the Language of Biblical Prophecy and Apocalyptic* (Downers Grove, Ill.: InterVarsity, 2002).

10. For a broader treatment of Old Testament texts surrounding the expectation of Messiah, see P. E. Satterthwaite, R. S. Hess, and G. J. Wenham, *The Lord's Anointed: Interpretation of Old Testament Messianic Texts* (Carlisle: Paternoster, 1995).

11. Indeed some have said that it is the most commented upon passage in the Old Testament.

12. For an account of King Ahaz's rule see 2 Kings 16.

13. See the following studies: G. Bostock, "Divine Birth, Human Conception," *ExpTim* 98 (1987): 331–33; G. P. Benson, "Virgin Birth, Virgin Conception," *ExpTim* (1987): 139–40; C. E. B. Cranfield, "Some Reflections on the Subject of the Virgin Birth," *SJT* 41 (1988): 177–89. See also G. Lüdemann, *Virgin Birth? The Real Story of Mary and Her Son Jesus* (Harrisburg: Trinity International, 1998); G. Machen, *The Virgin Birth of Christ* (New York: Harper and Brothers, 1930); B. Witherington, "The Birth of Jesus," in the *Dictionary of Jesus and the Gospels*, 60–74.

14. For other places where the word is used in the Old Testament, see Genesis 24:43; Exodus 2:8; 1 Chronicles 15:20; Psalms 46:2; 68:26; Proverbs 30:19; Song of Solomon 1:3; 6:8.

15. J. N. Oswalt suggests that the word can refer to a near fulfillment in Hezekiah and a distant fulfillment in the virgin. J. N. Oswalt, *The Book of Isaiah 1–39* (Grand Rapids: Eerdmans, 1986), 212–13. For differing opinions see H. Wildberger, *Isaiah 1–12: A Commentary*, T. Trapp, trans. (Minneapolis: Fortress, 1991), 279–318; O. Kaiser, *Isaiah 1–12: A Commentary*, OTL (Philadelphia: Westminster, 1972), 96–106.

16. Cf. K. Jobes and M. Silva, *Invitation to the Septuagint* (Grand Rapids: Baker, 2000), 45.

17. Note how the word is specifically connected to the word *bitulah*, which unequivocally means virgin in Isaiah 37:22 and 47:1.

18. B. Witherington, "The Birth of Jesus," in the *Dictionary of Jesus and the Gospels*, 64.

19. S. McKinnon, *Isaiah 1–39,* Ancient Christian Commentary on Scripture 10 (Downers Grove, Ill.: InterVarsity, 2004), xx.

20. NASB. See also the KJV, which records the ending of Micah 5:2 as "whose goings forth *have been* from of old, from everlasting"(emphasis added).

21. See Psalms 2:7; 45:7; 110:3; Isaiah 9:6. W. Kaiser, *The Messiah in the Old Testament,* 153–54.

22. Other Old Testament texts also prophesy the Lord's death. For texts on the betrayal of Jesus, see Psalm 69:25 and 109:8 in Acts 1:20. For the involvement of thirty pieces of silver in Jesus' betrayal, see Zechariah 11:12–13 in Matthew 26:15; 27:9–10. For Messiah's thirst during his death, see Psalm 69:21 in Matthew 27:34, 48; Mark 15:36; Luke 23:36; John 19:28. For the piercing of Messiah's side, see Zechariah 12:10 in John 19:37. His suffering at Gethsemane can be seen from Isaiah 50:4–9 in Mark 14:65; John 18:22; 19:3. For a further treatment of texts such as these, see W. Kaiser, *The Messiah in the Old Testament,* 100–22, 211–26; and C. H. Scobie, *The Ways of Our God: An Approach to Biblical Theology* (Grand Rapids: Eerdmans, 2003), 403–40.

23. J. B. Payne, *Encyclopedia of Biblical Prophecy* (New York: Harper and Row, 1973), 257.

24. For other passional psalms consider Psalms 35; 41; 55; 69; 109.

25. J. E. Smith, *What the Bible Teaches About the Promised Messiah* (Nashville: Nelson, 1993), 146. See also C. A. Briggs who makes a similar statement in *Messianic Prophecy* (New York: Scribner's, 1889), 326.

26. S. Tostengard, "Psalm 22," *Interpretation* 44 (1992): 170.

27. F. Delitzsch, *Biblical Commentary on the Prophecies of Isaiah* (Grand Rapids: Eerdmans, 1954), 2:303.

28. W. Kaiser, *The Messiah in the Old Testament,* 178.

29. The four servant songs in the book of Isaiah are as follows: 42:1–7 or 9 or 12; 49:1–6 or 7 or 13; 50:4–9 or 1–11; 52:13 –53:12.

30. C. H. Scobie, *The Ways of Our God,* 409.

31. G. P. Hugenberger, "The Servant of the Lord in the 'Servant Songs' of Isaiah: A Second Moses Figure," in *The Lord's Anointed,* 105–39.

32. See M. N. Hooker, *Jesus and the Servant: The Influence of the Servant Concept of Deutero-Isaiah in the New Testament* (London: SPCK, 1959); R. T. France, "The Servant of the Lord in the Teaching of Jesus," *TynBul* 19 (1968): 26–52; idem, *Jesus and the Old Testament: His Application of Old*

Testament Passages to Himself and His Mission (Grand Rapids: Baker, 1982); D. C. Allison, *The New Moses: A Matthean Typology* (Minneapolis: Fortress, 1993).

33. Other prophecies of Jesus' birth are found in Matthew 1–2. Prophecies surrounding the flight of Jesus' family from King Herod include Hosea 11:1 in Matthew 2:15, and Jeremiah 31:15 in Matthew 2:18. In Matthew 2:23 is found the prophecy that he will be called a Nazarene (from Isa. 11:1, or perhaps a combination of Old Testament texts).

34. Cf. C. Keener, *A Commentary on the Gospel of Matthew* (Downers Grove, Ill.; Leicester: InterVarsity, 1997), 59.

35. See further the explanation in D. Bock, *Jesus According to Scripture* (Grand Rapids: Baker, 2002), 70.

36. S. B. Frost, "Psalm 22: An Exposition," *Canadian Journal of Theology* 8 (1962): 113, 115.

37. It is perhaps possible that vindication is seen in Jesus' statement as well. The context of Psalm 22 and parallels with other early Jewish literature may support a secondary sense of vindication in Jesus' words. Cf. R. Watts, "The Psalms in Mark's Gospel," in *The Psalms in the New Testament*, ed. M. Menken and S. Moyise (London: T. and T. Clark, 2004), 41–44.

38. H. J. Kraus, *Theology of the Psalms* (Minneapolis: Augsburg, 1986), 189.

39. Note how the ideas of giving one's life for others from Isaiah 53 influences the statement by Jesus in Mark 10:45: "For even the Son of Man did not come to be served, but to serve, and to give his life as a ransom for many." See R. Watts, "Jesus' Death, Isaiah 53, and Mark 10:45: A Crux Revisited," in *Jesus and the Suffering Servant: Isaiah 53 and Christian Origins*, W. H. Bellinger and W. R. Farmer, eds. (Harrisburg, Pa.: Trinity International, 1998), 125–51.

40. (1) Matthew 16:21; Mark 8:31; Luke 9:22; (2) Matthew 17:22–23; Mark 9:31; Luke 9:44; (3) Matthew 20:18–19; Mark 10:33–34; Luke 18:31–33. He also alludes to it in the Parable of the Vineyard. C. H. Scobie, *The Ways of Our God*, 417–18.

41. See also Romans 10:16 which quotes Isaiah 53:1 and Romans 15:21, which quotes Isaiah 52:15.

42. For a greater exploration of the theme of prophecy and fulfillment in the New Testament see C. H. Scobie, *The Ways of Our God*, 105–927. The author traces the promise, fulfillment, and consummation of such themes

as God, creation, Messiah, Spirit, the adversary, the church, worship, ministry, and others.

43. Cf. Paul's argument in 1 Corinthians 15, which draws on the promises of the Old Testament and forecasts the resurrection of all flesh in the future. Cf. Isaiah 25:8 and Hosea 13:14 in 1 Corinthians 15:54–55. For further reading on prophecy in Revelation, see R. Bauckham, *The Climax of Prophecy: Studies on the Book of Revelation* (Edinburgh: T. and T. Clark, 1993).

44. The quotation is from M. Water, comp., *The New Encyclopedia of Christian Quotations* (Grand Rapids: Baker, 2000), 835.

45. Henry W. Baker, "Lord, Thy Word Abideth," from *The Pilgrim Hymnal* (Boston: Pilgrim Press, 1968).

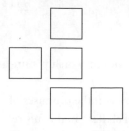

SELECT BIBLIOGRAPHY

For further reading on the use of the
Old Testament in the New Testament:

Adam, P. *Hearing God's Words: Exploring Biblical Spirituality.* NSBT. Leicester,
England: Apollos, 2004.

Alexander, T. D., and B. S. Rosner, eds. *New Dictionary of Biblical Theology.*
Downers Grove, Ill.: InterVarsity, 2000.

———. *The Servant King.* Downers Grove, Ill.: InterVarsity, 1998.

Bauckham, R. *The Climax of Prophecy: Studies on the Book of Revelation.*
Edinburgh: T. and T. Clark, 1993.

Beale, G. K. "Did Jesus and His Followers Preach the Right Doctrine from the
Wrong Texts?" *Themelios* 14 (1989): 89–96.

———, ed. *The Right Doctrine from the Wrong Texts? Essays on the Use of the
Old Testament in the New.* Grand Rapids: Baker, 1994.

Borland, J. A. *Christ in the Old Testament: OT Appearances of Christ in Human
Form.* 2d ed. Geanies House, Scotland: Christian Focus/Mentor, 1999.

Bruce, F. F. *The New Testament Development of Old Testament Themes.* Grand
Rapids: Eerdmans, 1968.

Carson, D. A., and H. G. M. Williamson, eds. *It Is Written: Scripture Citing
Scripture: Essays in Honour of Barnabas Lindars.* Cambridge: Cambridge
University Press, 1988.

Childs, B. *Biblical Theology: A Proposal.* Philadelphia, Fortress, 2002.

———. *Biblical Theology of the Old and New Testaments: Theological Reflection on the Christian Bible.* Minneapolis: Fortress, 1992.

Dumbrell, W. J. *Covenant and Creation: A Theology of the Old Testament Covenants.* Carlisle, England: Paternoster, 1984, 1997.

Ellis, E. E. *Paul's Use of the Old Testament.* Edinburgh: T. and T. Clark, 1957.

———. *Prophecy and Hermeneutic in Early Christianity: New Testament Essays.* Wissenchaftliche Untersuchungen zum Neuen Testament (hereafter WUNT). Vol. 18. Tübingen, Germany: J. C. B. Mohr (Paul Siebeck), 1978.

Elwell, W., ed. *Evangelical Dictionary of Biblical Theology.* Grand Rapids: Baker, 1996.

Evans, C. A., and J. A. Sanders, eds. *Paul and the Scriptures of Israel.* Studies in Scripture in Early Judaism and Christianity. Vol. 1. Sheffield: Sheffield Academic Press, 1993.

Ferguson, E. *The Church of Christ: A Biblical Ecclesiology for Today.* Grand Rapids: Eerdmans, 1996.

Fuller, D. P. *The Unity of the Bible.* Grand Rapids: Zondervan, 1992.

Goldsworthy, G. *According to Plan: The Unfolding Revelation of God in the Bible.* Downers Grove, Ill.: InterVarsity, 2002.

———. *Gospel and Kingdom: A Christian Interpretation of the Old Testament.* Carlisle, England: Paternoster, 1981.

———. *Preaching the Whole Bible as Christian Scripture: The Application of Biblical Theology to Expository Preaching.* Grand Rapids: Eerdmans, 2000.

Hafemann, S. J. *Biblical Theology: Retrospect and Prospect.* Downers Grove, Ill.: InterVarsity, 2001.

———. *The God of Promise and the Life of Faith: Understanding the Heart of the Bible.* Wheaton, Ill.: Crossway, 2001.

———. *Paul, Moses, and the History of Israel.* WUNT. Vol. 81. Tübingen, Germany: J. C. B. Mohr (Paul Siebeck), 1995.

Hanson, A. T. *The New Testament Interpretation of Scripture.* London: SPCK, 1980.

Hays, R. B. *Echoes of Scripture in the Letters of Paul.* New Haven: Yale University Press, 1989.

Jensen, P. *At the Heart of the Universe: What Christians Believe.* Downers Grove, Ill.: InterVarsity, 2003.

Kaiser, W. *The Messiah in the Old Testament.* Grand Rapids: Zondervan, 1995.

Köstenberger A., and P. O'Brien. *Salvation to the Ends of the Earth: A Biblical Theology of Mission.* Downers Grove, Ill.: InterVarsity, 2001.

Longenecker, R. *Biblical Exegesis in the Apostolic Period*. Grand Rapids: Eerdmans, 1975.

Menken, M. and S. Moyise. *The Psalms in the New Testament*. London: T. and T. Clark, 2004.

Poythress, V. *The Shadow of Christ in the Law of Moses*. Phillipsburg, N.J.: Presbyterian and Reformed, 1991.

Robertson, O. P. *The Christ of the Covenants*. Phillipsburg, N.J.: Presbyterian and Reformed, 1980.

Rosner, B. S. "'Written for Us': Paul's View of Scripture." In *A Pathway into the Holy Scripture*. Edited by P. Satterthwaite and D. Wright. Grand Rapids: Eerdmans, 1994, 92–96.

Scobie, C. H. *The Ways of Our God: An Approach to Biblical Theology*. Grand Rapids: Eerdmans, 2003.

Van Gemeren, W. *The Progress of Redemption: The Story of Salvation from Creation to the New Jerusalem*. Grand Rapids: Zondervan, 1988.

Vos, G. *Biblical Theology: Old and New Testaments*. Grand Rapids: Eerdmans, 1948.

SCRIPTURE INDEX